COOKING with
FRIENDS

COOKING with FRIENDS

Marie Nightingale and
Canada's Celebrated Cooks

A Collection of
Recipes and Stories

NIMBUS
PUBLISHING

Nimbus Publishing Limited
PO Box 9166
Halifax, NS   B3K 5M8
(902) 455-4286

Printed and bound in Canada

Design: Kate Westphal, Graphic Detail, Charlottetown, PE
Cover photo by: Jack LeClair

National Library of Canada Cataloguing in Publication

Nightingale, Marie
    Cooking with friends : Marie Nightingale
    and Canada's celebrated cooks / Marie
    Nightingale.

    Includes index.
    ISBN 1-55109-467-3

1. Cookery. 2. Nightingale, Marie. 3. Cooks—Canada—Anecdotes. 4. Food writers—Canada—Biography. I. Title.

TX619.N53A3 2003   641.5   C2003-905408-X

We acknowledge the financial support of the Government of Canada through the Book Publishing Industry Development Program (BPIDP) and the Canada Council for our publishing activities.

photo credits

On Citadel Hill with Joseph Howe Festival brochure: Bob Brooks. Used with permission.
newspaper ad: The Halifax Herald
Herald staffers: Len Lagg, Reprinted with permission from The Halifax Herald Limited
Herald retirement party: The Halifax Herald Limited
Margaret Carson: Tim Krochak, Reprinted with permission from The Halifax Herald Limited
Bonnie Stern and Audrey Grantham: Eric Wynne, Reprinted with permission from The Halifax Herald Limited
Margaret Dickenson: Rogers Communications
Mona Yuskiw: Peter Bolli, Bolli & Hutchinson Photographic Design Ltd.
Jean Pare: Company's Coming Publishing Limited. Photographer: Darren Jacknisky
Shae Griffith: Richard Griffith
Lucy Waverman: Jenna Muirhead-Gould
Hans Wicki: Heckbert Studio & Gallery (Charlottetown)
Margaret Fraser: Frank Grant
Julia Aitken: Mark Mainguy
Christophe Luzeux: Catherine Silver
Julian Armstrong: Allen McInnis
Sandi Richard: Ian Grant
Jean Hoare: Steve Wendelboe of The Studio Ltd. (Calgary)
Alex Clavel: Michael Creagen
Elaine Elliot: Julian Beveridge
Virginia Lee: Mel Lee
Monda Rosenberg: John Reeves
Lavinia Parrish-Zwicker: Focus Photography (Wolfville, NS)
Cheryl Tardif and Noel Woolgar: Katie Barteaux
Maurizio Bertossi: Tim Krochak, Reprinted with permission from The Halifax Herald Limited
Rose Murray: Andrew Stowicki
Margaret Howard: John Prettie
Heather Howe: Dianna Last

The completion of this book was done without the support of Laurie, my husband of forty-nine years. But somehow I think he knows and would approve.

So, to my family and all of my friends, old and new, especially those I have come to know during my twenty years of food writing for The Chronicle-Herald *and* The Mail-Star, *I dedicate this book. With an eye to my present association,* Saltscapes, Canada's East Coast Magazine, *you might forgive me if I consider that "the best" is yet to come..*

contents

acknowledgements

I could say that it took twenty years to write this book, but the baby you hold in your hands was a nine-month effort. It began by researching close to one thousand columns and thousands of recipes I've written and shared over those years. Many of the recipes belong to friends I have interviewed and whose cookbooks I have reviewed.

To all who have contributed to this book in any way, even when they didn't know they were doing it, I say thank you. A special thanks must go to the Herald editors who worked with my text and made it better, especially to the one who stuck it out with me for half of those twenty years, Margie MacKay. I miss her.

To Diane LeBlanc, whose friendship bridges the twenty years and beyond, my sincere thanks for painstakingly reading the manuscript, and offering her excellent editorial advice. Her gracious demeanor serves as an inspiration to me to be a better person. She's the best.

To Hughena Hubley and Jan Heighton for sharing and keeping the secret as the manuscript unfolded. They read each chapter as it was finished and encouraged me to keep going. I appreciate their friendship.

To Dorothy Blythe, publisher at Nimbus, who took immediately to the idea and gave the book a name and a face, and to editor Sandra McIntyre and her assistant Ali Symons, who gave it a body and brought it to life, it's been such a pleasure. Thank you also to Kate Westphal of Graphic Detail in Charlottetown.

Oh yes, and my thanks to Paul Heighton for his technical advice. He was a worthy opponent to my computer glitches. And he always won.

I am grateful, too, to my loyal readers who have graciously said that my recipes and writings were important to them. (I don't remember many complaints.)

I wanted to call this book What a Spread it Was, but was advised that people wouldn't understand. But it has to be said, and this is the spot to say it. Oh, what a spread it was!

Thank you, all.

introduction

There have been so many times in my life when I have thought it doesn't get any better than this. My teenage years, filled with excitement, loves, and intense friendships, were at the time the "best." They were followed by an exciting career in radio—the year in Windsor at CFAB then back to Halifax and CJCH were the best times, with many new friends made and cherished.

Then marriage and motherhood became the very best times of my life. Sure, there were challenges. How on earth could a family survive on one salary? And, how can you live in a house with a husband and three sons and only one bathroom? But, into that house on Greenwood Avenue, where we lived for twenty-five years, came friends, some old, some new, and all have left fond memories.

It was under the dining room chandelier in that house in Halifax's south end that I wrote *Out of Old Nova Scotia Kitchens*, almost ruining my eyesight in a process that took four years to complete. Publication in 1970 brought other bests, for with it came a small measure of fame and recognition.

But yet another best was on its way. Hard work, probably the hardest work of my life, and a wide circle of friends who helped, brought about the Joseph Howe Festival, a celebration of the great champion of the people of Nova Scotia. This best lasted four years

The late great photographer Bob Brooks took this photo of me on the ramparts of Citadel Hill holding a programme for the Joseph Howe Festival. The photo was part of a thirteen-page spread, in *Homemaker's* magazine, in September 1973.

for me, although the festival continued for another couple of years after I retired.

By now I had given my best to several projects organized by my sorority, Beta Sigma Phi, which in turn gave to me many of my best friendships, most of which have lasted more than fifty years.

After enjoying our family cottage at Indian Point, Halifax County, for twenty-five years, we turned it into a home to enjoy year-round. Some of our best parties were held there. But, with the boys grown and gone, time weighed heavy on idle hands. It was time to find another project. That's when I went to The Halifax Herald and presented the idea of a food section. Prior to that, an occasional recipe or two would appear on the social page, although there

At the microphone at CFAB, Halifax

was an annual cookbook insert, which was very popular. In the written presentation I left with Ken Foran, managing editor at the time, I boldly suggested the following:

You can live without comics, entertainment and art,
You can live without sports, at least, well, in part,
You can live without social, though readers keep lookin',
But civilized women can't live without cookin'.

I guess they realized the advantage, because I was hired and became food writer, first for *The Mail-Star* and shortly afterward, for *The Chronicle-Herald*, as well. The job, which started in March 1982, was to last twenty years. This was most definitely the best time of my life.

Old enough to be mother to most of my colleagues, I was accepted as one of them, and happiness, for me, was going to work each day. There were those who said the newsroom language toned down somewhat after my arrival, but I swear I didn't flinch if a reporter forgot and let out an expletive. It was usually one of two single words, but if it helped them to write their stories, it was alright with me. Forget appearances. These were not my children—they were my friends.

Forced into retirement when I turned sixty-five, in 1993, I went kicking and screaming into the next best.

As a freelancer, I continued to be the Herald's food writer, my second book, *Marie Nightingale's Favourite Recipes*, was published, and Cuisine Canada held its first Northern Bounty conference in Stratford, Ontario. Another world had opened up to me. So many new friendships started there. Through this association, I have inhaled the heady fragrance of the extensive herb beds of Ravenhill Farm, in Saanichton, British Columbia, while relaxing by the pool with Andrew Yeoman and Noel Richardson, the husband-and-wife team who own and operate the farm and make a business of writing about it. Still keen are the memories of visits to Sooke Harbour House where, just an hour's drive from Victoria, I entered a whole new world of gastronomy. There, in the highly rated dining room overlooking Juan de Fuca Strait, I willingly fell victim to the generous hospitality of innkeepers Sinclair and Fredrica Philip. There could be no greater compliment paid to me than the presentation of a special menu bearing my name.

These members of Alpha Master Chapter, Beta Sigma Phi, have been together for over fifty years, getting together for on-going events like our annual lobster party as well as twice-monthly meetings. Who knows you better than your sorority sisters of half a century? Good friends, all.

So many wonderful memories: a late morning breakfast at Diane Clement's funky Tomato Fresh Food Café in Vancouver; an appearance on *The Vicki Gabereau Show* to talk about Acadian cuisine; a Mennonite meal in Kitchener followed by a visit to Edna Staebler's cozy home on Sunfish Lake, where she wrote her *Food That Really Smecks* series of cookbooks; a cookout at the Cochrane Corral, near Calgary, where I enjoyed beef at its best. And in the wee small hours, a taxi in Stratford, shared with Judy and Ed Schultz, of Edmonton, turned out to be a carriage pulled by a horse emitting his own brand of gas. Such good times.

And the food! I've dined on such delicacies as dungeness crabcakes, sea urchins, gooseneck barnacles, smoked prairie oysters, ostrich, wild boar, buffalo hump, smoked buffalo tongue, pit roasted ribs, oxtail stew, beef jerky, pemmican, braised Angus grass-fed natural beef, Yukon Arctic char, West Coast herring spawned on hemlock branches, herring roe, oolicans (similar to smelts), Jerusalem artichokes, Taber corn, rainforest mushrooms, sea lettuce, and native soapberries whipped to a frothy dessert.

To quench my thirst, I've sipped tea with Mr. Twining himself, sampled many award-winning Canadian wines, both red and white, savoured ice wines, cream ale, lagers, and Rippin' Kickin' traditional ale. And I've felt the jolt of Kicking Horse coffee.

I've sampled groundcherries, black soy beans, golden beets, and red wattle pork at a Feast of the Fields, a roving picnic of fresh organic foods and ingredients held near Guelph, Ontario.

I've toured Prince Edward Island with food writers Julie Watson, Anita Stewart, Kasey Wilson, and Barb Ostmann for a week of lobster eating. I travelled Nova Scotia on a pork-eating adventure with Heather MacKenzie, Ray Foote, Steve Bone, and Elizabeth Baird. With three other Canadian food writers, including Susan Pedwell, of Toronto, I toured the impressive Gerber Baby Foods plant in Fremont, Michigan.

I've stood shoulder-high in a field of canola, climbed into the seat of a huge farm combine, toured a lobster processing facility, checked out a mussel-growing business, visited an Irish moss operation, and savoured seaweed pie. I stepped in among young chickens so crowded that there was hardly room for my feet. And I climbed a cherry tree to celebrate my sixty-fifth birthday.

For Herald interviews, I've talked with Jane Brody, the very slim *New York Times* personal health columnist and best selling author, who claimed to be fat before she started jogging and eating wisely. I questioned whether Kenny Rogers, in Halifax for a March 1989 concert, could really cook, or if he was just lending his name to Dole's cookbook, *Cooking with Kenny Rogers.* And I published the answer: sometimes he cooks at home, if it's informal. There was also Danny Kaye who, in October 1983, flew his own plane into Halifax for an event, and talked with me about his favourite cuisine: Chinese. With two kitchens in his Beverley Hills home, this man could cook! He claimed he could prepare an eight-dish meal for thirty days in succession without repeating himself.

I love the Body Break duo of Hal Johnson and Joanne McLeod. They caused quite a stir when, after our interview, I led them through the newsroom with the announcement, "Hey, everybody, it's body break time!" Some of the reporters were a bit ticked when Mark Tewksbury came to me to talk about beef, and not to the sports department to talk about the gold medal he won for swimming in the 1992 Summer Olympics. To compensate, Mark agreed to stop at every desk to let anyone who wished hold—or bite—his gold medal.

And to my collection of friends I've added cookbook authors, food writers, chefs, restaurateurs, farmers, producers, suppliers, and other foodies. There was Madame Jehane Benoit, who wrote a gracious introduction to the hardcover edition of *Out of Old Nova Scotia Kitchens* (1971). My last interview with her, in November 1987 was possibly her last, and she never got to read the story that started this way:

As the door opened into the Sheraton Hotel's Joshua Slocum suite, she sat there like a queen, composed, relaxed, and smiling. I didn't recognize her immediately, for Madame Jehane Benoit's face was framed with soft wisps of pure white hair. And she was smaller than when we last met, only a year ago.

There's Judy Schultz, food and travel editor for the *Edmonton Journal,* with whom I shared a breakfast table in 1984, when we both attended the Newspaper Food Editors and Writers Conference in Montreal. So caught up were we in our conversation that we lingered for two hours, missing the first speaker of the day, but having no regrets. There is Johanna Burkhard, who brought to my home a fine sampling of comfort foods, and stayed to chat. There's petite Anne Lindsay, home economist, food writer and consultant, whom I greatly admire, and whose bestselling cookbooks are excellent sources of healthful recipes and information. She brought food or flowers when she came calling. The Inn Chef Michael Smith came to talk about his future plans and shared the secret that he was planning to ask his Rachael to be his wife. (I didn't tell, but now she knows, and said yes.)

Other chef friends have come and gone from the area, but not from my heart. Steve Huston, such a talent! Mark Gabrieau, who now has his own bistro in Antigonish. John Haines, where are you? Ray Hammer and Richard Skinner, both former chefs at The Sheraton. Roland Glauser, who opened his own restaurant in Shelburne several years ago. Alex Clavel, taken from us all, in the prime of his life. Hans Wicki, now a chef instructor in Charlottetown. Dale Nichols, a wonderful friend, sadly missed since he left Halifax.

Some of my chef friends supplied favourite vegetable recipes to include in my third book, *Out of Nova Scotia Gardens,* published in 1997.

So many friends, far too many to mention. Some appear in little snippets within these pages, which contain recipes and story excerpts that appeared in my newspaper columns from 1982 to 1993. They are reprinted with permission from The Halifax Herald Limited. I am grateful for their support. But, don't consider this to be the last song the Nightingale sings. There's yet another best for me. I'm living it now in the food section of *Saltscapes* magazine.

Halifax businessman and former alderman Bob Stapells (seated) had just auctioned off Mayor Walter Fitzgerald's tie, which I am removing. Shirley Ellis helps to remove the next item to go—the mayor's coat. The auction was held to raise funds for the first Joseph Howe Festival, in 1973.

Arts reporter Elissa Barnard, columnist Peter Duffy, news editor Pam Sword, editor Frank DePalma, and restaurant critic Stephen Maher gather in a New Year's Eve toast.

In a Saskatoon Market

She adds
a flavour
all her own;
Food-Writer
Marie Nightingale...
Wednesday in
Living Today
263N5

Herald Retirement Party: The gathering in this photo might indicate that there would be no newspaper on the day I retired from my job as food writer for *The Chronicle-Herald* and the *Mail-Star*. In fact both editions were printed.

appetizers

During the holidays, whether in summer or winter, the wise host will be prepared by keeping an appetizer in the freezer, or at least by having a stash of ingredients on hand for quick finger foods.

Sliced salmon, shrimp, meatballs, and homemade cheese biscuits are among the summer mainstays in Joan Gurnham's freezer at Mason's Point, and she's seldom without bottled solomon gundy, which she serves on a lettuce-lined tray with smoked salmon and shrimp. "I like to use scallops when I can gt them, and when they'r not too expensive" Joan says. She sometimes serves scallops with shrimp and haddock as an accompaniment to pasta for a light meal. To prepare this, she cuts the fillets into large bite-size pieces, then dips the fish, scallops, and shrimp into a combination of olive oil and dried tarragon. The seafood is baked at 425F (220C) for 10 to 12 minutes, and served on the side with red pepper pasta.

Joan Gurnham (right) and Jean Milson

Rose-Marie McKibbin of Indian Point also relies on seafood when entertaining, especially frozen crabmeat and smoked salmon.

One of her favourite appetizers is crabmeat combined with low-fat cream cheese, a little horseradish and a dash of Tabasco sauce. She transfers the mixture to an oven-proof serving dish, puts it under the broiler for a couple of minutes, and serves it warm with crackers or pita triangles.

When serving shrimp, Rose-Marie makes an accompanying sauce of drained yogurt, a couple of tablespoons (30 ml) of mayonnaise, a touch of Dijon mustard and a pinch or two of dried tarragon.

"I enjoy cooking, but it's always a challenge to keep the fat down, so I often use drained yogurt in place of sour cream in dips or sauces to serve with fresh vegetables," she says. To drain yogurt, place a paper coffee filter in a sieve set over a bowl, spoon in the yogurt, cover, and place in the refrigerator overnight to drain. In the morning, the drained yogurt will have the consistency of sour cream, and can be substituted for sour cream in most recipes.

When it comes to winter entertaining, try little choux puffs made ahead and stored in the freezer, and a filling put together the night before. Your guests will wonder at your efficiency.

I never seemed to have much luck getting my granddaughters, Candice, Ashley, or Christa, to work with me in the kitchen. The grandsons were different. When Craig was younger, he would immediately head to my kitchen, asking "What can we cook today, Nan?" And Corey (shown here at age ten) was happy to help out on those occasions when I visited the family in Nashville. In fact, the boys each had special aprons.

Hazelnut Chicken Bites with Pineapple Mustard Sauce

Served with a salad, these delicious chicken morsels also make a nice light meal.

1 pound (500 g) boneless chicken breasts or thighs
1/2 cup (125 ml) fine dry breadcrumbs
1/2 cup (125 ml) finely chopped hazelnuts or pecans
1/2 teaspoon (2 ml) garlic powder
1/4 teaspoon (1 ml) paprika
Pinch each of salt and freshly ground pepper
1 egg
1 tablespoon (15 ml) water
Flour

Pineapple Mustard Sauce:
1/2 cup (125 ml) crushed pineapple with juice
1 tablespoon (15 ml) granulated sugar
2 tablespoons (30 ml) coarse grained mustard
2 tablespoons (30 ml) horseradish

Cut chicken into 32 one-inch (2.5 cm) pieces. In small bowl, mix together breadcrumbs, nuts, and seasonings. In another bowl, beat together egg and water. Lightly dust chicken pieces in flour; dip in egg mixture, and then in crumbs.

Conventional oven: Place coated bites on ungreased, nonstick baking pan. Bake at 425F (220C) about 15 minutes, until chicken is tender.

Microwave: Place 10 to 12 coated bites in circular pattern on microwave-safe rack. Cover with wax paper and cook at medium-high for 3 to 4 minutes. Let stand 2 minutes. Repeat twice for remaining pieces.

Sauce: In small saucepan or glass measure, combine pineapple with juice, granulated sugar, mustard and horseradish. Stirring occasionally, simmer over medium heat until thickened, about 10 minutes; or, microwave on medium-high for 4 to 5 minutes.

Serve bites with sauce. Makes 32 bites, or 16 appetizer servings.

Chef Stephen Huston

■ When Cuisine Canada, the national alliance of Canadian culinary professionals, held its Northern Bounty conference in Halifax in September 1998, chefs from each of the four Atlantic provinces were able to flex their "mussels" at the opening reception, held at the Maritime Museum of the Atlantic. Stephen Huston and Stefan Czapalay were two of those chefs. Steve's scallops and Stefan's mussels created quite a stir among the two hundred delegates.

Steve Huston's Seared Digby Scallops with Maple and Curry

1 pound (500 g) 20–30 count scallops
1 tablespoon (15 ml) mild curry paste
1/2 teaspoon (2 ml) lemon pepper
1/2 teaspoon (2 ml) Jamaican jerk paste
1/3 cup (75 ml) canola oil
1 tablespoon (15 ml) chopped parsley
1/2 cup (125 ml) chopped sundried tomatoes
1/2 teaspoon (2 ml) lemon juice
1/4 cup (50 ml) maple syrup
Pinch each of salt and freshly ground pepper

Garnishes:
Drizzle of good quality olive oil
Pinch each of chopped fresh basil and cilantro
1/4 cup (50 ml) finely diced red pepper

Combine all ingredients except garnishes. Add scallops and toss. Refrigerate one hour to marinate.

In hot sauté pan, fry scallops a few at a time to colour. Do not overcook. Remove scallops to cookie sheet to cool. (Some juice will come from scallops as they sit.) Put scallops and juice in mixing bowl; toss with a drizzling of good olive oil and a pinch each of chopped fresh basil and cilantro. Add diced red pepper to finish.

Serve cool (not cold) on toothpicks or on sea vegetable rice crackers. Averages 25 pieces.

Mussels Chef Stefan Czapalay Style

Chef Stefan Czapalay

2 tablespoons (30 ml) unsalted butter
1 shallot, finely minced
2 cloves garlic, finely minced
1 tablespoon (15 ml) finely minced gingerroot
1 rib celery, finely chopped
1/2 teaspoon (2 ml) chopped basil
5 fennel seeds
30 mussels
3 ounces (90 ml) white wine
1 small tomato
1 pinch curry powder
5 pink peppercorns
1/4 cup (50 ml) whipping cream

In saucepan, melt 1 tablespoon (15 ml) butter over medium heat. Add shallot, garlic, gingerroot, celery, basil, and fennel seeds, cover and cook gently until softened. Add mussels, wine, chopped tomato, curry powder and peppercorns. Cook until mussel shells open, 5 to 7 minutes. Remove mussels and arrange in a bowl. Return broth to high heat; boil until reduced by half. Add cream and return to a boil. Remove from heat, swirl in remaining butter and adjust seasoning. Pour over mussels. Serve with crusty bread. Makes 30 pieces.

Italian Puffs

3 eggs, well beaten
2/3 cup (150 ml) flour
3/4 cup (175 ml) milk
2 tablespoons (30 ml) chopped onion
1 tablespoon (15 ml) butter, melted
1/2 teaspoon (2 ml) salt
1/3 cup (75 ml) tomato sauce
1/2 teaspoon (2 ml) oregano
1/2 teaspoon (2 ml) basil
1/2 cup (125 ml) diced pepperoni
1/4 cup (50 ml) diced green pepper
1/2 cup (125 ml) shredded mozzarella cheese

In medium bowl, combine eggs, flour, and milk until smooth. Stir in onion, butter and salt. Pour into a lightly greased 9-inch (23 cm) square baking pan.

continued on next page

Maddie MacMillan

■ Whenever the MacMillan/ Morris families of Halifax get together for Christmas dinner, Maddie MacMillan is expected to bring everyone's favourite appetizer: lobster tarts. "I've been making them for about twenty-five years now, not only for Christmas, but for Thanksgiving and other special occasions as well, including birthdays. As soon as I come in the door, someone will ask 'did you bring our lobster treats?' It's the first thing they look for," Maddie says. Apart from the lobster, she says it's the pastry that makes the tarts so special. She always makes her own pastry, and her family of three grown children, now expanded to fourteen, wouldn't want it any other way. "I usually make the tart shells well ahead of time and keep them in the freezer until I need them. It's a great time saver when things get rushed."

In a small bowl, combine tomato sauce, oregano, and basil. Gently spread sauce on top of batter to produce marbled effect. Sprinkle with pepperoni and green pepper. Cover with mozzarella. Bake at 425F (220C) for 25 to 30 minutes or until puffed and golden brown. Cool 5 minutes before cutting into squares. Serve warm or chilled. Makes about 25 appetizers.

Maddie MacMillan's Lobster Tarts

Pastry:
2 cups (500 ml) sifted all-purpose flour
1 teaspoon (5 ml) salt
1 teaspoon (5 ml) granulated sugar
1 teaspoon (5 ml) baking powder
2/3 cup (150 ml) shortening
1/3 to 1/2 cup (75 to 125 ml) ice water

In large bowl, combine flour, salt, sugar and baking powder. Cut in shortening until mixture forms pea-size pieces. Sprinkle water by tablespoonfuls (15 ml) over mixture, stirring with a fork until dough can be patted lightly into a ball. Wrap in wax paper; chill if desired.

Roll pastry as for pies, cut with a 2 1/2 inch (6.5 cm) round cookie cutter; fit into small tart pans. Prick with fork to prevent puffing. Bake at 425F (220C) until lightly browned. Makes 24 small tart shells.

Lobster Filling:
1 can (11-ounce/320 g) frozen lobster meat, thawed, chopped
1/4 cup (50 ml) finely chopped celery
1/4 cup (50 ml) finely chopped green pepper
1/2 cup (125 ml) mayonnaise
Salt and pepper to taste
Stuffed olives, sliced

Combine lobster, celery, green pepper, and mayonnaise; season to taste. Just before serving, spoon into tart shells and serve cold, topped with a stuffed olive slice. If desired, these may be heated in the microwave and served hot.

Chef James MacDougall

■ Chef James MacDougall has been in charge of the kitchen in the family's La Perla restaurant in Dartmouth since 1988, leaving only for brief periods to upgrade his skills. Claiming he inherited his love of cooking from his mother and maternal grand-mother, James was drawn to the kitchen at an early age: "I can remember cooking and baking since I was five…I would drag out my mother's pots and pans and watch the Galloping Gour-met or anything to do with cooking," he says.

Though he says the two women in his life were "the best cooks in the world," it was his grandfather Wagner, a Louisbourg fisherman, who ate everything the little boy cooked, and always encouraged him. As he grew, the young cook began experimenting and adding his own creative twists. He'd substitute a spice or add an ingredient to satisfy his own demanding taste buds, a tradition he continues today at La Perla.

James MacDougall's Chicken Puffs

Choux Pastry:
1 cup (250 ml) water
1/4 teaspoon (1 ml) salt
1/2 cup (125 ml) butter, cut in pieces
1 cup (250 ml) all-purpose flour, sifted
4 eggs
1 beaten egg, for brushing
1/4 cup (50 ml) finely grated Swiss cheese

Chicken Filling:
2 tablespoons (30 ml) butter
2 tablespoons (30 ml) flour
1 cup (250 ml) milk
1/4 cup (50 ml) grated parmesan cheese
1 cup (250 ml) finely minced cooked chicken
Salt and pepper

Prepare pastry: Put water, salt and butter in a fairly large saucepan over high heat; bring to a boil. Remove from heat and add flour all at once. Stir vigorously until thoroughly combined; return to medium heat and stir until mixture forms a solid mass that comes away cleanly from sides of pan. Remove from heat; cool slightly.

Beat eggs into mixture one at a time, thoroughly blending in each. Beat until mixture is smooth and shiny and holds its own shape.

Fit piping bag with 1/2 inch (1 cm) nozzle; fill bag with pastry. Pipe miniature puffs, about 1-inch (2.5 cm) in diameter, onto a greased baking sheet; brush with beaten egg; sprinkle with Swiss cheese. Bake in a 400F (200C) oven until firm and crisp, about 30 to 40 minutes. When cooked, pierce each puff with a knife to release steam.

Chicken Filling: Make cheese sauce by melting butter over medium heat; then stir in flour and, whisking constantly, pour in milk. Gradually bring sauce to a boil. When boiling, remove from heat and stir in parmesan cheese. Let sauce sit; mix in minced chicken and season with salt and pepper.

Fit piping bag with 1/8 inch (3 mm) nozzle; fill bag with chicken mixture. Insert nozzle into base or side of each puff; force mixture into puffs.

To serve: heat puffs in 400F (200C) oven for 5 minutes. Makes 24 puffs.

Chef Margaret Carson

■ If there's been a decline in recent years in the number of holiday cocktail parties, Margaret Carson, proprietor and executive chef at Bonne Cuisine catering in Spring Garden Place, Halifax, hasn't heard about it. She says the old stand-bys are still the most popular appetizers "As long as you have a base, which could be as varied as a small herb tea biscuit, a dollar-size blini, a sliced French stick, or baked croutons that you made yourself, you're well on the way to making delicious and easy-to-prepare hors d'oeuvres."

Margaret's Cheese Sandwiches

Filling:
4 ounces (125 g) cheddar cheese, grated
2 tablespoons (30 ml) softened cream cheese
2 tablespoons (30 ml) softened unsalted butter

Biscuits:
8 ounces (250 g) sharp cheddar cheese, grated
1 cup (250 ml) all-purpose flour
1/2 cup (125 ml) softened butter
1 tablespoon (15 ml) Worcestershire sauce
1/2 teaspoon (2 ml) salt
1/4 teaspoon (1 ml) cayenne
1 egg white
Sesame seeds

To make filling: Combine ingredients to form a paste.

To make biscuits: Combine cheese, flour, butter, Worcestershire sauce, salt, and cayenne. Knead until dough is smooth and forms a ball.

On a lightly floured surface roll dough into four rolls, 5-inches (13 cm) long and 1-inch (2.5 cm) in diameter. Wrap separately in wax paper and refrigerate until firm.

Slice each roll into 1/8-inch (3 mm) slices; place on lightly greased cookie sheets, 1/2 inch (1 cm) apart. Brush lightly with beaten egg white; sprinkle with sesame seeds.

Bake at 375F (190C) for 8 to 10 minutes, until lightly golden. Remove to wire racks to cool. Split biscuits in half horizontally, and sandwich together with cheese filling. Makes 30 filled sandwiches.

Marie with Chef Robert Moore

■ When asked about catering a party, Robert Moore, one-time chef and owner of Pastaman in Halifax, now president of Halifax-based Pastaman Wholesale Inc, says that there are many appetizers that a busy host can prepare on a weekend and store in the freezer to pull out when needed. One of his favourites is spanakopita, a Greek-style spinach pastry: "You can get 180 pieces from one box of phyllo [pastry], so make up a whole batch, freeze them on cookie sheets, then store in plastic containers in the freezer. Take them out to thaw four to six hours in the refrigerator, and pop them into the oven when your guests start arriving."

Spanakopita

2 teaspoons (10 ml) olive or canola oil
1 small onion, chopped
1/2 clove garlic, finely chopped
6 ounces (170 g) fresh spinach, chopped
4 ounces (125 g) cream cheese
8 ounces (250 g) feta cheese
1 egg
1 cup (250 ml) chopped green onions, optional
salt and pepper to taste
8 ounces (250 g) frozen phyllo pastry sheets, thawed
cooking spray

In medium saucepan, over medium heat, heat oil; sauté onions and garlic until tender, about 5 minutes. Add spinach, cover, and cook gently for about one minute. Turn mixture into food processor. Combine cheeses. Add egg and green onion, if using. Process on and off until blended. Set aside.

Cut phyllo pastry sheets crosswise into five strips. Layer two strips and spray with cooking spray. Place one teaspoon (5 ml) cheese mixture at bottom of one double strip, fold corner up to form a triangle; continue folding in triangular shape until entire strip is used. Repeat procedure with remaining pastry and filling.

Place triangles on oiled cookie sheet; spray each with cooking spray. Bake at 375F (190C) for 15 to 20 minutes, until golden brown. Makes 90 bite-size triangles.

Camembert Almondine

Soft cheeses like brie and camembert are great on their own, but can be turned into festive party fare at a moment's notice.

1 tablespoon (15 ml) butter
1/4 cup (50 ml) sliced almonds
1 whole camembert (200 g) or brie (150 g) cheese
Chopped parsley
French bread slices or crackers

Melt butter in frypan and sauté almonds until golden. Spoon nuts on top of cheese. Bake in a 300F (150C) oven until centre is hot and melted, about 18 to 20 minutes. Garnish with parsley. Serve with bread or crackers. Makes 6 to 8 servings.

tip *Thai hot sweet sauce contains red chilies, sugar, garlic, vinegar and salt. Bonnie suggests using it on its own or in Asian-flavoured sauces, dips and marinades. You can find it at Asian markets. In North America usually only the leaves of fresh cilantro are used, but many Asian recipes call for the stems and roots, which add considerably more flavour.*

Bonnie Stern's Spicy Thai Shrimp

2 pounds (1 kg) extra-large shrimp (about 32), cleaned
3 cloves garlic
1 (1-inch/2.5 cm) piece fresh gingerroot, peeled
1 hot chili, seeded, deribbed
1/4 cup (50 ml) fresh cilantro leaves, stems and roots (see tip)
2 tablespoons (30 ml) hoisin sauce
1 tablespoon (15 ml) Thai fish sauce or soy sauce
1 tablespoon (15 ml) lime juice or lemon juice
1 tablespoon (15 ml) honey
1 tablespoon (15 ml) rice vinegar
1 teaspoon (5 ml) sesame oil
1/2 cup (125 ml) Thai hot sweet sauce

Pat shrimp dry; place in large bowl. In food processor or blender, combine garlic, ginger, chili, and cilantro; blend into a paste. Blend in hoisin sauce, fish sauce, lime juice, honey, vinegar and sesame oil. Combine marinade with shrimp; marinate for at least 30 minutes in refrigerator.

If using wooden skewers, soak them in cold water for 30 minutes before using. Thread shrimp on skewers from head to tail so shrimp are relatively straight. (Make sure shrimp are pushed right to the point of skewers so wooden tips don't burn.) Grill or broil shrimp for a few minutes on each side or until pink and opaque. Place dipping sauce in a small bowl; place in middle of serving platter. Arrange shrimp around sauce. Makes 32 appetizers.

Smoked Salmon Torta

2 (8-ounce/250 g) packages cream cheese, softened
1/2 cup (125 ml) butter, softened
Salt, to taste
Fresh dill weed
8 ounces (250 g) sliced smoked salmon
Assorted breads and crackers

Beat together cream cheese and butter; add salt to taste. Cut two 16-inch (41 cm) squares of cheesecloth. Moisten with water, wring dry and lay flat, one on top of the other, smoothing the cheesecloth out to avoid wrinkles.

Carefully line a 4-cup (1 L) straight-sided plain mould (loaf pan, terrine or charlotte mould) with the cheesecloth, pressing out any wrinkles as you work. Drape excess over rim and arrange 2 or 3 sprigs of dill on bottom of mould.

Carefully spread 1/3 of cheese mixture in mould to make an even layer. Chop enough dill weed to make 1/4 cup (50 ml); sprinkle half over cheese layer; top with half of the smoked salmon. Repeat layers, ending with cheese mixture. Fold ends of cheesecloth over torta and press down lightly to compact layers.

Chill overnight. To serve, lift mould from pan, loosen cheesecloth, invert onto a plate and carefully remove cheesecloth. Garnish as desired. Serve with bread or crackers. Makes about 4 cups (1 L).

Baby Cheddar Tarts

This recipe is from Jean Paré's Favourites.

Pastry:
1/2 cup (125 ml) butter or margarine, softened
4 ounces (125 g) cream cheese, softened
1 cup (250 ml) all-purpose flour

Filling:
1 cup (250 ml) grated cheddar cheese
1 egg
1/2 cup (125 ml) milk
1/4 teaspoon (1 ml) salt
1/4 teaspoon (1 ml) onion salt

To make pastry: Beat butter and cream cheese until smooth and light. Work in flour. Roll into a long thin roll. Mark off, and then cut into 24 pieces. Press into small tart tins to form shells.

Divide cheese evenly among tart shells.

To make filling: Beat egg until frothy. Mix in milk, salt and onion salt. Spoon into shells. Bake in a 350F (180C) oven for about 20 to 25 minutes until set. Makes 24.

Variations: For Baby Swiss Tarts, use grated Swiss cheese instead of cheddar. May be baked in a pie plate and served as a first course.

beverages

Samuel H.G. Twining, who you might say has been steeped in the tea industry of Britain, visited Halifax in October 1986 to introduce his newest blend and to revitalize the age-old tradition of sipping afternoon tea. While some people may measure an eon as the time it takes to use up a bottle of Tabasco sauce, others more wise in the ways of the British point to the tradition of serving afternoon tea as the truest test of time.

Since 1706, when Thomas Twining opened Tom's Coffee House and began selling tea as a novelty, nine generations of this famous tea family have been providing quality blends for teapots around the world. In fact, tea is consumed worldwide by more people in greater quantity than any other beverage except water. And Canadians are drinking their share: in 2002, Canadians filled their tea cups over seven billion times. Mr. Twining believes Canadians' increased interest in tea is caused by an overall change in our culinary lifestyle. And the beverage for all tastes and occasions is tea, he says, "because it offers an array of flavourful blends."

The tea merchant does not have a single favourite tea. It all depends on the weather, the time of day, and his mood. He says when he comes home his wife always asks, "What tea do you feel like today?" If it's a hot day, his choice will be Lapsang Souchong, taken in the garden with cucumber sandwiches. If the day is warm, he turns to Earl Grey, the worldwide favourite. On a cool day, he prefers light and refreshing Yunnan tea, "one of China's rarest and finest."

And if it's a real miserable day, he chooses Vintage Darjeeling, "a rare and very exclusive blend of the choicest Darjeeling flowery Orange Pekoe leaf teas."

But his tea preferences are not only governed by the weather. "In the evening, after I've had a heavy pudding and want to refresh my palate, I choose Earl Grey. If it's a heavy meal, I drink Jasmine, and Oolong is a very pleasant tea at the end of the day because it's light and gentle." As for caffeine, Mr. Twining says the strongest tea from Assam has only half the caffeine as coffee, but anybody who is really worried about caffeine should drink Gunpowder Green (the world's oldest known type, also the lowest in caffeine) or Jasmine (with only about two per cent caffeine; it's a great natural digestive, as well).

The visiting tea baron said Canadians, especially those on the East Coast, are returning to the tradition of afternoon tea, served graciously: "Afternoon tea is enjoying a comeback for a number of reasons," he said in an interview in his hotel suite, where tea was elegantly served. "Tea is both warming and cooling, and of course thirst quenching. I notice, in my travels around the world that more and more businessmen and women are finding it a nice way to end business discussions."

Barbara Shea taking tea with granddaughters Megan Kelly and Lesley Shea

■ Each Mother's Day, the home of Barbara Shea, of Halifax, is the scene of an afternoon tea held by Delta Master Chapter, Beta Sigma Phi sorority. Members honour their mothers and daughters in the timeless ritual of serving tea in a gracious manner. Even young granddaughters dress for the occasion and learn about the traditions of taking tea. Here, Barbara demonstrates the art of pouring tea to her granddaughters.

Hot Tea Glogg

4 cups (1 L) strong, hot tea
1 1/2 cups (375 ml) cranberry juice cocktail
3/4 cup (175 ml) frozen lemonade concentrate, thawed
1/4 cup (50 ml) raisins
1/4 cup (50 ml) slivered almonds

Combine all ingredients in a saucepan and simmer for about 5 minutes. Pour into warm mugs, distributing the raisins and almonds between the mugs. (Give each person a spoon to eat them up after they've had their drink.) Makes about 6 (8-ounce/250 g) servings.

Hot Tea Sangria

4 thick orange slices
8 whole cloves
2 cups (500 ml) dry red wine
2 cups (500 ml) strong, hot tea
1/2 cup (125 ml) orange juice
1/3 cup (75 ml) sugar

Stud each orange slice with two cloves. Combine all ingredients in a saucepan and simmer for 10 minutes to blend flavours. Pour into warm mugs and serve an orange slice with each. Makes about 5 (8-ounce/250 ml) servings.

Joy of Ginger authors Margaret Conrad and Heather MacDonald

■ *Chronicle-Herald* and *Mail-Star* readers already know of my love for ginger since I boldly indulged in the subject and provided several recipes in my column. History professor Margaret Conrad and home economist Heather MacDonald are two Nova Scotians who share my passion for this ancient rhizome. For two years, the pair got together on Friday evenings to talk of, cook with, and write about ginger in all its forms. The charming result was *The Joy of Ginger: A Winning Selection of Taste-Tingling Recipes.* Reading their book, I learned things about ginger that I never knew. Ginger can be used, for example, to cure indigestion, cramps and other stomach ailments. The authors say Ginger Syrup is an essential ingredient in every cook's kitchen. Not only does it make a fabulous flavouring for whipped cream, but a few tablespoons of syrup added to warm milk makes a divine Ginger Cream, "guaranteed to cure whatever ails you and to induce a sound night's sleep."

Ginger Syrup

| 1 cup (250 ml) grated gingerroot
| 2 cups (500 ml) brown sugar
| 2 cups (500 ml) water

Mix ginger and sugar in a small saucepan. Cover with water and bring to a boil. Boil gently, uncovered, for 25 to 30 minutes. When the liquid has reduced to about 2/3, remove from heat and press through a sieve, squeezing as much juice and pulp into the liquid as possible. The syrup can be stored, covered, in the refrigerator for 2 weeks or longer.

To make Ginger Cream, mix 2 tablespoons (15 ml) ginger syrup (or more to taste) in 1 cup (250 ml) of hot milk.

Hot Spicy Punch

This non-alcoholic punch was included in a six-week course, Cooking for the Health of It, held by the Halifax YWCA Preventative Medicine program in conjunction with the Halifax School Board continuing education department. The classes, featuring healthy, calorie-conscious recipes, were conducted by nutritionists Laura Kalina and Susan Robertson.

| 4 cups (1 L) cold water
| 2 tablespoons (30 ml) peeled, chopped fresh gingerroot
| 4 tea bags
| 2 sticks cinnamon, broken up
| 3 whole cloves
| 4 cups (1 L) boiling water
| 4 scant tablespoons (60 ml) sugar
| 1/2 cup (125 ml) lemon juice
| 1/2 cup (125 ml) orange juice
| 2 cups (500 ml) pineapple juice
| 4 cups (1 L) cranberry juice cocktail
| 4 cups (1 L) apple juice
| Thick slices of orange
| Whole cloves

Heat 4 cups (1 L) of cold water in a large kettle. Add ginger, bring to a boil, reduce heat, cover, and simmer for 15 minutes. Let stand until cool. Strain, and return liquid to pan; discard ginger.

Put tea bags, cinnamon and 3 cloves in a bowl. Add 4 cups (1 L) boiling water. Stir. Cover bowl and let tea steep for 10 minutes. Strain into ginger water.

Add all remaining ingredients except orange slices and cloves. Heat well and pour into a punch bowl. Stick a clove in the rind of each orange slice and float on top of punch. Ladle into punch cups to serve. Makes about 40 (4-ounce/125 ml) servings.

Hot Spiced Apple Cider

It's far better to serve crackers, cheese, and apple cider in a warm atmosphere than caviar, smoked salmon, and champagne with cold formality.

| 1 quart (1 L) apple cider or apple juice
| 1 quart (1 L) orange juice
| 1 cup (250 ml) freshly squeezed lemon juice
| 1/2 cup (125 ml) honey or brown sugar
| 4 cinnamon sticks, broken
| 12 whole cloves
| 12 whole allspice

Combine ingredients in a large Dutch oven or pot. Bring just to the boiling point. Reduce heat and simmer for 10 minutes, until hot and fragrant. Remove spices with a slotted spoon or strainer before pouring into glass mugs to serve. Makes about 18 (4-ounce/125 ml) servings.

Spiced Cranberry Cider

In this recipe, the juice of two Nova Scotian favourites—cranberries and apples—are combined to make a refreshing drink.

| 1 quart (1 L) apple cider
| 3 cups (750 ml) cranberry juice cocktail
| 1 tablespoon (15 ml) brown sugar
| 2 (3-inch/8 cm) sticks cinnamon, broken
| 3/4 teaspoon (3 ml) whole cloves
| 1/2 lemon, thinly sliced
| Additional cinnamon sticks, for stirrers (optional)

In a Dutch oven or large pot, bring to boil the apple cider, cranberry cocktail, brown sugar, broken cinnamon sticks, cloves and lemon slices. Reduce heat and simmer for 15 to 20 minutes. Strain cider, discarding spices and lemon. Serve hot with additional cinnamon sticks, if desired. Makes 7 cups (1.75 L).

Café au Lait Shake

Café au lait is made by pouring equal amounts of hot espresso and hot milk simultaneously into a heated bowl or large mug. But save the heating for cold wintry days. In summer, this coffee drink is better served cold.

1 tablespoon (15 ml) instant coffee
1 teaspoon (5 ml) sugar
2 cups (500 ml) cold milk
1/2 teaspoon (2 ml) vanilla
6 ice cubes

Combine coffee, sugar, milk, vanilla and ice cubes in blender. Blend until well mixed and ice is very finely broken up. Makes 2 servings.

Cranberry Liqueur

1 (12-ounce/340 g) package cranberries
1 orange
1 (750 ml) bottle vodka
1 1/2 cups (375 ml) granulated sugar
3/4 cup (175 ml) water

Chop cranberries coarsely. Pare orange with vegetable peeler, using only the thin orange part, no white.

Combine cranberries, orange parings and vodka in a glass or plastic one-gallon (4 L) container. Cover, and let steep at room temperature, for 3 to 4 weeks.

Strain into a clean container; filter or siphon off clear liquid if cloudy.

Combine sugar and water in a medium-size saucepan; bring to the boiling point. Boil 1 minute. Cool. Stir sugar syrup into cranberry-orange liquid. Taste. For a sweeter liqueur, more sugar syrup may be prepared and added. Makes about 5 cups (1.25 L).

Chef, author, and television host Bonnie Stern and Audrey Grantham, of Bedford

■ Some people have all the luck. Just ask Audrey Grantham of Bedford, who in September 2000 won a dinner for eight with Bonnie Stern, chef, author, and host of the television show *Bonnie Stern Entertains*. Early on the given day, Bonnie arrived at Audrey's door with assistant Rhonda Catlin, of Toronto, and Lynn Johnson, food and catering manager of the Italian Market in Halifax, who prepared most of the food and kept things going in the kitchen. Vanessa Quinn of Halifax was also there to help with preparations and serving. The feast started with Limencello Martinis (see Sunburst Martinis) and fabulous appetizers, including spicy Thai shrimp, served out on the deck on a lovely evening.

Sunburst Martinis

Since limencello liqueur is not listed in Nova Scotia liquor stores, Bonnie Stern offered Sunburst Martinis as an alternative to Limencello Martinis.

| 3 cups (750 ml) lemonade
| 1 1/4 cups (300 ml) vodka
| 1/4 cup (50 ml) orange liqueur

Shake (or stir), pour into martini glasses, add three fresh berries to the glass, and a slice of starfruit on the edge.

Blueberry Spritzer

On April 18, 1990, food and travel writers from Boston and surrounding areas were given a taste of Atlantic Canada at a luncheon aboard the Scotia Prince, *host ship of Seasell '90. The menu included steelhead salmon, cucumber salad, potato flan, fiddleheads with cranberries, and maple mousse. Pre-luncheon drinks were blueberry spritzers.*

| 1/4 cup (50 ml) blueberry syrup (recipe follows)
| 1/2 cup (125 ml) white wine
| 1 teaspoon (5 ml) lemon juice
| 1/2 cup (125 ml) soda water

Combine ingredients; pour over ice into tall glass or goblet. Garnish with a twist of lemon. Makes 1 (10-ounce/280 ml) serving.

Variation: Mix equal parts of white wine and blueberry cocktail. Add 1 teaspoon (5 ml) lemon juice, top with soda water and stir.

Blueberry Syrup

| 1 quart (1 L) fresh or frozen wild blueberries (equivalent to 600 g frozen pack)
| 1/3 cup (75 ml) water
| 1 1/2 cups (375 ml) granulated sugar
| 1/4 cup (50 ml) lemon juice

In saucepan, combine ingredients and bring to a boil. Reduce heat and simmer for 10 to 15 minutes. Cool. Strain, using fine sieve or cheesecloth. Cover and refrigerate. Makes 2 cups (500 ml).

soups

A bowlful of soup can be a comforting meal any day of the year. It can be served hot or cold—with a sandwich for lunch in April, a garden salad for supper in August, or on its own in February.

And it doesn't need to be made with homemade stock. Sure it's better to start from scratch if you have the time, but today's meal-makers often don't have time to make stock.

So, there are alternatives.

A healthful soup, packed with vegetables, legumes, grains, or a combination, can be made from scratch with water as the base.

Saved vegetable water is even more nutritious because of the nutrients that may have leached into the water when cooking the vegetables. Drain vegetables over a bowl, allow liquid to cool, then pour it into a plastic container and store in the freezer. Add to it each time you cook vegetables. Then, when you want to make soup, use it as a base.

Augment the stock water by saving peelings and vegetable scraps, such as celery leaves and onion skins, in a plastic bag in the freezer until you have enough to cook. Cover with water, bring to a boil, reduce heat and simmer for 30 minutes. Then strain, cool, and add to your vegetable water, or use it to make soup on the spot.

A good tomato soup can be made from tomato juice or vegetable juice cocktail. Or, combine a 28-ounce (796 ml) can of tomatoes, undrained, and a 10-ounce (284 ml) can of tomato soup, add seasonings to taste, and grated cheese for a satisfying and comforting bowl of "homemade" soup.

For a heartier nourishing soup, combine a 19-ounce (540 ml) can of undrained tomatoes, a 14-ounce (398 ml) can of beans baked in tomato sauce, and 1 cup (250 ml) of water, with chopped onions, seasonings and grated cheese.

But don't add salt when using canned tomatoes or soups—there's plenty of sodium in the canned goods, even if they're labeled "low-salt."

For "cream" soups, substitute low-fat milk or buttermilk for cream. To prevent curdling, add some of the hot soup mixture to the milk before adding it to the pot.

Canned broth is another alternative to homemade stocks. Although most cooks dilute the broth with an equal amount of water, I follow Toronto cooking school guru Bonnie Stern's example and use a 10-ounce (284 ml) can of broth with enough water to equal 4 cups (1 L) of liquid.

To reduce fat content, store canned broth in the refrigerator and remove congealed fat before using.

While there's nothing new to bouillon cubes, the new twist is that chicken and beef bouillons now come in instant-dissolving packets. That's another alternative to soup-making, although not for those on salt-restricted diets.

What constitutes a meal fit for a king? At least one person in Halifax once had the answer. After eighteen years in the food business, John Cooney, executive chef at the Nova Scotian Hotel, met his greatest challenge when he planned and executed a meal for the man who was raised to be king of England, and the woman whom fate had named his queen. Prince Charles and Princess Diana did not dine alone, of course; there were seven hundred invited guests who, along with their host, Prime Minister Pierre Trudeau, enjoyed the fruits of Chef Cooney's labour.

In planning the menu, the only instruction the chef had been given was to avoid poultry, shellfish, lamb, pork, and game. This had nothing to do with royal palates: the fear of contamination is ever in the forefront when planning meals for visiting royalty. "That pretty well left fish or beef," Cooney said. It was not difficult to make the choice. What was a concern was whether the fresh sole he had ordered a month ahead would be available on the precise day it was needed.

So, when his supplier phoned two days in advance to say the fish, all hand picked, separated from bones, packed in ice, and loaded into a refrigerated truck, was on its way from Glace Bay to Halifax, Chef Cooney was able to direct his energies elsewhere. By then, things had been planned, rehearsed and honed to perfection.

Health inspectors entered the hotel kitchen two days before the meal. Though royal tasters are a thing of the past, strict sanitary codes and conditions are enforced. Extra staff were hired. The twenty-five wait staff who would normally handle an event of these proportions were joined by another fifteen, and the cooking staff was increased by ten.

With everything ready, Chef Cooney directed the curtain to be raised on his performance. Did he get to hear the applause? No, he was too busy to take a bow. He didn't even get a peek at his royal patrons. After the last dish had been cleared away, Chef John Cooney sat down with a cup of tea. "Well, that's it," he said, simply. There was nothing to look forward to any more.

The menu for a royal couple consisted of the following: a first course of Liver Pâté with Moulin Rouge wine; second course: Annapolis Valley Fruit Soup; main course: Poached Sole Veronique with Parisienne Boiled Potato, Buttered Broccoli, Lemon Crown and Tomato Stuffed with Peas, L'Acadie Blanc wine; Green Leaf Salad; and for dessert,

Baked Apple Snow with Brut wine and Champagne.

The fruit soup recipe was developed by Chef John Cooney specifically for the occasion.

Fruit Soup

2 apples
1 pound (500 g) watermelon
1 pear
1/2 cantaloupe
1/2 honeydew melon
6 maraschino cherries (for colour)
2 tablespoons (30 ml) grenadine (for colour)
3/4 cup (175 ml) dry white wine
2 cups (500 ml) apple juice
1 kiwi fruit
1/8 teaspoon (.5 ml) ground allspice
Pinch of ginger
Pinch of nutmeg
Pinch of cinnamon
Pinch of mace
Garnish: Fresh lime slices

Peel and free all fruit of seeds. Add ingredients and seasonings to blender container and purée fine. Strain, pushing pulp through strainer as much as possible. Chill a few hours and serve in chilled cups. Garnish with a slice of lime. Makes 8 to 10 servings.

Note: All fruits are optional. Any can be omitted or added, according to taste or availability.

Tomato Onion Soup au Gratin

There's nothing wrong with getting a little help from canned chicken or beef bouillon, bouillon powder or bouillon cubes, but there's no need to add extra salt when using them—they contain plenty.

1/3 cup (75 ml) butter
4 cups (1 L) sliced onions
2 tablespoons (30 ml) flour
2 (10-ounce/284 ml) cans beef broth
2 cups (500 ml) water
1 (28-ounce/796 ml) can Italian-style tomatoes
Toasted French bread slices
2 cups (500 ml) shredded cheddar cheese

Melt butter in large saucepan; sauté onion slices until golden. Blend in flour, stirring, to cook for a minute or two. Gradually stir in beef broth and water. Cook, stirring, over medium heat, until mixture comes to a boil. Reduce heat, cover, and simmer for 10 minutes. Place tomatoes and juice in a blender container; cover and blend until smooth. Stir into ingredients in saucepan. Simmer 15 minutes longer.

Ladle into individual heat-proof bowls. Top with toast slices and sprinkle generously with cheese. Place under preheated broiler until cheese melts. Makes about 10 cups.

Real Mushroom Soup

5 tablespoons (75 ml) butter, divided
2 pounds (1 kg) fresh mushrooms, chopped
1 onion, chopped
1 tablespoon (15 ml) flour
8 cups (2 L) chicken broth
Salt and freshly-ground black pepper to taste

Use two frying pans to sauté mushrooms in a single layer, using 2 tablespoons (30 ml) butter in each pan.

Melt remaining 1 tablespoon (15 ml) butter in a large saucepan or soup pot. Add onion and sauté until limp. Stir in flour, reduce heat and cook, stirring for 2 to 3 minutes to cook the flour. Add cooked mushrooms.

Increase heat, gradually add broth and bring to the boiling point. Reduce heat again, cover, and let simmer gently for 20 to 25 minutes. Add salt and pepper to taste.

Optional: A little dry sherry and minced dill make this soup a culinary wonder.

Sauerkraut Soup

According to tradition, the Chinese accidentally discovered sauerkraut more than two thousand years ago, while the Great Wall was being built. The coolies' rations of cabbage and rice wine, when mixed together, eventually soured into something like sauerkraut. In Nova Scotia, sauerkraut is made commercially in several locations along the province's South Shore.

2 cups (500 ml) sauerkraut, drained and coarsely chopped
7 cups (1.75 L) beef stock or bouillon
1/3 cup (75 ml) diced bacon
1 large onion, coarsely chopped
1 large potato, peeled and grated
1 large apple, peeled, cored and grated
1 teaspoon (5 ml) paprika
2 tomatoes, peeled, seeded, and puréed
1/2 cup (125 ml) white wine, optional
1 teaspoon (5 ml) caraway seeds
1 (4-ounce/125 g) knackwurst sausage, thinly sliced
Garnish: 2 tablespoons (30 ml) minced fresh parsley

In a large saucepan, simmer sauerkraut in 4 cups (1 L) beef stock over medium heat. In a large deep skillet or Dutch oven, fry bacon over medium heat until it just begins to brown; add onion and cook, stirring, until golden, about 5 minutes.

Reduce heat to low, add potato, apple and paprika. Continue to cook, stirring, for 6 minutes. Gradually add remaining 3 cups (750 ml) stock. Add tomato purée, wine, sauerkraut mixture and caraway seeds. Stir until blended. Cover, bring to a boil, reduce heat and simmer gently for 45 minutes. Stir in knackwurst and heat through. Serve in soup bowls, garnished with parsley. Makes 8 to 10 servings.

Marie with Chef Linda Hatt

■ Linda Hatt, a talented chef who grew up in Lunenburg County, Nova Scotia, has never strayed far from her roots. She still lives there with her husband, Johnie, and nineteen-year-old son, Peter. A graduate of Nova Scotia Institute of Technology, she returned to the institute some years later to earn her chefs de cuisine status, an intensive course that sometimes knocks out more chefs than it qualifies: "It was one of the toughest things I've ever done, but it was worth it," she says. She's now pleasing palates at the Lunenburg Yacht Club. Known for her wonderful brunch buffets, Linda also excels at soups and traditional Lunenburg fare. She says her fiddlehead soup can be made with frozen fiddleheads, but for her it's a seasonal dish that she makes only when fresh fiddleheads are available.

Smoked Salmon Fiddlehead Soup

2 cups (500 ml) chicken stock
1 leek, washed and chopped
1 small onion, chopped
2 celery ribs, chopped
1 large carrot, chopped
8 ounces (250 g) fresh (or frozen) fiddleheads
4 ounces (125 g) smoked salmon, finely chopped
1 tablespoon (15 ml) dried dill weed
1/4 teaspoon (1 ml) white pepper
1 1/2 cups (375 ml) light cream (or milk)
Garnish: sour cream, chopped green onions

In large saucepan or soup kettle, combine stock, leek, onion, celery, carrot and fiddleheads. Cook until vegetables are tender; cool slightly.

In batches, purée in food processor or blender. Return to saucepan; add salmon, dill weed, pepper and cream. Heat gently. Taste and adjust seasoning. Serve in soup bowls, garnished with sour cream and green onions. Makes 8 (1 cup/250ml) servings.

Bean Chowder

Dried beans must be soaked for eight hours or longer, then cooked for an hour or more before they're ready to use in a recipe. One test for doneness is to remove a bean from the cooking water and blow on it. If the skin splits and curls back, the bean is cooked.

1/4 cup (50 ml) canola oil
1 cup (250 ml) chopped onion
1 cup (250 ml) chopped celery
1 clove garlic, minced
1/4 cup (50 ml) flour
1 bouillon cube
2 1/2 cups (675 ml) water
3 cups (750 ml) low-fat milk
5 cups (1.25 L) cooked Jacob's cattle or soldier beans
2 cups (500 ml) canned tomatoes
1 1/2 cups (375 ml) whole kernel corn
1 1/2 cups (375 ml) cut green beans (frozen or drained canned)
Dash of pepper
1 teaspoon (5 ml) salt (or less, to taste)

In soup kettle or Dutch oven, cook onion, celery and garlic in oil until soft. Blend in flour. Dissolve bouillon cube in water and add. Stir in milk and bring to a boil. Add cooked beans, tomatoes, corn and green beans. Heat to a gentle boil. Add pepper and salt. Makes 12 servings.

Note: For thicker chowder, purée 1 to 2 cups (250—500 ml) soup in blender and return to pot, stirring well. Leftovers can be frozen in portioned amounts.

Margaret Dickenson's Fast-Track Borshch

2 (12-ounce/340 ml) cans sliced beets
2/3 cup (150 ml) cold water
1 tablespoon (15 ml) crushed dark beef bouillon cubes
2 cups (500 ml) hot water
1 1/2 cans (12-ounce/340 ml) corned beef
2 teaspoons (10 ml) crushed fresh garlic
2/3 teaspoon (3 ml) crushed black peppercorns
2/3 teaspoon (3 ml) ground nutmeg
1 to 2 tablespoons (15 to 30 ml) chopped fresh dill
2 teaspoons (10 ml) white vinegar
Garnish: 1/2 cup (125 ml) sour cream
Fresh dill sprigs, optional

Drain juice from beets into a large saucepan; set aside. Cut 2/3 of drained beets into matchstick pieces; set aside. Place remaining beets in food processor, add 2/3 cup (150 ml) cold water and process into paste. Sieve purée into beet juice.

Dissolve crushed bouillon cubes in hot water; add to beet juice. Stir in corned beef, garlic, pepper, nutmeg and dill. Bring to boil over medium heat, cover, reduce heat to low, and barely simmer for 10 minutes. Add vinegar. Adjust flavour, adding a little more spice and vinegar or water.

Just before serving, heat cut beets in saucepan or microwave oven. Arrange beets in heated bowls and add enough hot soup to just cover beet sticks. Top with 1 to 3 teaspoons (5 to 15 ml) sour cream and a fresh sprig of dill if desired. Makes 4 to 6 main course servings.

Margaret Dickenson

■ Margaret Dickenson's degree in foods and nutrition from the University of Guelph has helped enormously in her role as an ambassador's wife. For over twenty-eight years she accompanied her husband, Lawrence T. Dickenson, in his foreign service postings around the world. Whether entertaining the prime minister at a formal dinner in Ottawa, an Indonesian buffet dinner for thirty, or an informal luncheon for four, Margaret follows her own blueprint for strategic planning. She tells how she did it all in *From The Ambassador's Table.*

Mitch Nauss

■ When tomato season kicks in, Mitch Nauss of East Chester gets out her electric food dehydrator and starts putting up a stash of dried tomatoes. While she uses whatever tomatoes are on sale at the time, she says the meatier plum tomatoes are a good choice for drying. She slices them 1/4 of an inch (5 mm) thick, lays them, seeds and all, on the dehydrator trays, plugs the machine in, and in about ten hours she has a good (and inexpensive) stock of dried tomatoes. She rehydrates them before using them in casseroles, sandwiches, scrambled eggs, on pizzas and burgers, or in soups, like Golden Squash and Tomato Soup.

Golden Squash and Tomato Soup

1 butternut squash (about 2 pounds/1 kg)
1 medium onion, sliced
1 tablespoon (15 ml) canola oil
2 1/2 cups (625 ml) water
1 cup (250 ml) dried tomato halves or slices
1 cup (250 ml) blend or milk
1 tablespoon (15 ml) chopped fresh basil or 1 teaspoon (5 ml) dried basil
Salt, to taste
Hot pepper sauce, to taste (optional)

Cut stem end from squash and halve lengthwise. Place cut sides down in a shallow microwave-safe dish and add 1/4 inch (5 mm) water. Cover with plastic wrap and microwave on high 12 to 14 minutes, until fork-tender, turning once. (Alternatively, you can bake the squash in a shallow baking pan with 1/2 inch/1 cm water in a 400F/200C oven for 45 to 60 minutes.)

In a 3-quart (3 L) saucepan over medium heat, sauté onion in oil about 5 minutes until limp. Add water and tomatoes, bring to a boil, reduce heat and simmer 5 minutes.

Discard squash seeds. Scoop squash pulp into food processor or blender. Add contents of saucepan; blend until smooth. Return to saucepan. Mix in milk and basil. Simmer 3 minutes. Thin with a little more water, if necessary. Season with salt and hot pepper sauce, if desired. Serve hot. Makes 4 to 6 servings.

Ron Downie's Hot Mediterranean Soup

1 (10-ounce/284 ml) can tomato juice
1 (10-ounce/284 ml) can beef bouillon
2 soup cans water
1(7.5-ounce/225 g) can tomato sauce
2 teaspoons (10 ml) sugar
1/2 teaspoon (2 ml) salt
1/4 teaspoon (1 ml) dried basil
1/8 teaspoon (.5 ml) thyme
1/2 inch (1 cm) piece of bay leaf, crumbled
freshly ground black pepper

Combine ingredients in soup kettle; simmer 15 minutes. Transfer to large tureen; serve in mugs. Makes 6 servings.

Add the following Pistou to the soup.

Pistou

3 cloves garlic
1/4 cup (50 ml) chopped fresh basil or 2 tablespoons (30 ml) dried
2 tablespoons (30 ml) chopped fresh parsley
1 tablespoon (15 ml) tomato paste
1/4 cup (50 ml) grated parmesan cheese
3 tablespoons (45 ml) olive oil

Use mortar and pestle or finely chop garlic, basil, and parsley. Gradually work in tomato paste and parmesan. Blend in olive oil, 1 tablespoon (15 ml) at a time. Thin out pistou with a little hot soup. Add to soup, a little at a time, to taste. (This recipe makes enough to flavour the quadrupled amount of soup.)

Variations:
* Add Tabasco sauce or horseradish and sprinkle with parsley and parmesan cheese.
* Add 1 teaspoon (5 ml) dried basil, 1 tablespoon (15 ml) chopped fresh parsley, 1/2 teaspoon (2 ml) minced garlic and 1/2 cup (125 ml) grated parmesan cheese.

Ron Downie

■ Halifax lawyer Ron Downie knows his way around the kitchen, and loves to try to out-guess the chefs while watching cooking shows. Experimenting may be part of the challenge that keeps him interested in cooking, but once he finds a good recipe he doesn't change it. His Hot Mediterranean Soup recipe is such a favourite that he wouldn't think of excluding it from the traditional gathering of family and friends on Christmas Eve. Ron's wife, Marie, does the rest: "…she makes a big Greek salad, homemade bread, and tourtieres, and sometimes we'll have spiced beef, if we remember to get it started ten days ahead of time," he says. "And, of course, we'll have a splash of rum punch or wine to go with it." The recipe serves six people, but the Downies quadruple it to accommodate their extended family of twenty-two.

Fred MacGillivray

■ There's nothing that will stop Halifax businessman Fred MacGillivray from doing the best that can be done. As an after-school carry-out boy, he early set his sights on—and was promoted to—top management in the grocery business. I didn't ask about his marks at Saint Mary's University, but he graduated, and has since received two honorary degrees. He excels as a volunteer and community leader, and has many awards and recognitions to show for his spirit and dedication. Count on two hands the number of boards on which he serves, and a full hand on those he chairs. But, closer to the subject of this book, there's something else that Fred is good at: the chowder he makes every Christmas Eve. He's so proud of it he's named it after himself!

Freddie's Lobster Chowder

2 medium potatoes, peeled and diced
1 medium onion, diced
2 cups (500 ml) water
1 1/2 cups (375 ml) milk
2 cans evaporated milk
1 teaspoon (5 ml) salt
1/4 teaspoon (1 ml) pepper
1 (11-ounce/320 g) can frozen lobster, broken or cut into bite-size pieces
1/4 cup (50 ml) butter
Seafood seasoning

Bring potatoes and onion to boil in water. Reduce heat and simmer, covered, until potatoes are just tender (do not drain). Add milk, evaporated milk, salt, pepper and lobster, including liquid. Bring to a simmer—do not boil. Add butter and seafood seasoning to taste. Serve with warm rolls. Makes 8 servings.

Quick Fish Chowder

There's nothing like a hearty chowder to warm you up after February's brisk winds and minus-degree temperatures have chilled you to the bone. Even when time is short, it just takes a little planning and a well-stocked pantry to get a comforting bowl of chowder quickly to the table.

1 tablespoon (15 ml) canola oil
1 onion, chopped in large dice
1 clove garlic, crushed
1 (28-ounce/796 ml) can tomatoes, chopped, undrained
Dash of Worcestershire sauce
Pinch of oregano
Pinch of black pepper
1 pound (500 ml) frozen fish fillets, cut in 1-inch (2.5 cm) pieces
Chopped green onion or parsley

In large saucepan, sauté onion and garlic in hot oil until onion is soft, about 5 minutes. Add remaining ingredients; bring to a boil. Reduce heat, cover and simmer for 15 minutes or until fish flakes easily with a fork. Sprinkle with green onions or parsley. Makes 4 servings.

Carole Regan

■ When Carole Regan, wife of Gerald Regan, former international trade minister, decided to invite several MPs' and senators' wives to a luncheon, she called on some of her guests to help bring the Maritimes to Ottawa— with resounding success. The forty to fifty women who attended, including Aileen Chrétien, were welcomed by a piper outside the door. Inside, a Cape Breton fiddler offered his own accompaniement to the hors d'oeuvres of cod cakes and Solomon Gundy. But it was Carole's seafood chowder that most impressed the guests. Today, Carole says she changes the ingredients to whatever is in season and not too expensive. "If it's for family, I might not use lobster. I save that for special occasions. If the haddock is fresh, I use that. I've even used salmon," she says.

Carole Regan's Seafood Chowder

2 cups (500 ml) diced potatoes
I cup (250 ml) chopped onion
1/2 cup (125 ml) diced celery
1/2 teaspoon (2 ml) salt
1/2 pound (250 g) scallops
1/2 pound (250 g) haddock
1/2 pound (250 g) halibut
I can evaporated milk
4 cups (I L) milk
I (2-ounce/57 g) can lobster paste (see note)
I (11-ounce/320 g) can frozen lobster
1/4 pound (125 g) shrimp
1/4 cup (50 ml) butter
salt and pepper, to taste
2 tablespoons (30 ml) sherry

Cover potatoes, onions, celery and salt with hot water and simmer for 20 minutes or until fork tender. At the same time, in a separate pot, steam scallops, haddock and halibut until fish flakes, about 10 minutes. Do not overcook. Combine fish and vegetable mixtures, including cooking water. Heat evaporated milk and homogenized milk and add to fish and vegetables.

Add lobster paste, lobster, shrimp and butter. Heat together and add salt and pepper to taste. Add sherry and serve. Fish can be used according to availability. Sometimes Carole makes the chowder using only haddock as the seafood.

Note: Lobster paste, available at most fish counters, is optional, but adds flavour and colour, Carole says.

sandwiches

The fourth Earl of Sandwich gets my vote as the most famous food-related name of all time. Too busy at the gambling table to stop to eat, John Montagu (1718–1792) ordered a portable lunch be brought to him so he could munch as he played. History tells us the meal that kept the earl gambling was nothing more than a slab of cold roast beef between two slices of bread. Since then, almost any filling placed between bread slices has been called a sandwich.

But how times—and sandwiches—have changed! Now there are hot sandwiches, cold sandwiches, club sandwiches, loaf sandwiches, French-toasted sandwiches, stacked sandwiches, rolled sandwiches—everything from dainty tea sandwiches to a hearty Reuben on rye. Betcha the earl would be impressed as his portable lunch continues to grow in popularity in many countries of the world. In fact, according to the Canadian Restaurant and Foodservice Association, sandwiches ranked seventh in the top ten menu items in 1995. But I wonder what the earl would think about his name being dropped as new forms have been adopted. Still, a sandwich is a sandwich, whether it's a hero, submarine, grinder, hoagie, po' boy, muffuletta, Croque Monsieur, a burger, or a wrap.

As people travel, they discover new food ideas and bring them home to their own kitchens. And so, regular white or brown bread is often replaced with the Mexican staple tortilla, the Greek phyllo, Italian focaccia, French croissant, Ukranian perogy or Middle-Eastern pita. All are good bases for the fast-food wrap, but especially the pliable tortilla

Brenda and Joe Treige sampling muffeletta in New Orleans

and pita. One of the oldest breads in the world, the tortilla is available in local supermarkets, both fresh and frozen. Traditionally made of cornmeal, but more popular here when made of wheat flour, the tortilla is an unleavened flat, round bread. It's fried on a griddle and is best served warm. It's used in many Mexican and Tex-Mex dishes, including fajitas, quesadillas, tostadas, burritos and, when fried until crisp and folded to make shells, tacos. However, in tune with the trend, tortillas are becoming a delicious replacement for bread as "roll-ups" and "wraps."

Pita bread also has many origins and uses. This "pocket" bread is a natural for those who like to take their meal with them to eat on the fly. Had the Earl of Sandwich been so lucky, he never would have missed a roll of the dice.

Smoked Turkey Wraps

8 ounces (250 g) light cream cheese, softened
1/4 cup (50 ml) light mayonnaise or salad dressing
2 tablespoons (30 ml) prepared mustard
8 flour tortillas (9-inch/23 cm)
16 slices smoked deli turkey
1 bunch green onions, chopped
8 lettuce leaves, washed and dried

Cream together cream cheese, mayonnaise and mustard. Spread on tortillas. Arrange two slices of turkey on each tortilla, leaving 1/2 inch (1 cm) border of cheese at top. Sprinkle with onion and top with lettuce. Roll up tightly, pressing firmly to seal. Wrap tightly and refrigerate until serving time. Cut in half diagonally. Makes 8 servings.

Mitch's Wraps

Large soft flour tortillas or pitas
Dijon or honey mustard
Black Forest ham
Swiss cheese slices
Romaine lettuce
Rehydrated dried tomatoes
Salt and pepper, to taste

Lightly spread tortillas or pitas with mustard. Layer with ham, cheese, lettuce and tomatoes. Season with salt and pepper. Roll up jelly-roll style. Insert toothpicks and cut on the diagonal into halves. Allow two halves per serving.

Mona Yuskiw

■ Mona Yuskiw, who lived for six years in Walton, Nova Scotia, before settling in Calgary, was one of those women who loved to cook and was good at it— good enough to have her favourite recipes gathered in a cookbook. For a time, *Cooking with a Touch of Class* appeared to be as much in demand as the hot cakes Mona made when she was a cook in a North Saskatchewan mining camp.

Not only did she meet the challenge of cooking everything from what has been called "the best perogy in the world" to Peking duck, but you couldn't fool her taste buds. She could eat a dish in a restaurant and go home and duplicate the recipe, without anyone telling her what was in it. Mona Yuskiw is gone now, but her Reuben sandwiches, served with her French onion soup and crunchy dill pickles, remains a family favourite.

Reuben Sandwiches

2 cups (500 ml) sauerkraut
1/4 of a green pepper, diced
2 green onions, diced
2 tablespoons (30 ml) canola oil
1/2 teaspoon (2 ml) salt
1/4 teaspoon (1 ml) pepper
16 slices rye bread
16 slices corned beef
8 slices mozzarella cheese
16 slices cold roast turkey
1/2 pound (250 g) butter, softened

Drain sauerkraut through a sieve, squeezing out all the juice. Turn sauerkraut into a bowl and add green pepper, onion, canola oil, salt and pepper. Mix well and refrigerate for an hour to blend flavours.

Lightly butter all 16 slices of bread. Divide sauerkraut evenly over buttered side of 8 bread slices, and top each with 2 slices of corned beef, a slice of cheese, and 2 slices of turkey. Cover with a slice of bread, buttered side down. Press down firmly.

Butter top of bread slices and place, buttered side down in frying pan over medium heat. Butter the other side of the bread, which is now on top, and cook (at 350F/180C if using an electric frying pan) to a golden brown. Turn and cook other side. Cut in half and serve with bowls of your favourite soup. Makes 8 servings.

Apple Raisin Peanut Butter

For many parents, the beginning of school means the start of the constant sandwich-go-round and the daily decision of what goes into the lunch box. We should be grateful to that St. Louis, Missouri, doctor who invented peanut butter in 1890. No matter which way you spread it, peanut butter is the hands-down packed-lunched favourite of children. And when combined with whole wheat bread, a glass of milk, and a piece of fruit, such as an orange or apple, it constitutes a well-balanced meal.

1/2 cup (125 ml) chunky peanut butter
1/2 cup (125 ml) unpeeled, diced apple
1/4 cup (50 ml) raisins
1/2 teaspoon (2 ml) ground cinnamon

Combine all ingredients in a small bowl. Spread between bread slices. Makes about 1 cup (250 ml) or enough for 4 sandwiches.

Seafarer's Submarine

Leftover fish can make creative lunches in a submarine bun or pita pocket. Letting children add their own ingredients, such as cheese, lettuce, tartar sauce, tomato, and other good things, might make them more open to trying something new.

| 1 pound (500 g) fish fillets, cooked
| 1/4 cup (50 ml) tartar sauce
| 4 submarine rolls, halved
| 1/4 cup (50 ml) butter
| 2 cups (500 ml) shredded lettuce
| 1/4 cup (50 ml) French dressing
| 2 tomatoes, sliced
| 1/2 cup (125 ml) grated Swiss cheese

Combine cooled, flaked fillets with tartar sauce. Spread both halves of rolls with butter. Scatter lettuce over each half and sprinkle with dressing. Spread fish mixture on bottom halves, using 1/2 cup (125 ml) for each sandwich. Top with tomato slices and cover with grated cheese. Close sandwich. Makes 4 servings.

Bourbon Street Po' Boy

| 6 tablespoons (90 ml) butter or margarine
| 6 tablespoons (90 ml) flour
| 1 large onion, sliced
| 1 small green pepper, sliced
| 2 cups (500 ml) beef broth
| 1 teaspoon (5 ml) Worcestershire sauce
| 3/4 teaspoon (3 ml) Tabasco pepper sauce
| 1/2 teaspoon (2 ml) dried leaf thyme, crumbled
| 1 pound (500 g) cooked, thinly sliced beef
| 4 hero rolls

In a medium saucepan, melt butter and stir in flour. Cook over medium heat, stirring constantly until flour browns, about 4 minutes. Add onion and green pepper; cook, stirring constantly about 5 minutes. Gradually stir in broth. Add sauces and thyme. Stir constantly until mixture boils and thickens.

Cut thin slice from top of each roll; scoop out insides. Arrange meat on rolls. Spoon gravy over and replace tops. Makes 4 servings.

Norma McCulloch

■ If you're tired of the same old sandwiches and think there's nothing new between the slices, you might like to turn the pages of an old recipe book that offers a different sandwich for every day of the year. The book, which has lost its cover and offers no clue of its age or place of publication, was found by Norma McCulloch, of Halifax, among her late mother's belongings.

Norma doesn't know where the book came from but says her mother had it since before the Second World War: "…possibly, she brought it with her or got it on one of her trips back to Barrie, Vermont, where she grew up." Clues such as the names of sandwiches—Alabama, Boston, and George Washington—indicate the book was printed in the United States. "There were some unusual combinations there," Norma says—olives, cheese, and anchovies, for instance; or peanut butter and tomato ketchup.

Egg and Smoked Salmon Sandwiches

Cut white bread in strips 4 inches (10 cm) long and 1 1/2 inches (4 cm) wide. Toast lightly on one side. Spread untoasted side with 1/2 cup (125 ml) softened butter to which has been added the mashed and sieved yolks of 2 hard-cooked eggs. Season with salt, a few grains of cayenne and 1/2 tablespoon (7 ml) finely chopped parsley. Spread an equal number of slices of bread the same size with anchovy paste. Cover with very finely minced smoked salmon moistened with mayonnaise. Put together in pairs, press lightly and arrange in a sandwich basket. Garnish each sandwich with a slice of gherkin. Serve with potato salad.

Chicken Sandwich Souffle

Cooked chicken is one of the greatest assets fast-lane cooks can have. To help with mid-week meals, it's worth a little time on weekends to cook a couple of chickens and freeze the meat in meal-size packages. Before leaving for work in the morning, take a package from the freezer and put it in the refrigerator to thaw. On arriving home, you can pull an entire meal together in under an hour.

12 bread slices, crusts removed
3 cups (750 ml) chopped cooked chicken
6 slices Swiss cheese
2 large eggs, beaten
1 can (10-ounce/284 ml) undiluted condensed cream of chicken soup
2 tablespoons (30 ml) chopped onion
3/4 teaspoon (4 ml) dry mustard
1 tablespoon (15 ml) fresh lemon juice
1/3 cup (75 ml) chopped pimiento
1/2 cup (125 ml) milk

Grease a 12x8-inch (30x19 cm) shallow baking dish. Lay 6 bread slices on bottom of dish, top with chicken, cheese and remaining bread slices.

Combine remaining ingredients and beat well. Pour sauce over sandwiches; let stand at room temperature for 10 minutes. Bake in a 350F (180C) oven for 40 minutes or until golden and puffy. Makes 6 servings.

Homemade Cheese Spread

If you like the convenience of a cheese spread, but you're skeptical about what the bottled variety contains, you can create your own. It tastes even better than the over-salted "real thing."

1/2 pound (250 g) medium cheddar cheese, shredded (about 2 cups/500 ml)
1 cup (250 ml) evaporated milk
1 1/2 tablespoons (22 ml) granulated sugar
1 1/2 teaspoons (7 ml) all-purpose flour
1/2 teaspoon (2 ml) dry mustard
2 teaspoons (10 ml) vinegar
1/4 teaspoon (1 ml) garlic salt
1/4 teaspoon (1 ml) salt
1/8 teaspoon (6 mm) Worcestershire sauce
1/8 teaspoon (6 mm) molasses

Combine ingredients in top of double boiler; cook, stirring, until cheese melts. Remove from heat and beat until smooth. Store in refrigerator. Makes about 2 cups (500 ml).

Great Canadian Sandwich

1 (9-inch/23 cm) round Italian or French loaf
2 tablespoons (30 ml) olive or canola oil
1 clove garlic, minced
1/4 teaspoon (1 ml) dried oregano
1 large tomato, sliced
1 cup (250 ml) thinly sliced cucumbers
1/4 cup (50 ml) chopped pitted olives
6 slices fully cooked back bacon
2 ounces (50 g) part-skim mozzarella cheese, thinly sliced
6 slices smoked chicken breast
1 sweet green pepper, cut into rings
1 sweet yellow pepper, cut into rings
1–2 tablespoons (15-30 ml) Dijon mustard

Mix oil, garlic and oregano; let stand 5 minutes. Cut bread in half horizontally; hollow out each side of each half, leaving a 1-inch (2.5 cm) border. Brush oil mixture over inside of bottom bread shell. Arrange half of tomato slices inside shell. Layer with cucumbers, olives, bacon, cheese, chicken, remaining tomato, green and yellow pepper. Brush top bread shell with mustard; sandwich on top of pepper rings. Wrap with plastic wrap. Refrigerate 1 hour or up to 8 hours. Slice in wedges and serve. Makes 8 servings.

salads

August is the peak season for much of the local produce. What better way to enjoy the bounty than by tossing it together in interesting combinations during the salad days of summer? You don't need a recipe or any great amount of ingenuity. Just seek out the freshest ingredients available and toss them together with gentle abandon. Lettuce is a good place to start. And using more than one variety heightens texture, colour, and flavour. The crispness of iceberg lettuce blends well with rich-green leaves of romaine, pale bibb, curly green or red-tip leaf lettuce, or dark, nutritious spinach. A handful of mixed fresh herbs, including parsley, chervil, mint, chives, and sweet basil leaves will perform wonders when added to the salad bowl.

Salad greens need tender care to protect the vitamins and minerals they contain. Here are a few tips:

Leaves should be separated, washed in cold water, drained, spun dry, and stored in perforated plastic bags in the refrigerator.

Spinach, chard, and kale should be washed just before using and may need two or three washings, plunging and lifting them several times to release trapped dirt.

All greens are at their most nutritious when used within a couple of days of picking.

Try not to discard the darker, outer leaves, which contain the most nutrients.

Never cut greens with a knife, which causes darkening.

Shred vegetables, such as cabbage, just before serving, since air destroys some of the vitamin C content.

Don't overlook beets. Peeled and shredded raw with half to 3/4 as much celery, tossed with a mustard-flavoured

Apart from his ten-year stint as chef at The Pines Resort, in Digby, Nova Scotia, Claude AuCoin is a multi-award winning chef who has earned his creditation as chef de cuisine, and recently added international sommelier to his achievements. He and his wife, Diane, manage a large herb and edible flower garden at the resort.

vinaigrette, covered and refrigerated for at least six hours or up to four days, they make a delicious and unusual salad or side dish.

Make use of parsley. It can be chopped and added to almost any salad. Or mix a whole bunch with tomatoes, cucumbers, and scallions, dress with oil and lemon juice, and chill before serving.

Use a vegetable peeler to remove bitter-tasting fibrous strands of celery.

For a low-fat, creamy dressing, season buttermilk or low-fat yogurt with herbs and thicken with a little calorie-reduced mayonnaise. And, remember, a little dressing goes a long way. To keep the fat out of the salad, try using half your normal amount of dressing.

Garden Patch Rice Salad

2 1/2 cups (625 ml) water
1 cup (250 ml) converted rice
1 teaspoon (5 ml) salt
8 ounces (250 g) fresh green beans, cut in 1-inch (2.5 cm) pieces
8 to 10 cherry tomatoes, halved
1/2 cup (125 ml) sliced red onion
1/4 cup (50 ml) canola oil
1/4 cup (50 ml) vinegar
2 cloves garlic, minced
1/4 to 1/2 teaspoon (1—2 ml) pepper
1/2 cup (125 ml) coarsely crumbled blue cheese

In a medium saucepan, bring water to boil. Stir in rice and 1/2 teaspoon (2 ml) salt. Cover tightly, reduce heat and simmer for 20 minutes. Remove from heat; let stand covered until all water is absorbed, about 5 minutes. Transfer to a large bowl; cool to room temperature.

Cook green beans until tender-crisp; immediately rinse with cold water; drain. Add to rice along with cherry tomatoes and onion.

Combine oil, vinegar, garlic, pepper and remaining 1/2 teaspoon (2 ml) salt in small bowl; whisk well. Stir dressing into rice mixture. Cover and chill. Just before serving, gently stir in blue cheese. Makes 6 servings.

Super Buffet Macaroni Salad

1 cup (250 ml) elbow macaroni
8 cups (2 L) boiling water
2 teaspoons (10 ml) salt
1 small head of lettuce, thinly sliced
1 cucumber, sliced
1 green pepper, seeded and sliced
1 cup (250 ml) celery, sliced
2 red onions, sliced
3/4 cup (175 ml) mayonnaise
3/4 cup (175 ml) low-fat plain yogurt
1/2 cup (125 ml) grated cheddar cheese
3 slices bacon, cooked and crumbled

Gradually add macaroni and salt to boiling water so that water continues to boil. Cook uncovered, stirring occasionally, until tender. Drain in a colander. Rinse under cold water; drain and chill.

continued on next page

Arrange shredded lettuce over bottom of glass bowl. Add a layer of macaroni and each of the other vegetables. Mix together mayonnaise and yogurt and spread over salad. Cover and refrigerate overnight. Just before serving, garnish with cheese and bacon bits. Makes 8 servings, more as a buffet offering.

Oriental Pasta Salad

Besides containing no cholesterol and being rich in monounsaturated fats, peanuts and peanut butter are an economical source of protein and supply many vitamins and minerals.

12 ounces (350 g) dry fettuccine or linguine, preferably tri-colour
3 green onions, sliced
1 1/2 cups (375 ml) sliced mushrooms
1/3 cup (75 ml) shredded basil or chopped coriander
3 tablespoons (45 ml) chopped peanuts

Dressing:
1/4 cup (50 ml) soy sauce
2 tablespoons (30 ml) peanut butter
2 tablespoons (30 ml) white wine vinegar
2 tablespoons (30 ml) water
1 1/2 tablespoons (22 ml) granulated sugar
1 1/2 tablespoons (22 ml) finely chopped peeled ginger
1 tablespoon (15 ml) peanut oil
1/2 teaspoon (2 ml) sesame oil
Couple of drops of hot pepper sauce

Bring a large saucepan of salted water to boil. Add pasta and cook until tender, 4 to 8 minutes, depending on pasta. Drain well and rinse under cold running water. Drain very well. Turn into a large bowl. Toss with onions, mushrooms, basil and peanuts.

Whisk dressing ingredients together until blended. Toss pasta with dressing. Taste and adjust seasoning, if necessary. Salad can be covered and refrigerated for up to 3 days. Makes 4 servings.

Thai Chicken Salad

3 cups (750 ml) cooked, cooled converted rice
1 1/2 cups (375 ml) shredded cooked chicken
1 cup (250 ml) torn fresh spinach
1 medium-size red pepper, julienned
1/2 cup (125 ml) sliced fresh mushrooms
1/4 cup (50 ml) chopped unsalted peanuts
2 green onions, sliced
1 tablespoon (15 ml) chopped fresh basil
2 tablespoons (30 ml) chopped fresh coriander
1/3 cup (75 ml) hot water
3 tablespoons (45 ml) rice vinegar
2 tablespoons (30 ml) peanut butter
2 tablespoons (30 ml) soy sauce
1 tablespoon (15 ml) sesame oil
1 clove garlic, minced
Pinch red pepper flakes
Garnishes: chopped fresh coriander, chopped unsalted peanuts

Combine rice, chicken, spinach, red pepper, mushrooms, peanuts, green onions, basil, and coriander in large bowl.

Combine water, vinegar, peanut butter, soy sauce, sesame oil, garlic, and red pepper flakes in small bowl. Just before serving pour dressing over salad and toss. Garnish with coriander and peanuts. Makes 6 servings.

■ Ralph Hatt, of M.A. Hatt & Son Ltd. in Lilydale, Lunenburg County, has been making sauerkraut since 1971, when he joined his father's twenty-five-year-old business. Following an expansion in 1974, the operation puts out over one hundred tons of sauerkraut every year, most of which is marketed in Nova Scotia. But does Ralph go for the old wives' suggestion to cut the sauerkraut when the moon is waxing, so the brine will rise and impart a better flavour to the 'kraut? He has heard the tale, but for him, sauerkraut-making is a year-long operation. He can't wait for any moon! As for drinking sauerkraut juice to cure a hangover, he's heard that one too, but couldn't say if it really works.

Crunchy Sauerkraut Salad

2 cups (500 ml) cooked, cooled sauerkraut, drained
1 can (14 –ounce/398 ml) garbanzo beans, drained
1/4 cup (50 ml) diced pimiento, drained
1 cup (250 ml) chopped onion
1 cup (250 ml) chopped celery
1/2 cup (125 ml) granulated sugar
1/2 cup (125 ml) herbed vinegar
1/2 cup (125 ml) herbed olive oil
lettuce leaves (optional)

In a large bowl, combine sauerkraut, garbanzo beans, pimiento, onion and celery. In a small saucepan, combine sugar and vinegar; bring to a boil. Stir in oil; remove from heat. Pour over sauerkraut mixture; cover and chill overnight. Serve on a bed of lettuce, if desired. Makes about 6 servings.

Strawberries and Cucumbers

When looking for an interesting summer salad, could anything be more refreshing than the combination of cool cucumbers and strawberries? This is especially nice when served with fish.

2 medium cucumbers
24 large strawberries
Salt and pepper to taste
2 to 4 tablespoons (30 to 60 ml) dry white wine or white vinegar

Peel and thinly slice the cucumbers. Wash, hull, drain, and thinly slice the strawberries. Beginning at the outer edge, arrange the slices in a shallow serving dish, alternating and overlapping the strawberries and cucumbers in rows. End with a centre of strawberries. Season lightly with salt and pepper, and sprinkle with wine or vinegar. Chill in refrigerator before serving.

■ At a potluck affair, a friend talked about the wonderful crunchy salad she had brought. The recipe came from her daughter, with the stipulation that it wasn't to be passed around. Too bad, I thought, it would have been a good one to share with my readers. Shortly after that, I visited my son Bob and his family in Edmonton. While there, I attended a cooking class in the well-equipped kitchen of food consultant and cookbook author Eleanor Clark. There on the menu was the same salad I had enjoyed at the potluck back home. Fate must have brought it to me!

Cauliflower and Broccoli Crunch Salad

Dressing:
1/2 cup (125 ml) mayonnaise
1/4 cup (50 ml) cider vinegar
1 package seasoning from Ichiban soup mix or Mr. Noodles Oriental
1/4 cup (50 ml) granulated sugar

Salad:
1 head broccoli
1 small cauliflower
4 carrots, diagonally sliced
1 red onion, diced
Noodles from Ichiban soup mix or Mr. Noodles Oriental, crushed
8 slices cooked bacon, crumbled
1/2 cup (125 ml) cup sunflower seeds
1/2 cup (125 ml) raisins
1 box cherry tomatoes, halved

Combine dressing ingredients in jar with tight-fitting lid; store in refrigerator. Combine salad ingredients. Before serving, shake dressing, pour over salad and toss. Makes 8 to 10 servings.

Cool Taco Bean Salad

A serving of beans is higher in fibre than an apple, a baked potato, or a serving of bran flakes, cabbage, or broccoli.

Taco Filling:
1 pound (500 g) ground beef
1/2 cup (125 ml) barbecue sauce
1/4 cup (50 ml) water
2 teaspoons (10 ml) chili powder
1/2 teaspoon (2 ml) seasoned salt
Pinch of garlic powder
Pinch of cayenne pepper
1 can (14-ounce/398 ml) beans with pork in tomato sauce

Salad mixture:
1/4 cup (50 ml) chopped green onion
1 cup (250 ml) diced cucumber
1 cup (250 ml) sour cream
1 head iceberg lettuce, finely shredded
2 cups (500 ml) chopped tomatoes
2 cups (500 ml) grated cheddar cheese
Garnish: 1 cup (250 ml) tortilla chips

Prepare filling: In skillet, cook beef until browned; drain. Add barbecue sauce, water, chili powder, seasoned salt, garlic powder, cayenne pepper and beans. Simmer over low heat for 10 minutes. Cool completely.

Prepare salad: In medium bowl, combine onion, cucumber and sour cream; set aside. In large glass salad bowl, spread half of shredded lettuce in a layer. Follow with a layer of half of each of taco filling, tomatoes, grated cheese and sour cream mixture; repeat layers. Arrange tortilla chips on top. Chill 30 minutes before serving. Makes 6 to 8 servings.

Waldorf Supreme Salad

2 cups (500 ml) diced, unpeeled apples
1 cup (250 ml) thinly sliced celery
1/2 cup (125 ml) chopped walnuts
1/2 cup (125 ml) diced seedless raisins
1/2 cup (125 ml) diced oranges or pineapple
1 1/2 tablespoons (22 ml) chopped parsley or green onion
2 cups (500 ml) diced cooked chicken, turkey or ham
1/4 teaspoon (1 ml) curry powder (optional)
(about) 1/2 cup (125 ml) mayonnaise or lemon dressing (recipe follows)

Combine all ingredients and toss until well coated with dressing. Add salt and pepper to taste. Chill before serving. Makes 6 to 8 side salads.

Lemon Dressing:
1 cup (250 ml) reconstituted lemon juice
1 cup (250 ml) canola oil
1 tablespoon (15 ml) salt
1 teaspoon (5 ml) pepper
1/2 cup (125 ml) granulated sugar
4 tablespoons (60 ml) honey

Blend ingredients together. Makes 2 cups.

Seven Layer Jellied Salad

Be sure each layer of Jell-O is firm but still a bit tacky so the next layer will adhere without seeping through to the previous one. To help unmould the salad, first rub pans with paper towel sprinkled with a small amount of cooking oil. (Use just a little oil so the flavour isn't affected.) Alternatively, rinse the pan with cold water without drying it before you pour in the first layer.

1 package (85 g) each cherry, lime, lemon, orange, mixed fruit or lime,
    watermelon and strawberry jelly powders
1 (385 ml) can evaporated milk

For first layer, dissolve cherry jelly powder in 3/4 cup (175 ml) hot water. Stir in 3/4 cup (175 ml) cold water. Pour into a 13x9x2-inch (33x23x5 cm) pan, two ring moulds, two 8-inch (20 cm) square pans, or two 9x5-inch (23x13 cm) loaf pans. Refrigerate until firm.

continued on next page

For second layer, dissolve lime jelly powder in 1/2 cup (125 ml) hot water. Add 1/2 cup (125 ml) cold water and 1/2 cup (125 ml) evaporated milk. Pour over first layer and refrigerate until firm.

Repeat process with other jelly powders, adding milk to fourth and sixth layers, and letting each layer firm before adding the next.

With a knife, carefully loosen jelly from sides of pan. Turn onto large, flat serving tray. Shake gently to release. Slice crosswise about 1-inch (2.5 cm) in width, and cut each slice into three. Makes 39 servings.

Main Dish Fruit Salad

1/2 cup (125 ml) mayonnaise
1 tablespoon (15 ml) lemon juice
2 teaspoons (10 ml) granulated sugar
2 medium bananas, sliced
1 1/2 cups (375 ml) cantaloupe balls
1 medium peach, peeled and cubed
1 cup (250 ml) cubed fresh or canned pineapple
1 cup (250 ml) seedless green grapes, halved if large
1 cup (250 ml) fresh strawberries, halved
1 1/2 cups (375 ml) watermelon balls
Lettuce leaves
3 cups (750 ml) cottage cheese
6 fresh strawberries

Combine mayonnaise, lemon juice and sugar; stir well and set aside. Combine fruit, tossing gently. Spoon into six individual lettuce-lined serving dishes, and top each with 1/2 cup (125 ml) of cottage cheese. Slice 6 strawberries lengthwise, keeping stem end intact; fan out on top of each salad. Serve with mayonnaise dressing. Makes 6 servings.

Lemon Cheddar Salad

1 (3-ounce/85 g) package lemon jelly powder
1 cup (250 ml) boiling water
1 (14-ounce/398 ml) can crushed pineapple and juice
1 cup (250 ml) whipping cream
1 cup (250 ml) grated cheddar cheese

Combine jelly powder and boiling water in a bowl. Stir to dissolve jelly powder. Stir in crushed pineapple and juice. Chill until mixture is the consistency of egg white.

Whip cream until stiff. Fold into thickened jelly. Fold in grated cheese. Pour into your prettiest bowl. Chill. Garnish with orange slices, if desired. Makes 10 servings.

Variation: One cup (250 ml) of miniature marshmallows can be added with the whipped cream and cheddar cheese.

Red Pepper Slaw

When buying peppers, choose those that are firm and glossy, with no wrinkling or soft spots. Store, unwashed, in a perforated plastic bag in the refrigerator, for up to five days. Once cut, they deteriorate quickly.

3 small red bell peppers, 1 whole, 2 thinly sliced
1/2 medium head of green cabbage, finely shredded
1 small onion, thinly sliced
1/2 cup (125 ml) thinly sliced sour gherkins or other pickles
1 garlic clove, minced
1/3 cup (75 ml) mayonnaise
2 teaspoons (10 ml) white wine vinegar
Salt and freshly ground black pepper

Roast whole red pepper under broiler, turning until charred all over, about 5 minutes. Place in paper bag; set aside for 10 minutes to steam. When cool enough to handle, peel pepper and remove core, seeds, and ribs. Slice in thin strips.

In large bowl, combine cooked and uncooked peppers with cabbage, onion, gherkins, garlic, mayonnaise and vinegar. Season with salt and pepper. Cover and refrigerate until ready to serve. (Can be made up to a day ahead.) Makes 4 servings.

Jean Paré

■ Just four years after the first "Company's Coming" cookbook appeared, Alberta author Jean Paré and her company had sold one million copies. "Come join us in celebrating a milestone in Canadian publishing," read the invitation that went out to friends, business associates, and media across the country. She's been called a publishing phenomenon and "the supermarket recipe queen." But to me she is just a regular person, and I miss her since she stopped doing promotional book tours—we always found a lot to talk about when we got together for lunch or an interview. Jean told me once that it was beyond her comprehension that her name was a household word in her hometown of Vermilion, Alberta, let alone across the globe. But Canadians know and love her best, and prove it by collecting her dozens of cookbooks, known for their good, easy, every-day recipes.

breakfast/brunch

There have been a lot of changes in the way we think of food since we took our three daily meals at mother's dining room or kitchen table. Back then, there wasn't much talk about vitamins, protein, or carbohydrates. Certainly no one used the word cholesterol. Nor did they give much thought to fat. We ate a lot of butter and fried pork scraps, and wouldn't have had it any other way. How did we survive?

For one thing, we started the day with a good breakfast. In those days, especially in winter, breakfast meant hot oatmeal porridge, cream of wheat, or Red River cereal, preceded by an orange and followed by buttered whole wheat toast with homemade jam or marmalade. For a beverage, there was milk for children and coffee for adults. Whether we ate breakfast because we were hungry or just to get rid of the taste of the cod liver oil that started our day is of little concern.

Many breakfasts have gone under the nose bridge since those days. And the metamorphosis is almost complete. We've just about come the full circle. Didn't our mothers tell us to eat our porridge? Our fruits and vegetables? And whole grain breads? She did. And if she referred to fibre (she called it roughage), it was only a passing interest. But I don't remember her ever saying anything about cholesterol or triglycerides, and fat was something poured into a jar after the bacon was cooked. Who ever heard of saturated, polyunsaturated, or monounsaturated anything back then?

With the current focus on the link between diet and health, there's a familiar ring to what nutritionists are telling us are the right kinds of food—foods that are nutrient-dense, high in fibre and complex carbohydrates, and low in fat.

It didn't take me long to realize that Mary Elizabeth Stewart, of Dartmouth, Nova Scotia, is an efficient person whose organizational skills would serve Cuisine Canada well. She hesitated only briefly when I asked that she let her name stand for regional director. At that level, others recognized her value and she was eventually elected chair of the national organization. After thirteen years with the Beef Information Centre, Mary Elizabeth has retired to open two new businesses. She now provides communications and marketing services to the agri-food industry through Stewart Communications and Marketing, and is also the proprietor of the newly opened garden accessories and gift shop, The Secret Garden, in downtown Halifax.

Sunflower-Prune Oatmeal

1 1/2 cups (375 ml) water
2/3 cup (150 ml) rolled oats
Pinch of salt
6 pitted prunes, chopped
Pinch ground cinnamon
1 tablespoon (15 ml) unsalted raw sunflower seeds
1 tablespoon (15 ml) honey

Bring water to boil in a medium-size saucepan. Stir in oats, salt, prunes and cinnamon. Reduce heat and simmer 4 to 5 minutes until thick. Stir in sunflower seeds and honey. Serve with orange juice to pour over cereal. Makes 2 servings.

Multigrain Cereal Mix

Nutritionists tell us that many Canadians need to double their intake of fibre and complex carbohydrates, and that there's no better opportunity to get started on the daily supply than with whole-grain, bran and other high-fibre cereals and fruit, preferably with edible skin intact. You can vary your cereal choices—a hot cereal today, a cold one tomorrow—and sprinkle a little whole bran cereal on top. If you're not used to bran cereal, it's wise to start with a tablespoon or two (15 to 30 ml) and slowly increase it. This will help prevent stomach cramps while your body adjusts.

1 cup (250 ml) quick-cooking rolled oats
1 cup (250 ml) oat bran
1 cup (250 ml) whole-grain cereal (i.e. Red River)

Combine ingredients and store in a tightly sealed container. Makes 3 cups (750 ml). Each serving equals 1/2 cup (125 ml).

Hot Multigrain Cereal

1/4 cup (50 ml) cereal mix (above)
3/4 cup (175 ml) water
Dash maple or vanilla extract

Microwave method: In microwave-safe bowl, combine ingredients. Microwave, uncovered, on high 2 minutes; stir. Microwave on low 3 minutes. Let stand 2 minutes. Stir, serve. For more than one serving, choose deep bowl or 2-cup (500 ml) glass measuring cup to prevent boiling over.

Stove-top method: Combine ingredients in saucepan. Cook on medium-low heat 3 to 5 minutes or until desired consistency; stir occasionally. Cover and remove from heat; let stand a few minutes. Stir and serve.

Options: Add 1 teaspoon (5 ml) raisins, chopped dried apples or apricots. Replace maple or vanilla extract with a pinch of ground cinnamon or nutmeg.

Make Ahead French Toast

8 slices day-old bread (white enriched, whole grain or raisin)
6 eggs
1 cup (250 ml) milk
3 tablespoons cinnamon sugar or honey
1 teaspoon (5 ml) vanilla extract

Grease well a rimmed cookie sheet and arrange bread slices so that they do not touch. Beat together eggs, milk, sweetener and vanilla. Spoon and spread half the mixture evenly onto bread. Turn slices and spoon remaining mixture on other sides. For each side, allow time for mixture to absorb.

Bake in a 425F (220C) oven about 10 minutes. Turn and bake another 10 minutes. Let cool and then wrap tight. Freeze in portions required for breakfast.

To serve, unwrap and heat in toaster or toaster oven.

Brunch-or-Breakfast-in-a-Pan

Entertaining for brunch can be easy when the main dish is assembled the night before. Perfect for breakfast, brunch, or lunch, it also is a handy dish to serve on those television sports days, like The Grey Cup.

16 slices white bread, crusts removed
8 slices ham or back bacon, cooked
8 slices sharp cheddar cheese or 1 cup (250 ml) grated
6-8 eggs
1/2 teaspoon (2 ml) salt
1/2 teaspoon (2 ml) pepper
1/2 teaspoon (2 ml) dry mustard
1/4 cup (50 ml) minced onion
1/4 cup (50 ml) chopped green pepper
1 teaspoon (5 ml) Worcestershire sauce
2 1/2 cups (625 ml) whole milk
3 drops Tabasco sauce
1/2 cup (125 ml) butter
1 cup (250 ml) Special K or cornflake crumbs

Generously butter a 13x9-inch (34x23 cm) glass baking dish. Cover bottom of dish with slices of bread, followed by slices of ham or back bacon, then cheese. Cover with another layer of bread.

In a mixing bowl, beat eggs and add all other ingredients except butter and cereal crumbs. Pour over bread layer, cover, and let stand in refrigerator overnight.

Half and hour before you're ready to bake the dish, remove from refrigerator and bring to room temperature. Melt the butter, pour over top, then sprinkle with cereal crumbs. Bake, uncovered, in a 350F (180C) oven for 50 to 60 minutes. Let sit for 10 minutes before serving. Makes 8 servings.

Dawn Loner of Halifax reads "the food page" as she prepares to munch on a bar or two taken with a glass of milk.

Fruity Nut Breakfast Bars

There are days, let's face it, when you just don't have time for breakfast. Rather than resort to the usual fast-food offering, keep a supply of these tasty, high-fibre, and nutritious breakfast bars on hand to take with you. They'll supply enough energy to last until lunch time.

1 cup (250 ml) whole wheat flour
3/4 cup (175 ml) Bran Buds or All-Bran cereal
1/2 cup (125 ml) rolled oats
2 tablespoons (30 ml) sesame seeds
1 teaspoon (5 ml) baking powder
1/4 teaspoon (1 ml) baking soda
1/4 teaspoon (1 ml) salt
1 teaspoon (5 ml) grated lemon rind
6 tablespoons (90 ml) frozen orange juice concentrate, thawed
1/4 cup (50 ml) raisins
1/2 cup (125 ml) shredded coconut
1/2 cup (125 ml) chopped walnuts
1/2 cup (125 ml) soft butter
1 cup (250 ml) firmly packed brown sugar
1 egg

Combine flour, Bran Buds, rolled oats, sesame seeds, baking powder, soda, salt and lemon rind; set aside. Mix together orange juice, raisins, coconut and walnuts; set aside.

Cream butter and sugar; add egg and beat until light and fluffy. Stir in flour mixture. Press half of the dough into a greased 8-inch (20 cm) square pan. Spread fruit mixture over the dough, then press remaining dough on top. Bake in a 350F (180C) oven about 30 minutes, or until done. Cut into bars to serve. Makes 12 (3x1 1/2 inch/7.5x3.75 cm) bars.

Oatmeal Breakfast Cookies

Incorporating as little as two to three tablespoons (30 to 45 ml) of combined oat and wheat bran is usually enough to take advantage of the substantial benefits that bran has to offer.

3/4 cup (175 ml) soft margarine
1 cup (250 ml) brown sugar
2 eggs, beaten (or 3 egg whites)
3 tablespoons (45 ml) molasses
1/2 cup (125 ml) low-fat milk
1 cup (250 ml) whole wheat flour
1 cup (250 ml) bran
3/4 teaspoon (3 ml) baking soda
1 teaspoon (5 ml) salt
2 cups (500 ml) quick-cooking oats
1 to 2 cups (250 to 500 ml) raisins

Blend margarine, sugar, eggs, molasses and milk. Add flour, bran, baking soda and salt. Mix well. Blend in oats and raisins. Drop large tablespoonfuls (20 ml) onto greased cookie sheet. Bake in a 375F (190C) oven 10 to 12 minutes, Makes 4 dozen cookies.

Sunshine Breakfast

To freeze bananas, simply mash them, add a little lemon juice to retard discolouration, pour into containers, and place in the freezer for up to two months. Or spoon banana purée into ice cube trays—one tablespoon (15 ml) per cube. When the cubes are well frozen, remove them and pack them in a plastic bag. Three cubes equal half a banana.

3/4 cup (175 ml) orange juice
1 small carrot, sliced
1/2 banana
1 egg
1/3 cup (75 ml) skim milk powder
1 teaspoon (5 ml) honey

Pour orange juice into blender container, add carrot and process at high speed until carrot is liquefied. Add remaining ingredients, cover and process until smooth, about 10 seconds. Makes 2 servings of about 1 cup (250 ml) each.

pancakes, griddle cakes, crepes

If you don't flip over griddle cakes, but adore French crepes, Chinese egg rolls, Russian blini, Italian cannelloni, Mexican tortilla, or Jewish blintzes, you can still be counted among the world's pancake aficionados. Most countries have their own version of pancakes, considered to be the oldest form of bread. Even before the discovery of fire, grain would be pounded, mixed with water, and spread on a hot rock to dry. Times, thankfully, have changed, but stories of pancakes are still recorded in history.

As with so many famous food innovations, Crepes Suzette are said to have been the result of an accident. Chef Henri Carpenter was preparing crepes for King Edward VII when the contents of the pan accidentally caught fire. Not one to keep a king waiting, the chef carried the flaming pan to the table and when the fire died, he served the little pancakes to the king and his companions. He called them Crepes Suzette after his host's daughter.

But more than any other day, Shrove Tuesday has kept the tradition of pancakes alive and cooking. On the eve of Ash Wednesday and the beginning of Lent, it was necessary to get all animal food and perishables eaten up. Somebody had the bright notion to combine these ingredients with flour and, in so doing, cleared the larder of such "impurities."

History dubs pancake day a celebration. In central European and Latin nations it was even considered a carnival. The German word for the festival is fastnacht, "even of the fast." In old Russia, the people feasted on blini (small yeast-raised pancakes) served with butter, sour cream, smoked salmon, and pickled herring. In Olney, England, women turned out for the pancake race , running a 415-yard course while carrying a griddle and flipping a pancake along the way. The Austrians had their Kaiser-schmarren, Hungarians their palacinta,

the Swedes their flaaskpannkaka, the Dutch their pannekoekan or the thinner flensjes, the Indian their chapatti, and the Scots their oatcakes. In Canada, the flapjack helped to settle the west, where it was served almost daily with thin beef steaks and eggs for breakfast. But no matter how you flip it, a pancake is still a pancake.

She leads a double life, triple if you count her home life, and more considering the help she gives her husband in running their greenhouse operation. Dorothy Long is administrator for Saskatchewan Bounty, home economist for Canolainfo, and executive director for Cuisine Canada. Every year she puts on what she calls "Canola Camp," which brings twelve or more people from Canada, the United States, Mexico, and abroad to Saskatoon to learn about the canola industry. Not the least of these events centres around eating some of the wonderful Saskatchewan bounty.

Craig wasn't cooking with me yet, but he showed an early interest in food and how it was prepared. This photo, taken by his Uncle Gary, was one of three that appeared with a *Chronicle-Herald/Mail-Star* story.

Power Packing Pancakes

1 cup (250 ml) whole wheat flour
1 cup (250 ml) all-purpose flour
1 tablespoon (15 ml) baking powder
1/2 teaspoon (2 ml) salt
3 eggs, separated
2 tablespoons (30 ml) sugar
1 cup (250 ml) orange juice
1 cup (250 ml) milk
1/4 cup (50 m L) butter or margarine, melted
3 oranges, peeled and diced
1/3 cup (75 ml) dried currants
3/4 cup (175 ml) coarsely chopped pecans

Sift together whole wheat and all purpose flours, baking powder and salt. In large mixer bowl beat egg yolks. Add sugar, orange juice, milk and melted butter; beat until smooth. Add dry ingredients and stir just until moistened. (Batter should be slightly lumpy.) Stir in diced oranges and currants. Fold in beaten egg whites.

Heat frying pan or griddle and grease lightly. Pour about 1/4 cup (50 ml) batter for each pancake onto griddle. Sprinkle with pecans. When bubbles appear on top and pancake is puffed, turn and brown other side. Makes about 36 pancakes (6 to 8 servings.)

Sybil's Pancakes

■ Boondock Pancake House in Earltown, Nova Scotia, used to serve Sybil's Pancakes on weekends from mid-March to the end of the maple sap season. Under the new ownership of Scott Whitelaw and Quita Gray and now called Sugar Moon Farm, the restaurant serves Sybil's Pancakes year round— with some adjustments to the recipe—under the maple syrup produced on the premises.

2 cups (500 ml) flour (whole wheat, all-purpose, or combination)
2 teaspoons (10 ml) baking powder
1 teaspoon (5 ml) baking soda
2 tablespoons (30 ml) canola oil
1 egg
buttermilk
hot water, about 1/2 cup (125 ml)

In a bowl, combine dry ingredients. In a 2-cup (500 ml) measure, combine oil and egg; whisking lightly with a fork. Add buttermilk to come to the 2-cup (500 ml) level. Combine with dry ingredients, adding about 1/2 cup (125 ml) hot water.

For each pancake, pour about 1/3 cup (75 ml) batter onto a hot griddle; cook until bubbles appear on top, then flip to cook other side. Serve with pure maple syrup and baked beans, if desired.

Vera Schwartz

■ When Vera Schwartz of Halifax makes pancakes, breads, and biscuits, she begins with the sourdough her parents, Elaine and Edward MacHardy, of MacLellan's Mountain, Nova Scotia, started using more than thirty years ago. "Dad used to experiment with starter made with potato water and kept trying to duplicate the flavour" Vera recalls. When Elaine joined the search, she found a recipe in a trappers' magazine, and the couple began to unravel the intricacies of a sourdough starter. The culture they made in 1970 is still active today.

Several years ago, Vera brought some of the starter home and has been using it for her own family, replenishing it with 1/2 cup (125 ml) of flour and 1/2 cup (125 ml) of water to keep it active.

Vera's Mother's Sourdough Pancakes

2 eggs, lightly beaten
1 1/2 cups (375 ml) milk
3 tablespoons (45 ml) melted butter
1 1/2 cups (375 ml) flour
1 tablespoon (15 ml) sugar
3/4 teaspoon (3 ml) salt
2 teaspoons (10 ml) baking powder
1/2 teaspoon (2 ml) baking soda
1 cup (250 ml) sourdough

In a small bowl, combine lightly beaten eggs, milk and melted butter.

In a large bowl, combine flour, sugar, salt, baking powder, and baking soda. Make a hole in the centre and add sourdough and milk mixture. Stir until mixed. Batter should have the consistency of heavy cream. To thin, add liquid or to thicken, add flour. Ladle batter onto a hot lightly greased griddle and cook until bubbles cover top. Turn to brown other side. Makes 12 large pancakes.

Blueberry Pancakes

At their best, pancakes are light and fluffy. To accomplish this, the batter should be mixed only until ingredients are dampened. Yes, it will be lumpy, but don't worry, it will smooth out during cooking. The batter improves if made an hour or two in advance.

2 eggs
2 1/4 cups (550 ml) milk
1 tablespoon (15 ml) canola oil
2 cups (500 ml) all-purpose flour
2 tablespoons (30 ml) sugar
3 teaspoons (15 ml) baking powder
1/2 teaspoon (2 ml) salt
Blueberries

Beat eggs, add milk and oil. Add dry ingredients which have been sifted together (mixture will be a little lumpy). Ladle a scant 1/4 cup (50 ml) batter onto moderately-hot, lightly greased griddle. Sprinkle a few blueberries on top of each pancake and cook until brown underneath and bubbly on top. Turn to brown other side. Makes about 20 pancakes.

Fresh Strawberry Puff Pancake

1/4 cup (50 ml) butter
3 eggs
1 1/2 cups (375 ml) milk
1/2 cup (125 ml) sugar
3/4 cup (175 ml) all-purpose flour
1/4 teaspoon (1 ml) salt
3 cups (750 ml) strawberries, halved
Sour cream
Brown sugar

Place butter in a 9-inch baking dish or ovenproof frying pan. Put in a preheated 425F (220C) oven until butter melts and bubbles, about 10 minutes.

Measure out 2 tablespoons (30 ml) of the sugar and set aside. In a bowl, combine remaining sugar with eggs, milk, flour and salt; beat until smooth.

Remove pan from oven and immediately pour batter into hot pan. Return to oven and bake for 30 minutes, or until edges are puffed and browned.

Combine strawberries and reserved 2 tablespoons (30 ml) of sugar. Spoon strawberries into centre of hot pancake. Cut into wedges and pass sour cream and brown sugar. Makes 4 servings.

Raisin Rice Griddle Cakes

The sauce can be made ahead and reheated.

I cup (250 ml) milk
I cup (250 ml) cooked rice, cooled
2 eggs, separated
I tablespoon (15 ml) melted butter or margarine
1/2 teaspoon (2 ml) vanilla
1/2 teaspoon (2 ml) salt
1/2 teaspoon (2 ml) ground cinnamon
I cup less 2 tablespoons (250 ml less 15 ml) all-purpose flour
1/3 cup (75 ml) raisins
Orange Marmalade Sauce (recipe follows)

In large bowl, mix milk, rice, egg yolks, butter, vanilla, salt, and cinnamon to blend thoroughly. Sprinkle flour over rice mixture; mix to blend well.

In another bowl, beat egg whites until stiff peaks form; fold into rice mixture. Gently mix in raisins. On a hot, greased griddle or skillet over medium heat, bake quarter-cupfuls until browned, turning once. Grease griddle and repeat as necessary. Serve hot with Orange Marmalade Sauce. Makes 12 griddle cakes.

Orange Marmalade Sauce: In small saucepan over low heat, stir 1/2 cup (125 ml) orange marmalade until melted. Add 1/4 cup (50 ml) butter or margarine and 1/2 cup (125 ml) orange juice. Stir until butter is melted. Serve slightly warm. Makes about I cup (250 ml).

■ The eight-day celebration of Hannukkah, Festival of Lights, is a time for rejoicing and eating latkes, the much-loved potato pancakes traditionally served with applesauce and/or sour cream. While the traditional recipe directs the cook to grate pounds of potatoes by hand (a little skin from the knuckles makes it even more authentic), some cooks, like Bea Zemel of Halifax, have turned to the food processor for help. The resulting smooth batter means sacrificing the lacy appearance, but the flavour remains.

Bea Zemel's Food Processor Latkes

4 medium potatoes, pared
1 onion
2 eggs
1/3 cup (75 ml) all-purpose flour
1 teaspoon (5 ml) baking powder
3/4 teaspoon (3 ml) salt
Freshly ground black pepper, to taste
Oil for frying

Using steel knife, cut potatoes in chunks and onion in half. Place in food processor with eggs; process until puréed, 20 to 30 seconds. Add remaining ingredients except oil; process a few seconds to blend smooth.

Pour oil to a depth of 1/8 inch (6 mm) into large skillet. When hot, drop in potato mixture by large spoonfuls to form pancakes. Brown well on both sides. Drain well on paper towels. Makes about 2 dozen.

Note: These freeze well. To reheat, place frozen latkes in single layer on ungreased, foil-lined baking sheet. Bake uncovered, at 450F (230C), 7 to 8 minutes, until crisp and hot.

Light and Crisp Belgian Waffles

Traditionally, Belgian waffles were baked between two heavy iron plates. The plates were usually decorative and stamped with family emblems or religious scenes. Modern versions are streamlined with deeper wells and grids—the better to hold all those delectable toppings.

2 egg yolks
2 cups (500 ml) milk
2 cups (500 ml) all-purpose flour
1 tablespoon (15 ml) baking powder
1/2 teaspoon (2 ml) salt
1/3 cup (75 ml) canola oil
2 egg whites, stiffly beaten

Preheat waffle maker.

Put in mixer bowl egg yolks, milk, flour, baking powder, salt and oil; combine on low speed until moistened. Increase speed to medium and mix until smooth. Using a rubber spatula, gently fold beaten egg whites into batter.

Pour 1/2 cup (125 ml) batter over centre of heated grids. Close waffle maker and bake about 2 1/2 minutes, or until golden. Repeat until all batter is used. Serve hot with desired topping. Makes 18 waffles.

Chicken and Mushroom Crepes

Here's a savoury rather than sweet filling for crepes.

2 eggs
I cup (250 ml) milk
I cup (250 ml) all-purpose flour
1/4 teaspoon (I ml) salt
I tablespoon (15 ml) canola oil
No-stick cooking spray
I tablespoon (15 ml) butter or margarine
3 tablespoons (45 ml) finely chopped onion
1/2 cup (125 ml) finely chopped celery
1/4 pound (125 g) mushrooms, thinly sliced
3 tablespoons (45 ml) flour
1/4 teaspoon (I ml) salt
one and three quarter cups (425 ml) chicken broth
1/2 teaspoon (2 ml) dried thyme, crumbled
2 cups (500 ml) diced cooked chicken
2 tablespoons (30 ml) chopped fresh parsley
I pound (500 g) fresh asparagus, trimmed and chopped

To make crepes: Combine eggs, milk, I cup (250 ml) flour, 1/4 teaspoon (I ml) salt and oil; beat until well blended. Chill I hour.

Spray a small skillet or crepe pan, 5 to 6 inches (13 to 15 cm) in diameter, with cooking spray. Heat over medium heat. Pour batter, 2 to 3 tablespoons (30 to 45 ml) at a time, quickly rotating pan to spread batter evenly. Cook over medium heat to brown lightly, about one minute on each side. Slide onto a plate; when cool, stack with wax paper in between.

To make filling: Spray a medium saucepan with cooking spray. Add onion, celery and mushrooms; cover pan. Cook over medium heat, about 3 minutes. Add butter and heat just until melted. Stir in 3 tablespoons (45 ml) flour and 1/4 teaspoon (I ml) salt; cook I or 2 minutes. Gradually stir in chicken broth. Cook, stirring constantly until sauce thickens and bubbles. Add about I cup (250 ml) of sauce to chicken; mix well.

Place about 2 tablespoons (30 ml) filling on each crepe; roll up and place, seam side down in sprayed pan. Spoon remaining sauce over crepes; bake in a preheated 375F (190C) oven for 15 minutes to heat through. Makes 8 servings.

eggs

It appears that the good old egg isn't such a bad egg, after all. A Harvard School of Health study indicates all the fitful clucking about what lies just inside that shell—namely fat and cholesterol—is outdated and overstated. Due to better laying hens and more nutritious feed, today's egg has twenty-three per cent less fat and thirty-one per cent less cholesterol than at the beginning of the 1980s. For years, this nutrient-rich and highly available food has posed a dilemma for health professionals.

On the positive side, the egg is recognized as one of the most nutritious foods. In one little package you can get more than six grams of protein, twenty-nine per cent of the daily recommended intake of vitamin B12, fifteen per cent of folacin and pantothenic acid, fourteen per cent of riboflavin, and nine per cent of the vitamin E the body needs daily. And since eggs are also a source of zinc, phosphorus, niacin, and vitamins A and D, how could nutritionists not recommend them?

The negative factor is their perceived high fat content, a substance to be avoided by people suffering from or at risk of cardiovascular disease. And the old count of 274 milligrams of cholesterol must have sounded almost lethal to those with high blood cholesterol. (The 1999 nutrient analysis indicates that cholesterol values have dropped to 190 mg). But Harvard's fourteen-year study of 118,000 people concludes the risk of cardiovascular problems doesn't increase whether you eat less than one egg a week or more than an egg a day. In other words, says Halifax Registered Dietitian Pam Lynch, "eating up to one egg a day poses no risk for healthy adults."

Registered Dietitian Pam Lynch

Pam says that she's always thought the egg has been much maligned over the years: "It's a good meat alternative choice, especially for vegetarians who have difficulty getting enough protein in their diets." With the average consumption at 3.5 eggs a week, she says an egg a day would be reasonable for men and women who don't have diabetes, high cholesterol, or risk for heart disease. "That would include, of course, eggs used in cooking."

Devilled Eggs

To hard-cook eggs, place in a single layer in a saucepan. Add enough water to cover eggs by at least 1 inch (2.5 cm). Quickly bring to a full boil. Remove pan from heat, cover and let stand for 19 minutes. Immediately run cold water over eggs until completely cooled. Hard-cooked eggs will keep in the refrigerator, in or out of the shell, for up to 1 week.

12 hard-cooked eggs
1/2 cup (125 ml) mayonnaise
2 tablespoons (30 ml) soft butter
1 1/2 tablespoons (22 ml) Dijon mustard
Dash of cayenne
Salt, pepper, and lemon juice to taste
Garnish: Paprika

Cut eggs in half lengthwise; remove yolks into a bowl. Mash yolks with a fork. Add mayonnaise, butter, mustard, cayenne, salt, pepper, and lemon juice. Pipe yolk mixture into whites. Garnish with a sprinkling of paprika. Makes 24 appetizers.

Mushroom Egg Foo Yung

Yolk colour indicates what a chicken eats, not its nutritional value. A hen laying eggs with dark, yellow-orange yolks is corn-fed. A pale yolk means the chicken is fed wheat. Dark or light, eggs are a powerhouse of nutrition.

Sauce:
3/4 cup (175 ml) chicken stock
1 tablespoon (15 ml) soy sauce
1 tablespoon (15 ml) cornstarch
2 tablespoons (30 ml) cold water
Omelettes:
6 eggs
1 teaspoon (5 ml) salt
1 cup (250 ml) bean sprouts
1 cup (250 ml) chopped mushrooms
1/2 cup (125 ml) finely chopped green onion

Prepare sauce: Dissolve cornstarch in water. In a medium-size saucepan bring stock to a boil. Add soy sauce and cornstarch mixture; cook over low heat until thickened. Keep warm.
Prepare omelettes: In a medium-size bowl, beat together eggs and salt until blended.

Add bean sprouts, mushrooms and onions. Pour 1/4 of the mixture into a lightly greased frying pan over medium-high heat. Cook about 1 minute until lightly browned on the bottom, then turn and cook on the other side for another minute. Transfer omelette to a heated serving plate and keep warm. Repeat with remaining egg mixture. Serve sauce over omelettes. Makes 4 servings.

Maritime Morning Eggs

2 English muffins
Mayonnaise
4 slices cooked ham
4 eggs, poached
4 slices cheese, cut into strips

Split muffins in half with fork; spread each half generously with mayonnaise. Top each half with a slice of ham. Place muffins in a covered baking dish and warm them in a 350F (180C) oven about 15 minutes. Top each muffin with a well-drained poached egg; arrange cheese strips in lattice design on top. Return to oven and bake, uncovered, until cheese melts. Makes 4 servings.

Egg and Chicken Scramble

2 slices bacon
1/4 cup (50 ml) sliced green onions
1 small garlic clove, minced
1/2 teaspoon (2 ml) basil leaves, crushed
1 (10-ounce/284 ml)) can condensed cream of chicken soup
8 eggs, slightly beaten
1 cup (250 ml) cubed cooked chicken
1/4 cup (50 ml) chopped pimiento

In frying pan, cook bacon until crisp; remove and crumble. Pour off all but 2 tablespoons (30 ml) drippings. Cook onions with garlic and basil in drippings until tender. Combine soup and eggs. Pour into frying pan. Cook over low heat. As mixture begins to set around edges, gently lift cooked portions with large turner so that thin, uncooked portion can flow to the bottom. Add remaining ingredients. Continue gently lifting cooked portions until eggs are completely set, but still moist (about 8 minutes). Garnish with bacon. Makes 4 servings.

Shae Griffith in the kitchen at Fairfield Farm Inn

■ It's always nice to pick up a newly published book and see a local connection. Such was the case when in May 1999 I started thumbing through *Rise and Dine Canada*, by Marcy Claman. Not only is this book a guide to some of Canada's cozy bed and breakfast inns, but it contains three hundred tempting and appealing recipes. Included among several of Nova Scotia's B&Bs is Fairfield Farm Inn, Middleton, where Shae and Richard Griffith take pride in offering warm hospitality and wholesome country breakfasts like Maritime Morning Eggs.

Egg Strudel

1 (10-ounce/300 g) package frozen chopped spinach, thawed, and squeezed dry
1 cup (250 ml) finely chopped almonds (optional)
1 onion, chopped
1 garlic clove, crushed
1/2 cup (125 ml) melted butter, divided
8 eggs
1 1/2 cups (375 ml) grated Swiss cheese
1 teaspoon (5 ml) ground nutmeg
1/2 teaspoon (2 ml) ground allspice
Salt and pepper to taste
1 (16 ounce/454 g) package strudel pastry (phyllo), thawed

In a bowl, combine spinach and almonds, if using. In a skillet, sauté onion and garlic in 1 tablespoon (15 ml) butter. Add to spinach and almonds.

In another bowl, beat eggs. Add cheese and seasonings. Line a greased 13x9-inch (33x23 cm) pan with 1 sheet of pastry, brush with some melted butter; repeat until there are 8 buttered pastry sheets.

Cover pastry with spinach mixture. Pour in egg and cheese mixture. Top with 4 more buttered sheets of pastry. Roll up edges and seal.

Slit top of strudel. Brush with melted butter. Bake at 400F (200C) for 30 to 40 minutes, until pastry is golden and crisp.

Cut strudel into thick slices; serve warm. Makes 8 servings.

Bernard Benoit's Favourite Omelette

1 teaspoon (5 ml) butter or bacon fat
1/2 cup (125 ml) cooked ham, diced
1 small onion, chopped fine
1/4 cup (50 ml) red or green pepper, slivered
Salt and pepper to taste
1 3-Egg Omelette (page 62)

Place butter or bacon fat in a 1-cup (250 ml) glass measuring cup or a microwave-safe bowl and melt 1 minute at high. Add ham, onion, and red or green pepper. Stir well. Microwave 2 minutes at high, stirring once. Add salt and pepper to taste. Add a small pinch of sugar. Make the omelette.

Marie and Madame Benoit

■ Canada's culinary grand dame, Madame Jehane Benoit, is gone, having died of a heart attack in November 1987, but her legacy lives on, not only because of her pioneering work with the microwave, but through the library of her work compiled by her husband. Bernard Benoit was in Halifax in late 1990 to introduce two cookbooks he was instrumental in publishing after his wife's death. Jehane's Favourite 3-Egg Omelette and Bernard Benoit's Favourite Omelette are from *The Best of Madame Benoit's Illustrated Encyclopedia of Microwave Cooking.*

Jehane's Favourite 3-Egg Omelette

3 eggs
3 tablespoons (45 ml) sour cream
Salt and pepper to taste

Break eggs into a bowl. Add sour cream, salt and pepper; mix all together. Butter generously a 9-inch (23 cm) ceramic pie plate and pour in egg mixture. Cover with wax paper. Microwave 2 minutes at medium. Stir lightly, moving the outer portions of omelette to centre of plate. Microwave another 2 minutes at medium.

Place your choice of filling or sauce in middle and fold omelette over. Microwave 30 seconds more at medium-low. Serve. (No standing time necessary.)

Tuna Frittata with Peas

A frittata is an open-faced unfolded version of the omelette. Vegetables, cheese, meat or other filling ingredients are combined with eggs, placed over direct heat until the underside is browned, and then put in the oven or under the broiler, or covered with a lid, to set the top. Frittatas, served hot or cold, can be cut into wedges and served as a light meal, or cut into 1- to 2-inch (2.5–5 cm) squares for appetizers.

2 tablespoons (30 ml) butter or margarine
1 small onion, chopped
1 rib celery, chopped
3 eggs
1/4 cup (50 ml) milk
1/4 teaspoon (1 ml) salt
Pinch pepper
1/2 cup (125 ml) frozen peas, thawed
1 (170 g) can tuna, drained, flaked
1 tablespoon (15 ml) grated parmesan cheese

In two 6-inch (15 cm) or one 10-inch (25 cm) ovenproof frying pans, melt butter over medium heat. Sauté onion and celery for 3 minutes.

Whisk together eggs, milk, salt and pepper. Stir in peas and tuna. Pour into frying pan(s). (To make handle ovenproof, wrap completely in foil.) Bake in preheated oven at 350F (180C) for 4 minutes. Sprinkle with cheese. Bake 3 or 4 minutes longer or until set. Cut into wedges to serve. Makes 2 servings.

No Crust Low Calorie Quiche

I've been using this recipe since 1976, and it still holds up as an easy-to-prepare yet nutritious and delicious meal.

1 pound (500 g) spinach
1 tablespoon (15 ml) lemon juice
1 teaspoon (5 ml) margarine
4 eggs
1 cup (250 ml) plain yogurt
1/2 cup (125 ml) milk
1/2 teaspoon (2 ml) salt
1/4 teaspoon (1 ml) nutmeg
1/4 teaspoon (1 ml) pepper
1/4 cup (50 ml) grated parmesan cheese
1/4 cup (50 ml) chopped parsley

Wash spinach thoroughly. Cook, covered, in a large saucepan or wok with just the water that clings to it, about 2 to 3 minutes. Sitr in lemon juice. Drain well, pressing out water. Chop very fine or purée in a blender. Grease a 10x8-inch (25x20 cm) baking dish.

Beat eggs, add yogurt, milk, salt, nutmeg, pepper, 2 tablespoons (30 ml) of the parsley, and the puréed spinach. Also add 2 tablespoons (30 ml) of the grated cheese. Pour into baking dish, sprinkle top with remaining cheese and parsley. Place dish in a larger pan of water and bake in a 375F (190C) oven for 35 minutes, or until custard is set. Let quiche stand for 10 minutes before serving. Makes 4 to 6 servings.

cheese

It used to be that when you thought about cheese, you thought of Switzerland, France, Italy, Holland, even Wisconsin. But over the past couple of decades (or more), those in the know have been heading their list with the many varieties of Canadian cheese.

Although cheddar remains the most popular, there are now almost one hundred types of specialty cheeses on the market—all made in Canada. The sudden rise of specialty cheeses has been attributed to the massive influx of European immigrants into Canada after the Second World War. During the late 1950s, Italian immigrants in Canada were hungry for their mozzarella and pizza cheeses; Dutch new-comers wanted edam and gouda; Greeks sought feta; the Swiss wanted emmental and gruyere; the Danes, havarti; Norwegians, jarlsberg; the Germans, muenster, limburger, and quark cheeses, the French looked for camembert and brie; and the British wanted stilton.

Where there is consumer demand, industry will rise to the challenge. It wasn't long before enterprising businesses were answering the calls for all the specialty cheeses. What resulted is Canada's flourishing and diverse cheese industry with something for virtually everybody. By 1986, cheese production in Canada had reached 250,000 tonnes.

Most Canadian cheeses fall into the categories of fresh, soft, semi-soft, firm, or hard. During the initial stage, all cheeses are fresh, unripened and unfermented. All fresh cheeses are made with pasteurized skimmed milk, whey, whole milk, or cream. The fat content can vary between .5 and 30 percent, depending on the milk used. Fresh cheeses include cottage, quark, ricotta, baker's (white cheese), neufchatel, and cream. All fresh cheeses should be eaten shortly after purchase. If you do need to store them, keep them refrigerated.

Canadian soft cheeses are neither pressed nor cooked and they have bloomy rinds. They are surface-ripened, which means they begin to age from the exterior of the cheese to the interior, and throughout the body. Bloomy rinds develop after curdling, natural draining, and salting. The cheese is then surface-ripened with a penicillium culture. At their peak, soft cheeses with bloomy rinds have a smooth, creamy texture that is not runny. Included are brie, double-cream, and camembert.

Semi-soft cheeses are slightly firmer than the soft varieties. Some, such as mozzarella, are unripened. Others, including muenster, havarti, and monterey jack are interior-ripened. Yet others, like limburger and feta, are surface-ripened and have more pronounced flavours.

The largest category of Canadian cheeses are the firm ones, notably cheddar, brick, colby, edam, emmental, swiss, marble, farmer's, and gouda. With fat content varying between 20 and 31 per cent, they keep well and can be easily cut or sliced. Hard cheeses, such as romano and parmesan keep well over long periods and have a distinct texture that is usually dry and grainy, best used for grating.

Mexican Rice and Bean Skillet with Cheese

2 teaspoons (10 ml) canola oil
1/2 cup (125 ml) chopped celery
1/2 cup (125 ml) chopped onion
1/2 cup (125 ml) chopped green pepper
1 cup (250 ml) uncooked rice
1 cup (250 ml) water
1 cup (250 ml) canned tomatoes, drained and chopped
1 (19-ounce/540 ml) can red kidney beans, undrained
2 teaspoon (10 ml) chili powder
1 teaspoon (5 ml) cumin
1 teaspoon (5 ml) oregano
1 1/4 cups (300 ml) shredded mozzarella cheese

In a large skillet, heat oil; sauté vegetables and rice for 3 minutes. Stir in water, tomatoes, beans, and seasonings; bring to a boil. Reduce heat, cover and simmer 20 to 25 minutes or until liquid is absorbed. Sprinkle with cheese; cover, heat for 2 minutes, until cheese melts. Makes 4 servings.

Ham and Cheese Strata

16 slices white bread
2 cups (500 ml) cubed ham
1 pound (500 g) cheddar cheese, shredded
1 1/2 cups (375 ml) shredded Swiss cheese
6 eggs, beaten
3 cups (750 ml) milk
1/2 teaspoon (2 ml) onion salt
1/2 teaspoon (2 ml) dry mustard
3 cups (750 ml) cornflakes, crushed
6 drops hot pepper sauce
1/2 cup (125 ml) butter or margarine, melted

Remove crusts from bread; cut bread into cubes. Spread half of the cubes evenly in a greased 13x9x2-inch (33x23x5 cm) baking dish. Add ham and both cheeses; top with remaining bread cubes.

In a bowl, combine eggs, milk, onion salt and mustard. Pour over casserole. Cover and refrigerate overnight.

Combine cornflakes, hot pepper sauce and butter. Sprinkle evenly over casserole. Bake in a 375F (190C) oven for 40 minutes. Let stand 10 minutes before cutting into 3-inch (8 cm) squares. Makes 12 servings.

Prosciutto and Mushroom Strata

Unlike sandwiches, which are best made at the last minute, stratas can be made the night before. Simply remove them from the refrigerator half an hour before popping them into the oven.

2 tablespoons (30 ml) butter or margarine
1 medium onion, chopped
1/2 pound (250 g) portobello, cremini, or white mushrooms, sliced
1/4 pound (125 g) thinly sliced prosciutto or ham, cut into 1/4 inch
   (6 mm) strips
1/4 cup (50 ml) chopped fresh parsley
1 1/2 teaspoons (7 ml) dried basil
6 cups (1.5 L) cubed stale French bread (1/2-inch/1 cm cubes)
2 cups (500 ml) shredded Swiss cheese
6 large eggs
2 cups (500 ml) milk
1 tablespoon (15 ml) Dijon mustard
1/4 teaspoon (1 ml) salt
1/4 teaspoon (1 ml) pepper

In large skillet over medium-high heat, melt butter or margarine. Add onion and mushrooms. Sauté until liquid from mushrooms has evaporated, about 5 minutes. Remove from heat. Stir in prosciutto or ham, parsley and basil.

In a greased 13x9-inch (33x23 cm) baking dish, arrange half of the bread; top with half of the prosciutto or ham mixture and half of the cheese. Repeat layers.

Beat together eggs, milk, mustard, salt and pepper until just blended. Pour over strata. Cover with foil and refrigerate at least 2 hours or overnight.

Bake strata covered with foil in a 350F (180C) oven for 20 minutes. Remove foil and bake 20 to 25 minutes longer, or until centre is set and top is golden. Makes 6 to 8 servings.

Spinach Cheese Strata

1 loaf day-old French bread
1 cup (250 ml) chopped onion
2 tablespoons (30 ml) butter
3/4 cup (175 ml) cooked, chopped spinach (8 cups fresh) or 1
  (10-oz/300 g) package frozen chopped spinach, thawed
1 teaspoon (5 ml) dill weed
Salt and pepper to taste
1 1/2 cups (375 ml) shredded Swiss cheese
3 eggs
2 1/2 cups (625 ml) milk

Cut bread into thin slices; line bottom of a buttered shallow 11x7-inch (28x18 cm) baking dish with half the slices.

In a large skillet, sauté onion in butter for 5 minutes. Squeeze spinach dry and add to pan with dill, salt and pepper. Stir just to combine.

Spread spinach over bread in pan; sprinkle with 1 cup (250 ml) cheese. Arrange remaining bread overlapping on top.

Beat eggs in medium-size bowl; stir in milk and a little salt. Pour over bread. Sprinkle with remaining cheese. Cover and chill at least one hour, but overnight is better.

Bake uncovered in a 375F (190C) oven for 45 minutes, or until puffed and golden. If bread is browning too quickly, cover with foil. Remove to wire rack. Let stand 10 minutes before serving. Makes 6 servings.

Hans Wicki

■ When Hans Wicki was chef/ owner of Darlington's on Duke, a cozy little Halifax restaurant, he featured some of the traditional dishes of his homeland, Switzer-land. The origin of fondue, a timeless creation of the fun-loving and congenial Swiss, is given over to romantic legend. One story claims the invention ended a war, when two opposing armies ran out of food. One army had nothing left to eat but bread, the other only milk and a little cheese. To avoid starvation, they joined forces, combined the milk and cheese and dunked bread into what might have been the first fondue. Over time, the milk was replaced by wine, and a combination of cheeses, often Emmentaler and Gruyère, became traditional. Hans is now a chef instructor at the Culinary Institute of Canada, in Charlottetown, Prince Edward Island.

Swiss Fondue

1 clove garlic
1 cup (250 ml) dry white wine
200 g (about 7 ounces) Emmentaler cheese, grated
200 g (about 7 ounces) Gruyère cheese, grated
1 teaspoon (5 ml) cornstarch
1 1/2 tablespoons (22 ml) Kirsch (cherry brandy)
Salt and freshly ground pepper, to taste
Grated nutmeg, to taste
1 baguette, cut in three-quarter-inch (2 cm) cubes

Rub inside of caquelon (fondue pot) with mashed garlic; add wine and bring to a boil. While still on medium heat, gradually add grated cheese, stirring vigorously with a wooden spoon until melted and smooth.

Dissolve cornstarch in Kirsch; add to boiling cheese and stir until thickened. Season with salt and pepper. Place caquelon on rechard (food warmer). Serve with cubed baguette. Makes 2 servings.

Mushroom Quiche

1 1/2 cups (375 ml) grated Swiss cheese, divided
1 tablespoon (15 ml) flour
1 1/2 teaspoons (7 ml) dry mustard
1 chilled, unbaked 9-inch (23 cm) pie shell
2 cups (500 ml) sliced mushrooms (about 8-ounces/250 g)
1 tablespoon (15 ml) butter
4 eggs, beaten
1 1/2-cups (375 ml) milk
Salt and pepper, to taste

Combine 1 cup (250 ml) grated cheese with the flour and dry mustard. Sprinkle over bottom of pie shell.

Sauté mushrooms in butter until lightly browned, about 5 minutes. Combine mushrooms with eggs, milk and seasonings. Pour over cheese mixture. Top with remaining cheese. Bake in a 400F (200C) oven for 15 minutes; reduce heat to 325F (160C), and continue baking 15 minutes longer. Let stand 5 to 10 minutes before serving. Makes 6 servings.

Savoury Salmon Cheesecake

Crust:
1/2 cup (125 ml) melted butter
1 1/2 cups (375 ml) crushed crackers
2 teaspoons (10 ml) Dijon mustard
1 tablespoon (15 ml) finely chopped fresh dill

Filling:
1/4 cup (50 ml) butter
1 onion, chopped
2 pounds (1 kg) cream cheese
4 eggs
1/2 cup (125 ml) light cream
8 ounces (250 g) smoked salmon, finely chopped
2 tablespoons (30 ml) finely chopped fresh dill

Grease a 10-inch (25 cm) spring-form pan or 13x9-inch (33x23 cm) baking pan with 1 tablespoon (15 ml) melted butter.

Crust: In a bowl, combine remaining melted butter, cracker crumbs, Dijon mustard and 1 tablespoon (15 ml) dill. Mix well and spread in bottom of prepared pan. Pat down gently. Chill.

Filling: Heat 1/4 cup (50 ml) butter in small frying pan on medium-high heat. Sauté onion until softened but not brown, about 2 minutes. Reserve.

Beat cream cheese in food processor or mixer until smooth. Blend in eggs and cream; continue beating until smooth. Add onion, salmon, and 2 tablespoons (30 ml) dill; mix just until blended.

Pour filling into prepared pan. Bake at 325F (160C) for 1 hour and 15 minutes (1 hour in rectangular pan) or until cheesecake is firm to the touch.

Turn oven off, leaving cheesecake in oven another hour with door ajar. Remove from oven; cool to room temperature. Cut into wedges and serve with cucumber salad as first course, or cut in squares for hors d'oeuvres. Serves 12 as an appetizer; 15 as hors d'oeuvres.

Lucy Waverman

■ Well-known food writers Julia Aitken, Anita Stewart, Julian Armstrong, Carol Ferguson and Lucy Waverman have each contributed to the new Canadian cuisine, wherein traditional foods meet with modern culinary twists. "To become truly soverign, a nation must nurture its culinary arts," says Anita. Carol agrees that Canadian cooking is defined by its diversity: "We're country-style cosy and city-street sassy. We're butter tarts, Nanaimo bars, chili sauce, and figgy duff. And the evolution continues today." In her cookbook, *Dinner Tonight*, Lucy puts it this way: "As we travel the world and the world comes to us, the foods and techniques of other countries have made their way into our lives." Lucy's delicious savoury cheesecake is one I serve to friends on occasion.

p a s t a

Although we're fortunate to have imported produce in the off-season, we sometimes need a little help to present foods that have traveled far to get to our tables. To help us, there's pasta. Used as a base for many types of sauces, pasta can make even tired vegetables shine.

Made of Canadian-grown durum or other high-quality hard wheat, pasta is a nutritious energy food and an excellent source of complex carbohydrates. It has little fat, no cholesterol, and virtually no salt. And when served with vegetables, such as tomatoes, squash, celery and mushrooms, it provides a good source of vitamins A and C.

A meal can be as simple as heating up leftover vegetables in a store-bought spaghetti sauce and tossing it with pasta. Or, heat up some bottled salsa, add some chopped tomatoes, sweet peppers and sliced zucchini, toss with freshly cooked pasta and it's ready to eat. When fresh tomatoes come in, you may want to prepare your own salsa and toss it without heating into the freshly cooked pasta.

Pasta's versatility makes it a natural for new taste combinations. And it can be a life-saver when every second of the day counts. Just choose an appropriate shape, add a compatible sauce, toss in a few stir-fried vegetables, and you've got a meal prepared in less than half an hour. Delicate angel hair pasta, or vermicelli, for instance, should not be inundated with a heavy sauce. Go with something lighter, such as a simple garlic and oil sauce, made by cooking three thinly-sliced garlic cloves with three tablespoons (45 ml) of extra-virgin olive oil for two minutes, then adding 1/2 cup (125 ml) of the pasta cooking water. Toss with drained pasta and serve immediately. Wider shapes, like long and flat fettuccini, can handle the heavier cheese, meat, or tomato sauces, while those with holes or ridges, such as rigatoni, work well with chunkier sauces. Shapes like penne (straight tubes of pasta cut diagonally) or twisted fusilli are good choices for salads; large shells and cannelloni are perfect for stuffing, and small pasta, like rice-shaped orzo, is ideal for soups.

Herb Fettuccine Provencal with Mussels and Shrimp

1 package (375 g) fettuccini with herbs
1/4 cup (50 ml) olive or canola oil
16 large raw shrimp, peeled and deveined
3 cloves garlic, chopped
1 onion, finely chopped
1/2 cup (125 ml) dry white wine
3 tomatoes, skinned, seeded and chopped
20 mussels, cleaned
1/4 cup (50 ml) chopped parsley
Salt and fresh ground pepper

Cook fettuccini according to package directions.

In large saucepan, heat oil; add shrimp and sauté until just cooked, 3 to 4 minutes. Remove shrimp and set aside.

To remaining oil in saucepan, add onion and garlic; sauté until tender. Stir in wine and cook for 3 to 4 minutes or until most of the liquid is absorbed. Add tomatoes and cook 2 to 3 minutes. Add mussels, cover and simmer for 5 to 7 minutes or until they open. (Discard any that do not open.) Return shrimp to saucepan and heat through. Stir in parsley and season to taste with salt and pepper. Toss drained fettuccini with mussel mixture. Makes 4 servings.

Guilt-free Fettuccini Alfredo

With less calories and fat, everyone's favourite pasta dish is just as delicious—and it only takes 5 minutes to prepare.

1/2 pound (250 g) fettuccini
3/4 cup (175 ml) 2 percent cottage cheese
1/3 cup (75 ml) sour cream
1/4 cup (50 ml) grated parmesan cheese
1 egg
1/4 teaspoon (1 ml) grated nutmeg
1/4 teaspoon (1 ml) pepper
Garnish: chopped parsley, optional

Cook fettuccini according to package directions. In food processor or blender, process cottage cheese until smooth. Add remaining ingredients, blending until smooth. Drain fettuccini well. Add sauce and toss to coat. Serve immediately, garnished with chopped parsley if desired. Makes 4 servings.

Ashley Nightingale with Grandmother Marie

■ In May 1999, my column featured recipes that three young people would serve to their mothers on Mother's Day: bruschetta from Allison Gurnham, a salmon casserole from Branden Butler-Fox, and a pasta dish from my granddaughter Ashley Nightingale. Ashley, who was thirteen at the time, was a pastamaniac. As soon as she could talk she would order noodles for breakfast, lunch, and dinner. At age twelve, she got her own pasta machine, along with *The Pasta Machine Cookbook* by Gina Steer. Since her mother, Sarah, shares her passion for pasta, Ashley prepared fresh pasta and her mother's favourite fresh tomato sauce for a Mother's Day lunch. "It's easy and delicious," she said.

Basic Pasta Dough

2 1/2 cups (625 ml) all-purpose flour
Pinch of salt
3 medium eggs, room temperature
1 tablespoon (15 ml) virgin olive oil

In a large bowl, combine flour and salt. Make a well in centre. Break eggs, one by one, into well and beat with a fork until eggs are evenly mixed together. Add oil to eggs. With fork, gradually mix flour into eggs, working flour from centre until eggs are no longer runny. Then, use hands to bring flour up over egg mixture, working until all flour is mixed into the egg. Mix to form a stiff dough, adding a little water, if necessary. Dough should feel moist but not sticky.

Holding dough with one hand, fold it over with the fingers of the other hand. Knead dough with the heel of your palm, rotating it each time with a quarter turn. Knead by pushing dough down and away from you.

Continue kneading until dough is very smooth. Wrap in plastic wrap and let rest 20 minutes before rolling out and using. Follow manufacturer's directions for rolling and cutting pasta dough by machine.

Fresh Tomato Sauce

1 1/2 pounds (750 ml) fresh plum tomatoes
1/2 small fennel bulb (about 2 tablespoons/30 ml) chopped
3 tablespoons (45 ml) olive oil
1 onion, peeled, chopped
2 to 3 garlic cloves, peeled, minced
Few sprigs of oregano
2 to 3 tablespoons (30 to 45 ml) tomato paste
1 1/4 cups (300 ml) water
Salt and ground black pepper

Make a small cross in the top of each tomato and place in a large bowl. Cover with boiling water; let stand 2 minutes. Drain off water and peel tomatoes. Cut in half, chop roughly. Trim fennel, discarding damaged outer leaves, then chop fine.

In a large pan, heat oil; gently sauté fennel, onion, and garlic for 5 minutes, or until soft but not browned. Add tomatoes and oregano sprigs; sauté 3 minutes more.

Blend tomato paste with a little water. Bring to a boil, reduce heat and simmer for 10 to 12 minutes, until reduced to sauce consistency. Remove oregano sprigs and add seasoning to taste.

Meanwhile, cook 1 pound (500 ml) fresh pasta in salted boiling water for 1 to 2 minutes or until al dente. Drain pasta thoroughly; add to sauce with 1 to 2 teaspoons (5 to 10 ml) chopped fresh oregano.

Makes 2 1/2 cups (625 ml); enough for 4 servings.

Pizza Pasta

Toss extra cooked pasta in a little oil to prevent it from sticking together, and store it in a plastic bag or a covered container in the refrigerator for up to three days. To reheat pasta, place in a colander and immerse in rapidly boiling water just long enough to heat through (about two minutes), or microwave until hot. Unsauced leftover pasta can be a base for salads, side dishes, soups, casseroles, omelettes and other egg dishes.

2 1/2 cups (625 ml) wagon wheel or elbow pasta
4 tablespoons (60 ml) butter, divided
1 medium onion, chopped
2 medium tomatoes, chopped
1 small green pepper, chopped
1 1/2 cups (375 ml) sliced mushrooms
3/4 cup (175 ml) sliced pepperoni
1/2 teaspoon (2 ml) salt
1/2 teaspoon (2 ml) dried basil
1/2 teaspoon (2 ml) dried oregano
1 cup (250 ml) grated mozzarella cheese

Cook pasta according to package directions; drain well and return to saucepan.

Meanwhile, in large frying pan over medium-high heat , melt 2 tablespoons (30 ml) of butter. Sauté onions until tender, about 2 minutes. Add remaining 2 tablespoons (30 ml) butter and all other ingredients except cheese. Sauté for 4 or 5 minutes or until vegetables are tender.

In saucepan, combine cooked pasta with vegetable mixture. Add cheese and stir until melted. Serve immediately. Makes 4 servings.

Johanna Burkhard

■ One of Canada's leading food writers, Johanna Burkhard, visited Halifax in 1997 to promote her first cookbook, *The Comfort Food Cookbook*. As part of the promotion Johanna appeared on a call-in radio show to answer questions about favourite comfort foods. Almost half of the calls pertained to macaroni and cheese, which was a clear indication to her about the popularity of this old-fashioned dish. "Comfort foods tell a lot about who we are," she told me after the show. "We love Granny because she always made such wonderful cookies. But what was important was that she was making them especially for us." Johanna was concerned that fears about food may have led us to give up some of our favourite things.

Tomato wedges dress up the old favourite in Acadian Macaroni and Cheese.

Acadian Macaroni and Cheese

3 cups (750 ml) uncooked elbow macaroni
2 tablespoons (30 ml) butter
2 cups (500 ml) cubed cheddar cheese
1 teaspoon (5 ml) Dijon mustard
1/4 teaspoon (1 ml) pepper
2 1/2 cups (625 ml) milk

Topping:
3 tablespoons (45 ml) fresh grated parmesan cheese
1 cup (250 ml) soft breadcrumbs
2 tablespoons (30 ml) butter, melted
1 medium tomato, cut in wedges

Cook macaroni according to package directions; drain and return to saucepan. Add butter, cheese, mustard and pepper; mix well. Turn into a greased 2-quart (2 L) casserole. Pour milk over mixture.

Topping: Reserve 1 tablespoon (15 ml) parmesan cheese. Combine remaining parmesan, breadcrumbs, and melted butter; sprinkle evenly over top of macaroni. Bake at 350F (180C) for 30 to 35 minutes or until top is nicely browned.

Arrange tomato wedges on top and sprinkle with reserved parmesan. Continue baking 5 to 10 minutes, until tomatoes are hot. Remove from oven and serve. Makes 4 servings.

Shells with Thai-Style Shrimp

If you're having guests for dinner on short-notice, you can make it a snap with this Thai-style dish. Just pick up some shrimp on the way home from work and prepare this delicious up-scale meal in just 25 minutes. Your guests can relax with a drink while you prepare this dish. Or, if you're not intimidated by an audience, have them come to the kitchen and watch.

4 cups (1 L) large shell pasta
3 cloves garlic, minced
1 small green jalapeno pepper, seeded and finely chopped
2 teaspoons (10 ml) finely chopped fresh ginger
2 tablespoons (30 ml) peanut oil
1 pound (500 g) medium shrimp, peeled and deveined
1 tablespoon (15 ml) chopped fresh coriander or cilantro
1 tablespoon (15 ml) hoisin sauce
1 tablespoon (15 ml) cornstarch
3/4 cup (175 ml) chicken broth

Cook shells according to package directions.

In skillet, sauté garlic, jalapeno pepper and ginger in oil until tender, about 5 minutes. Add shrimp and sauté for 4 minutes. Add coriander and sauté for 3 minutes or until shrimp are cooked through. Remove shrimp and keep warm.

Whisk hoisin sauce and cornstarch into broth. Add mixture to skillet and cook until just thickened. Return shrimp to skillet and heat through. Toss shrimp mixture with shells. Makes 4 servings.

Pasta with Peppers

It's not surprising that pasta's appeal as the food of the '80s continues to grow. Pasta is versatile. It can be served plain, tossed with butter and parmesan cheese, or you can fancy it up. This recipe is not only a colourful addition to your favourite pasta, but is quick to prepare.

2 tablespoons (30 ml) good quality olive oil
2 red onions, sliced
2 cloves garlic, minced
5 red or green peppers, halved, seeded, and cut into 1-inch (2.5 cm) strips
1 cup (250 ml) peeled, seeded, chopped tomatoes, fresh or canned (drained)
1/2 cup (125 ml) dry white wine
3 tablespoons (45 ml) capers, drained
2 tablespoons (30 ml) chopped fresh parsley or fresh basil
Salt and freshly ground pepper to taste
1/2 cup (125 ml) grated parmesan cheese
1 pound (500 g) tubular pasta (rigatoni, macaroni, penne)
1 teaspoon (5 ml) salt
5 quarts (5 L) boiling water

Heat oil in a large skillet and add onions and garlic. Cook a few minutes until onions wilt and mixture becomes very fragrant. Do not brown onions or garlic. Add peppers and cook about 5 minutes. Add tomatoes and wine and reduce until slightly thickened. Add pasta and salt to boiling water and cook until tender. Drain well and combine with sauce. Toss well. Serve immediately. Makes 8 servings.

Zesty Lemon Spaghetti and Meatballs

Meatballs:
1 pound (500 g) lean ground beef
1/4 cup (50 ml) fine dry breadcrumbs
1 egg, slightly beaten
1/4 teaspoon (1 ml) grated lemon rind
1/4 teaspoon (1 ml) salt
1 tablespoon (15 ml) canola oil

Sauce:
1 small onion, finely chopped
1 (14-ounce/398 ml) can tomato sauce
1 tablespoon (15 ml) lemon juice
1/2 teaspoon (2 ml) dried basil leaves
12 ounces (375 g) spaghetti

Combine beef, breadcrumbs, egg, lemon rind, and salt. Mix well and form into 1-inch (2.5 cm) balls. In frying pan, heat oil over medium-high heat. Sauté meatballs until browned. Drain fat. Stir in onion, tomato sauce, lemon juice, and basil. Bring to a boil, reduce heat and simmer, uncovered, for 15 minutes, stirring occasionally. Cook spaghetti, drain and serve with sauce. Makes 4 servings.

rice

Rice has long been the staple food of 2/3 of the world's population. Now, its use is growing in Canada. With the convenience of always having the base of a meal in the cupboard or prepared ahead, one wonders why it took us so long to appreciate the value of this nutritious and inexpensive grain.

Since Canada grows no rice at all (wild rice doesn't count because it's really an aquatic grass), we look to our neighbour to the south for over 70 per cent of the rice we consume. The different types of American-grown rice include long-grain, medium-grain, short-grain, sweet, aromatic, and Arborio.

Long-grain rice is a slender kernel four or five times longer than it is wide. When cooked, the grains remain separate and are light and fluffy, making it the perfect rice for salads, side dishes, or main-dish recipes. Medium-grain rice is plump, but not round, about two to three times longer than it is wide. When cooked, the grains are more moist and tender and have a greater tendency to cling together than long-grain. It's ideal for recipes with a creamy consistency, such as puddings, custards and risottos. It's also used in sushi.

Short-grain rice is a plump, almost round kernel. When cooked, the grains cling together, making it great for sushi, rice pancakes, and desserts. Sweet or glutinous rice is short, plump and waxy with a chalky white, opaque kernel. Very sticky when cooked, it's traditionally used in Asian cuisine as well as desserts. Aromatic rice, which has a flavour and aroma similar to roasted nuts or popcorn, is growing in popularity. The most popular of U.S.-grown aromatic rices include della, jasmine, and basmati. Della cooks dry, separate and fluffy. Jasmine cooks more moist and clings together. Basmati cooks into very long, slender grains that are dry, separate and fluffy. Arborio is a large, bold rice with a characteristic white dot at the centre of the grain. Handled carefully, this rice develops a creamy texture around a chewy centre and has an exceptional ability to absorb flavours. It is typically used in risottos.

Tomato and Lemon Risotto

4 cups (1 L) chicken broth
1 tablespoon (15 ml) olive oil
1/3 cup (75 ml) finely chopped shallots
1 cup (250 ml) uncooked arborio or medium grain rice
1 cup (250 ml) cherry tomatoes, halved
1/2 cup (125 ml) lemon juice
1 tablespoon (15 ml) lemon zest (grated rind)
Freshly grated parmesan cheese

In a medium saucepan over medium heat, heat broth until it starts to boil; reduce heat to low and keep warm.

Meanwhile, in a large saucepan over medium heat, heat oil. Add shallots; cook 2 to 3 minutes or until soft. Add rice; stir 2 to 3 minutes. Increase heat to medium-high; stir in 1 cup (250 ml) broth. Cook, stirring frequently, until broth is absorbed. Continue stirring and add remaining broth, 1 cup (250 ml) at a time, allowing it to be absorbed before adding more. Cook until rice is tender and mixture is creamy, about 25 to 30 minutes. Stir in tomatoes, lemon juice and zest. Top with parmesan cheese. Serve immediately. Makes 6 servings.

Maple-Rice Pudding

3 cups (750 ml) cooked long-grain rice
2 eggs, beaten
1 cup (250 ml) pure maple syrup
1 cup (250 ml) milk
2 apples, peeled and diced (2 cups/500 ml)
1 teaspoon (5 ml) ground cinnamon
1/4 teaspoon (1 ml) nutmeg
Dash of salt
Sprinkle of cinnamon and sugar

Combine rice with eggs, maple syrup and milk. Mix well. Add apples and spices. Mix until blended. Transfer to a well-greased 1-quart (1 L) baking dish. Sprinkle with cinnamon sugar. Bake at 350F (180C) for 50 to 60 minutes, or until set. Drizzle with butter and syrup. Makes 4 to 6 servings.

Baked Rice with Tomatoes, Peppers and Smoked Ham

4 small ripe tomatoes
1 sweet red pepper
1 cup (250 ml) chopped smoked ham
1/3 cup (75 ml)olive oil, divided
4 cloves garlic, minced
1 teaspoon (5 ml) Spanish paprika
1/2 teaspoon (2 ml) hot pepper flakes
1 1/2 cups (375 ml) Arborio or other short-grain rice
1 (6-ounce/170 ml) jar quartered artichoke hearts, rinsed and drained
4 ounces (125 g) green beans, cut in 2-inch (5 cm) pieces
3 cups (750 ml) hot chicken stock
Dress with: drizzle of olive oil
Serve with: baby greens, dressed with lemon juice and olive oil

Finely chop two tomatoes and half of the red pepper. Finely chop smoked ham. Heat 1/4 cup (50 ml) olive oil in large skillet over medium-high heat. Add chopped tomatoes, red pepper and ham. Stir in garlic, paprika, and hot pepper flakes. Cook, stirring occasionally, 5 minutes or until most of the liquid has evaporated. Remove from heat.

Spread rice in shallow 12-cup (3 L) baking dish. Arrange artichokes and green beans on rice. Spoon skillet mixture evenly over rice mixture. Carefully pour hot stock onto rice mixture.

Cut remaining tomatoes into thin slices and remaining half of red pepper into thin strips; arrange over rice mixture. Drizzle with remaining 2 tablespoons (30 ml) olive oil. Bake uncovered in 350F (180C) oven 50 minutes or until rice is done. Makes 4 to 6 servings.

Mushroom-Rice Casserole

1 cup (250 ml) rice
1 teaspoon (5 ml) salt (or less)
1/2 pound (250 g) mushrooms, sliced
1/2 cup (125 ml) sliced green onions (white part only)
1/4 cup (50 ml) butter or margarine
2 cups (500 ml) chicken broth

Place rice and salt in a greased 2-quart (2 L) casserole dish; set aside. In a large saucepan, sauté mushrooms and onions in butter until tender, stirring occasionally.

Add broth and bring to a boil. Pour over rice; stir. Cover, and bake in a 350F (180C) oven 25 to 30 minutes or until rice is tender and liquid is all absorbed. Let stand, covered, for 5 minutes. Fluff with fork before serving. Makes 4 to 6 servings.

Whisk ingredients together until well combined.

Marie with Chef Kevin Belton of the New Orleans School of Cooking

■ When vacationing in Louisiana, the usual introduction to New Orleans cooking is a visit to K-Paul's Louisiana Kitchen in the city's famed French Quarter. This is where renowned chef Paul Prudhomme and his wife, Kay, established the now-famous restaurant where Cajun food is the order of the day. To learn more, I took in a session at the New Orleans School of Cooking, where Chef Kevin Belton demonstrated Cajun cooking while joking about his 400-pounds plus and what put it there.

Chef Kevin's Jambalaya

1 1/2 pounds (750 g) chicken breasts
3/4 pound (375 g) Cajun sausage
4 tablespoons (60 ml) canola oil
2 cups (500 ml) chopped onions
1 cup (250 ml) chopped celery
1 cup (250 ml) chopped green pepper
2 teaspoons (10 ml) chopped garlic
1 1/4 cups (300 ml) chicken or vegetable stock
1 1/4 cups (300 ml) tomato juice
1 teaspoon (5 ml) Cajun seasoning, or more to taste
2 tablespoons (30 ml) paprika
2 cups (500 ml) long grain rice
1 cup (250 ml) chopped green onions or tomatoes (optional)

Remove excess fat from chicken breasts; rub pieces with mixture of salt and garlic powder. Let stand 15 minutes for seasoning to penetrate. Cut chicken and sausage in bite-size pieces.

In large stainless steel pot or Dutch oven, brown chicken in 2 tablespoons (30 ml) oil over medium-high heat. Turn once to brown both sides. Add sausage; sauté with chicken until both are cooked. Remove from pot. Wipe pot with paper towels to remove food particles.

Add remaining oil to pot; sauté onions, celery, green pepper and garlic, for 2 minutes, or until tender. Return chicken and sausage to pot. Add stock, tomato juice and Cajun seasoning. Bring to boil.

Stir in paprika. Add rice and return to boil. Cover; reduce heat to simmer and cook for 10 minutes. Remove cover and quickly turn rice from top to bottom completely. Cover; continue cooking for 10 minutes, or until liquid is absorbed. Add green onions or chopped tomatoes, if desired. Heat through. Makes 6 servings.

fish and seafood

Nova Scotia seafood is much loved in Japan. More recently, that popularity has been spreading to Hong Kong and other Asian locales. The per capita consumption of seafood in Asian countries is much higher than it is in North America. That's because in Asia, fish is very symbolic, signifying plenty; it is considered to be a gift from God. No self-respecting Asian would consider a ten-course banquet of the Chinese New Year complete without at least one serving of fish.

And, if cooking show host Stephen Yan had his way, he'd be sending planeloads of Nova Scotia seafood to Asia every day of the week. Yan, of Burnaby, British Columbia, is the wok-cooking host of CBC's *Wok with Yan*. Since his personal tastes run to Nova Scotia seafood, notably lobster, salmon, and scallops, Yan has been featuring these delicacies on his cooking show for the past few years. It is only natural that he would want to share his culinary passions with other chefs. That opportunity arose recently when, at the Hong Kong Festival of Flavours in Vancouver, Yan acted as host to five award-winning chefs from Hong Kong. Not only did the visiting chefs demonstrate their own cooking skills, but they learned a great deal about cooking Canadian fish and shellfish.

"I felt that this food festival offered a unique opportunity to combine fantastic food ingredients with distinctive Chinese gourmet cooking techniques," said Yan, who had developed special recipes for the guest chefs. Three of the nine dishes featured his favourite Nova Scotia seafoods—Nova Scotia Scallops in Szechuan Sauce, Cashew Nut Atlantic Salmon, and Nova Scotia Lobster with Chinese Donut, which was a platinum prize winner at the Hong Kong Festival.

When asked what he liked about Nova Scotia lobster, he said it speaks for itself: "I don't have to say much. Everyone knows that Nova Scotia has one of the best lobster productions in the world. Its geographic location is so ideal. It is totally unpolluted." His first taste of Atlantic salmon was "unforgettable…I was really amazed to see and taste how good the Nova Scotia salmon is," he said, adding that the product is firmer and "a little bit tastier" than Pacific salmon. "And I can't believe how good the scallops are. They're completely white and big and free of sand. And they're so easy to handle and so attractive."

In Asia, Yan said, dried scallops are so popular that consumers there will pay up to $500 a pound for them. "I hope that some day we can sell these beautiful Nova Scotia scallops, both in fresh and dried form, in Asia," he said. This man should be a spokesperson for The Taste of Nova Scotia. Could anyone say it better?

Stephen Yan's Nova Scotia Scallops in Szechaun Sauce

1 pound (500 g) Nova Scotia scallops
1 egg white
1 tablespoon (15 ml) cornstarch
1 teaspoon (5 ml) salt
Dash pepper
3 tablespoons (45 ml) cooking oil
2 slices ginger, shredded
1 tablespoon (15 ml) minced garlic
2 stalks green onion, chopped
1/4 cup (50 ml) green pepper, cut into squares
1/4 cup (50 ml) red pepper, cut into squares
1 onion, sliced
2 tablespoons (30 ml) cooking wine
2 teaspoons (10 ml) granulated sugar
1 teaspoon (5 ml) soy sauce
1 teaspoon (5 ml) vinegar
1/2 teaspoon (2 ml) chili sauce
1 tablespoon (15 ml) cornstarch, dissolved in
1/4 cup (50 ml) water

Wash and dry scallops. Combine egg white, 1 tablespoon (15 ml) cornstarch, salt and pepper; add scallops and marinate for 20 minutes.

Heat cooking oil in a wok or large frying pan; stir-fry ginger, garlic, green onion, green and red peppers. Add scallops and stir-fry for 5 minutes. Add onion, wine, sugar, soy sauce, vinegar, chili sauce and starch solution. Continue to stir-fry for another minute. Serve hot.

Scallops Jacqueline

When Bernard Meyer was executive chef at Digby Pines, he created this dish to honour a former Scallop Queen, whose name was Jacqueline.

8 large scallops per person	Garniture for Julienne:
Bouillon:	white of leeks only
one-half leek	fresh herbs: thyme and
2 carrots	rosemary (a small bouquet)
2 bay leaves	
2 shallots	
2 celery sticks	
2 slices ginger root	
salt and pepper to taste	

Prepare a bouillon with about three litres of water, leeks, carrots, bay leaves, shallots, celery and ginger root. Let simmer for at least half an hour.

Wash scallops well, remove the nerve or muscle on the side, and place in the top of a steamer. Steam over the bouillon to let the scallops infuse the vegetable and ginger fumes for 3 or 4 minutes. Season to taste. Prepare a julienne of leek (white only) and steam them with scallops just before the scallops have finished cooking.

Place the scallops on a warm plate, and place a cordon of beurre blanc (recipe follows) around the scallops. Sprinkle the scallops with julienne of leeks and fresh herbs. Makes 6 servings.

Beurre Blanc
1 cup dry white wine
4 to 5 good sized shallots, peeled and finely diced
one half teaspoon crushed white peppercorns
one third cup white wine vinegar
one third cup whipping cream, unwhipped
12 ounces unsalted butter, at room temperature (cool enough to hold finger imprint, but not soft melted consistency), cut into half-inch cubes.

Combine wine, shallots, pepper, and wine vinegar in a saucepan. Bring to a boil over high heat. Lower heat and simmer until mixture is reduced to slightly more than one-third cup. This may take about 25 minutes. If reduction happens too quickly, add a little water.

Over low heat, add cream. Mixture will be lukewarm. Add butter, piece by piece (adding the second piece just before the first has completely disappeared, and so on…). Beat rapidly with a wire whisk after each addition. Continue adding butter and beating over low heat in this manner until all of the butter has been added. Serve immediately over scallops. Enough for six servings.

Heather MacKenzie of Cuisine Canada presents Marie with the Edna Staebler lifetime achievement award in 1998.

■ *The Taste of Nova Scotia Cookbook* goes well beyond its 110 recipes. It takes readers along the trails of the province, picking up the threads of traditional cooking and weaving in the modern influences that gave form to Nova Scotia's strong culinary heritage. The book, co-authored by Heather MacKenzie, executive director of The Taste of Nova Scotia, and Charles Lief, original owner of Halliburton House, one of Halifax's fine restaurants, includes this wonderful grilled scallop recipe.

Grilled Scallops with Lemon Chive Butter

1 1/2 teaspoons (7 ml) butter
1 clove garlic, peeled and minced
1 teaspoon (5 ml) freshly squeezed lemon juice
1/4 cup (50 ml) butter
1/2 teaspoon (2 ml) grated lemon rind
1/2 teaspoon (2 ml) white pepper
1/4 cup (50 ml) finely minced chives
Salt, to taste
1 pound (500 g) Digby scallops
1 tablespoon (15 ml) butter

Lemon Chive Butter: In small skillet over low heat, melt 1 1/2 teaspoons (7 ml) butter. Add garlic; sauté 3 minutes or until soft but not brown. Add lemon juice and cook 1 minute. Set aside.

In small bowl, cream butter, lemon rind, pepper, chives, salt and garlic mixture; blend until smooth. Cover and refrigerate at least 2 hours or overnight. Shape into a roll or press into a mould for serving. Return to refrigerator until serving time.

Scallops: In skillet over medium heat, melt 1 tablespoon (15 ml) butter. Add scallops and sauté until fork-tender, about 3 minutes, depending on size. Do not overcook. Place on warmed plate with several pieces of lemon chive butter on top. Makes 4 servings.

Scallops Baked in Wine

Looking to cut the calories? This is an easy, yet delicious way to do it: Each serving contains only 165 calories.

1 tablespoon (15 ml) soft high polyunsaturated margarine or oil
1/4 cup (50 ml) dry white wine
Juice of 1 lemon
1/2 teaspoon (2 ml) dried thyme
1 pound (500 g) scallops

Heat margarine or oil, wine, lemon juice and thyme. Pour over rinsed scallops. Marinate 15 to 20 minutes at room temperature. Bake in a 450F (230C) oven for 5 to 6 minutes. Do not overcook. Makes 4 servings.

Vince Snyder

■ Vince Snyder, long-time chef at the Park Place Ramada Plaza Hotel in Dartmouth enjoys cooking with beer, especially in dishes that traditionally call for wine. "I experimented with different beers to determine which best suited the dish," Vince told me after preparing a dinner based on beer for one hundred people. His menu included Schooner Steamed Mussels with Seaweed Twists, Cheddar and Ale Soup, Spring Rolls, Beer Beef Steak Stroganoff, Salmon Poached in Keith's Pale Ale with a Honey Lemon Vinaigrette, and Beer Barbecued Chicken. Each course was accompanied by a Keith's, Oland's, or Labatt's beer.

Vince said he particularly likes beer for braising or stewing. "And beer batter has been popular for a long time. There's something about the carbonation creating the bubbles that lighten the batter." But don't try to use beer when flambéing, he said. "Beer doesn't have a high enough alcohol content to flame. For that, it's best to stick with brandy."

Steamed Mussels

1 pound (500 g) mussels
2 tablespoons (30 ml) butter
1 large shallot, diced
1/2 cup (125 ml) mixed julienned carrots, zucchini, leek, red pepper
1/4 cup (50 ml) fresh basil, cut in fine strips
1/4 cup (50 ml) lager beer

Wash mussels thoroughly in cool water; remove beards. In a large saucepan over medium heat, melt butter; lightly sauté diced shallot. Add mussels, vegetables, basil and lager. Cover pot; turn heat to maximum. Cook 3 to 5 minutes, until mussels open. (Discard any that do not open.)

Put mussels in serving dishes with some of the broth and spoon vegetables over top. Makes 2 appetizer servings.

Stir-Fried Shrimp

Gary Nightingale

■ Once, when my son Gary and I visited Walt Disney World, we dined at Tangaroa Terrace in the Polynesian Village Resort, and had a stir-fried shrimp dish that was good enough to include in my column.

3/4 cup (175 ml) uncooked rice
6 tablespoons (90 ml) canola oil, divided
1/4 cup (50 ml) sliced onion
1/4 cup (50 ml) sliced celery
1/4 cup (50 ml) carrots, thinly sliced diagonally
2 tablespoons (30 ml) sliced water chestnuts
2 tablespoons (30 ml) bamboo shoots
1/2 cup (125 ml) sliced mushrooms
4 cherry tomatoes, halved
12 sugar peas, halved
1/4 cup (50 ml) thinly sliced raw, unpeeled zucchini
3/4 pound (375 g) medium, peeled raw shrimp
1/4 cup (50 ml) bottled ginger sauce
16 pimiento-stuffed olive slices

Cook rice as directed on package. Keep hot.

Heat 3 tablespoons (45 ml) of the oil in a large skillet or wok and stir-fry onion, celery, carrots, water chestnuts, bamboo shoots and mushrooms. Add cherry tomatoes, sugar peas and zucchini to sautéed vegetables and keep hot.

In another skillet, heat remaining oil and stir-fry shrimps until they turn pink. Add ginger sauce.

Divide rice on four plates, spoon over equal servings of shrimp and top with vegetables. Garnish wilth olive slices. Or, if desired, serve Chinese-style: Put rice in a bowl and shrimp and vegetables in another bowl and let everyone help themselves. Makes 4 servings.

Cy's Lobster Newburg

There was a time when my husband Laurie and I would plan our car trips so that we would be in Moncton at meal time. Whether it was for lunch or dinner, it didn't matter, we always stopped at Cy's Seafood Restaurant. This recipe from Cy's will serve eleven people, so do your friends a favour and invite them in for lunch.

2 pounds (1 kg) cooked lobster meat
3/4 cup (175 ml) melted butter
1 green pepper, chopped fine
1 cup (250 ml) all-purpose flour
1 teaspoon (5 ml) salt
5 cups (1.25 L) hot milk
1 cup (250 ml) dry white wine
1/4 cup (50 ml) cherry juice
patty shells or cooked rice

Cut lobster meat into bite-size pieces; set aside. In a large saucepan, sauté green pepper in melted butter for a moment or two. Gradually blend in combined flour and salt. Cook for 5 minutes over very low heat. Gradually add hot milk, stirring constantly and heating well after each addition, until thickened. Stir in wine and cherry juice. Add lobster meat and serve in warm patty shells or on hot cooked rice. Makes 11 servings.

Rigatoni with Lobster and Smoked Turkey

2 tablespoons (30 ml) olive oil
8 ounces (250 g) rigatoni, ziti or penne pasta
4 cloves garlic, crushed
1/4 cup (50 ml) chopped whites of green onion
1/4 cup (50 ml) seeded, skinned, chopped tomato
2 tablespoons (30 ml) finely chopped yellow pepper
1/2 cup (125 ml) dry white wine
2 tablespoons (30 ml) chopped fresh basil
1/2 teaspoon dried red pepper, crushed
3/4 cup (175 ml) heavy cream or blend
Salt and pepper
1 1/2 cups (375 ml) chopped cooked lobster meat
6 ounces (175 g) smoked turkey or smoked salmon, cut in half-inch
    (1 cm) squares
1/4 cup (50 ml) freshly grated parmesan cheese

Bring a large pot of salted water and 1 tablespoon (15 ml) olive oil to boil. Add pasta; cook 8 minutes or until al dente. Drain, rinse under running water, drain again.

Heat remaining tablespoon (15 ml) olive oil in a large, heavy saucepan over medium-high heat. Add garlic and onion; sauté for 2 minutes. Add tomato, yellow pepper and wine; cook 2 minutes more. Add basil, red pepper and cream; continue cooking until liquid is reduced by half (about 5 minutes). Taste, and season with salt and pepper, if desired.

Add lobster, turkey and pasta and gently sauté until heated, 1 1/2 to 2 minutes. Place on a serving platter or four individual plates; top with parmesan. Place under preheated broiler for about 30 seconds to brown cheese. Serve immediately. Makes 4 servings.

Julie Watson's Rigatoni with Lobster and Smoked Turkey recipe is from her *Fine Catch Seafood Cookbook*.

■ There was a flurry of excitement in mid-May 1994, as a brigade of Atlantic Canadian chefs hustled around the kitchens of Moncton's Hotel Beausejour. They were preparing a gastronomic feast to honour Paul Bocuse, recognized as the greatest French chef alive.

Accompanied by eight of his peers and a large contingent of French journalists and restaurateurs, the grand chef was in Moncton as part of Homard Nouveau, a program aimed at raising the image of Canadian lobster in France.

"It's the best," said one of the restaurant critics. "Vive le homard!" But all ears were tuned to the great Bocuse, who said Canadians must learn to appreciate their excellent lobster. "You have a complex here. You should treat your lobster with respect. I am sure the French will eat lots of it."

Basil and Garlic Crusted Cape Breton Snow Crab Cakes

In July 1994, John Haines, then chef at the Halifax Club, and Steve Huston, chef at the Prince George Hotel, combined their talents to prepare a luncheon for four visiting chefs from Japan. This dish is one that impressed the Japanese delegation.

1 pound (500 g) snow crab meat
1 teaspoon (5 ml) chopped fresh parsley
1 cup (250 ml) cold mashed potato
1/4 cup (50 ml) finely chopped onion
1 cup (250 ml) fine breadcrumbs
2 teaspoons (10 ml) fresh basil or 1/2 teaspoon (2 ml) dried (see note)
1 clove garlic, minced
1 teaspoon (5 ml) olive oil
1/2 cup (125 ml) cornmeal
Canola oil for frying

Combine crab, parsley, potato and onion; shape into 8 small patties. Chill for 30 minutes.

In a food processor, mix breadcrumbs, cornmeal, garlic, basil, and olive oil. Dip crab cakes into crumb mixture, patting and moulding gently. Chill for 30 minutes.

Heat 2 tablespoons (30 ml) canola oil in a frying pan. Add crab cakes; cook, turning once, until crisp and hot. Makes 4 servings.

Note: John Haines said once you've used fresh basil, you'll never want to go back to dried. Basil (and other fresh herbs) can be frozen with excellent results. Once thawed, the herbs will be limp, but the flavour remains intense.

Whole Stuffed Salmon

1 (4 tp 5-pound/2 kg) salmon
1 onion
4 ribs celery
1 green pepper
1/2 pound (250 g) mushrooms
3 cloves garlic
1/4 cup (50 ml) butter
6 slices stale bread, cubed
1/4 cup (50 ml) soy sauce
1/4 cup (50 ml) sherry
2 cups (500 ml) cooked rice
1 cup (250 ml) water chestnuts
1 cup (250 ml) raisins
1 tablespoon (15 ml) rosemary
1 teaspoon (5 ml) thyme
1 teaspoon (5 ml) basil
1/4 teaspoon (1 ml) paprika
1/4 teaspoon (1 ml) pepper
1/2 teaspoon (2 ml) salt

When buying salmon, have it scaled. Rinse salmon and pat dry.

Chop onion, celery and green pepper. Slice mushrooms and crush garlic cloves. In a large pot, sauté vegetables in butter until soft, about 5 minutes. Add bread to vegetables and cook until bread soaks up all the butter.

Mix together soy sauce, sherry, rice, chopped water chestnuts, raisins and spices; add to vegetables. Stir to combine. Fill cavity of salmon with stuffing. Close and wrap in foil. Put wrapped salmon on large baking sheet; cook at 450F (230C) for 10 minutes per inch of stuffed thickness. Makes 10 to 12 servings.

Note: Extra stuffing can be baked in a casserole dish along with the salmon, or recipe can be halved.

Poached Salmon

Poaching is not only the most traditional method for cooking salmon, but it's also one of the healthiest because there's no need for added fat. The easiest way to poach a whole salmon is in a fish poacher (a long, narrow pan with a removable tray and cover), but a small roaster, a Dutch oven, or a large skillet will do nicely for half a salmon or salmon steaks. Wrap larger pieces in cheesecloth (or a J-cloth) before cooking for easy removal from the pan, or carefully lift them with a wide slotted spatula. For poaching, cooking time is 10 minutes per inch of thickness, measured at the thickest part.

4 salmon steaks, 1-inch (2.5 cm) thick
1 large onion, sliced
6 sprigs fresh parsley
2 fresh celery tops with leaves
2 fresh limes, sliced
1/2 teaspoon (2 ml) whole peppercorns
1/2 teaspoon (2 ml) salt
4 cups (1 L) water
2 tablespoons (30 ml) butter or margarine
1 1/2 tablespoons (22 ml) freshly squeezed lime juice
1/4 teaspoon (1 ml) paprika
Lime slices for garnish, optional

In large skillet, combine onion, parsley, celery, lime slices, peppercorns and salt. Add water; bring to a boil. Arrange salmon on vegetables. Cover with wax paper. Return to boiling; reduce heat so water is just below simmering. Cook salmon 10 minutes or until it flakes easily with a fork.

Meanwhile, in small saucepan, melt butter; add lime juice and paprika. With slotted spatula, remove salmon to serving platter. Pour butter mixture over fish. Garnish with additional lime slices and parsley, if desired. Makes 4 servings.

Pam Collacott's Fish Fillets with Vegetables

Pam suggests serving rice or pasta with this healthy, low-fat dish and good rye bread to soak up the delicious juice.

Pam Collacott at The Herb Garden, Almonte, Ontario

■ If anyone has come close to matching Madame Jeanne Benoit and her skills with the microwave oven, it is Pam Collacott of North Gower, Ontario. This busy and talented home economist wrote the definitive microwave cookbook, *The Best of New Wave Cooking* (1992), as well as three other cookbooks on the topic. But microwave cooking is only one of Pam's talents. She owns and conducts classes at the Trillium Cooking School, which she operates in her renovated 160-year old log house, does regular TV cooking shows, and writes articles for *Canadian Living* and other magazines. Her recipes have appeared in several cookbooks.

1 cup (250 ml) tomato juice
3 tablespoons (45 ml) fresh lemon juice
2 carrots, peeled, in thin julienne strips
1 rib celery, in thin diagonal slices
1/4 cup (50 ml) finely chopped onion
2 tablespoons (30 ml) minced parsley
1/2 teaspoon (2 ml) dried oregano or thyme
1/4 teaspoon (1 ml) pepper
1 pound (500 g) haddock fillets
4 teaspoons (20 ml) parmesan cheese

Combine all ingredients except fish in an 8-inch (20 cm) baking dish. Microwave on high for 9 minutes, or until carrots are just tender and liquid is boiling. Stir twice.

Arrange fillets on top of vegetable mixture in a circle with the thickest part of fish facing the outside edge of dish. Spoon some vegetable mixture over fillets. Sprinkle with parmesan.

Cover dish with plastic wrap and microwave on high for 3 to 4 minutes, or until fish is opaque and flakes easily with a fork.

Spoon some sauce over each serving. Makes 4 servings.

Crisped Trout for Campers

6 trout
1/3 cup (75 ml) flour or cornmeal
1/2 teaspoon (2 ml) salt
Ground pepper to taste
1/2 cup (125 ml) bacon drippings or butter
1 cup (250 ml) granola or chopped almonds
1 tablespoon (15 ml) lemon juice

Clean fish. Combine flour and seasonings and coat fish. Sauté in two batches over medium heat, no more than 5 minutes per side, using half of fat per batch. Remove fish. In the same pan, heat granola or almonds. Remove from heat, add lemon juice, and pour over fish. Makes 6 servings.

Baked Trout Dinner

2 trout, 12 ounces (375 g) each
4 strips bacon
6 small new potatoes
1 onion, peeled and sliced
1/2 cup (125 ml) fresh sliced mushrooms
1/2 cup (125 ml) white wine (or water plus lemon juice)
Red pepper
Chopped dill
2 tablespoons (30 ml) butter, divided
1/4 cup (50 ml) breadcrumbs

Clean, rinse and drain fish. Place bacon in cold skillet and cook slowly until light golden; drain on paper and set aside.

Grease a baking pan with some bacon fat, reserving remainder in skillet. Parboil potatoes separately. Place sliced onion in greased baking pan. Lay fish on onions (tuck a few onion slices in cavities), and add sliced mushrooms. Pour wine or lemon water over fish; season with red pepper and chopped dill.

Heat 1 tablespoon (15 ml) butter in skillet with reserved bacon fat; add breadcrumbs and stir to combine. Sprinkle crumbs over fish and place a slice of bacon on each. Bake in a 350F (180C) oven for about 20 minutes.

Meanwhile, peel and thinly slice parboiled potatoes; brown in pan with remaining butter and bacon, diced. Serve with fish. Makes 2 servings.

Fish Stir Fry

1 pound (500 g) fish fillets
1/2 teaspoon (2 ml) powdered ginger
1/4 cup (50 ml) soy sauce
1/4 cup (50 ml) canola oil
1/2 pound (250 g) fresh bean sprouts
1 cup (250 ml) diagonally sliced celery
1/4 cup (50 ml) sliced green onion
2 tablespoons (30 ml) cornstarch
1 teaspoon (5 ml) sugar
1/2 cup (125 ml) chicken bouillon
1 pound (500 g) spinach, washed, drained and torn into bite-size pieces
Hot cooked rice

In a plastic bag, make a marinade with ginger and soy sauce. Cut fish into 2-inch by 1/2 inch (5 cm x 1 cm) strips, add to the marinade and marinate at least 15 minutes, turning once. Drain and reserve marinade.

In a wok or large frying pan, heat 2 tablespoons (30 ml) of the oil. Add fish and stir-fry, turning carefully until fish flakes easily. Remove and keep warm.

Heat remaining 2 tablespoons (30 ml) oil and stir-fry bean sprouts, celery and onion until tender crisp.

Combine cornstarch, sugar, chicken bouillon and marinade. Add to vegetables in wok, stirring gently. When thickened, stir in spinach and fry quickly until leaves begin to wilt. Return fish to pan and mix lightly. Serve with hot rice. Makes 6 servings.

■ "The lowly mackerel is one of the better fish. Cooked properly, it's the best fish there is," a South Shore fisherman once told me. Others agree. Some like it because they know mackerel contains large amounts of the valuable omega-3 fatty acids believed to lower blood pressure, a major risk factor for heart attack and stroke. Others—like my mother, who lived her last thirty years on the West Coast—like the fish simply for its taste. During a visit "home" some years ago, she told me all she wanted to eat was mackerel. British Columbia waters just didn't produce the fish she so fondly remembered, and she was determined to eat her fill while she had the chance.

So I cooked mackerel for her. I pan-fried it, barbecued it, baked it, even steamed it. And one day when I tried to put a chicken dish in front of her, she asked, "Where's my mackerel?" "It's swimming in the bay for tomorrow's breakfast," I replied. Supply was no problem, since we lived on the shores of St. Margaret's Bay, and the mackerel kept nudging our boat and latching on to our hooks. And yes, Mother had mackerel for breakfast the next morning. She liked it best pan-fried.

Pan-Fried Mackerel

To pan-fry, clean fish, remove head (and tail, if necessary to fit it into the frying pan). Dip in milk, then in flour. Melt a good-size piece of butter in a hot but not smoking frying pan. Add fish and sauté until nicely browned on one side. Turn and brown the other side. Remove to a hot platter and season with salt and pepper and chopped parsley, if desired.

Soused Mackerel

- 2 pounds (1 kg) fresh mackerel
- 1 cup (250 ml) vinegar
- 1/2 cup (125 ml) water
- 1 teaspoon (5 ml) salt
- 1 tablespoon (15 ml) mixed pickling spices
- 2 thin slices onion

Fillet and skin fish and cut into serving-size pieces. Place in a baking dish; cover with remaining ingredients. Cover dish and bake at 350F (180C) for 15 minutes. Remove from oven; cool fish in liquid. Drain. Makes 3 to 4 appetizer servings.

Finnan Farmhouse Scramble

- 1 pound (500 g) finnan haddie (smoked haddock)
- 1 cup (250 ml) milk
- 1/4 cup (50 ml) butter
- Salt, to taste
- Dash of cayenne
- 1/4 cup (50 ml) finely chopped parsley
- 4 eggs, slightly beaten
- 2 tablespoons (30 ml) lemon juice
- 4 slices bread, toasted
- 1 tablespoon (15 ml) cornstarch
- 2 tablespoons (30 ml) water
- 1/4 cup (50 ml) grated cheddar or Swiss cheese, optional

Cover fillets with milk. Simmer, covered, for 10 minutes or until flesh is opaque and flakes easily. Drain, reserve milk. Flake fish. Melt butter in the same pan; add fish, salt, cayenne and parsley. Pour eggs over fish, and cook, stirring constantly, until set. Pour lemon juice over fish mixture. Serve over toast.

Reheat poaching milk. Thicken with cornstarch mixed with water. Add cheese, if using. Cook and stir until thick and smooth. Spoon sauce over fish mixture. Makes 4 servings.

Jasper White's Old-Fashioned Salt Cod Cakes

■ Renowned chef Jasper White, whose restaurant, Jasper's, was one of Boston's most famous, took a busman's holiday in October 1991 to cook at a charity fund-raising event at the Halliburton House Inn, in Halifax. Jasper, who loves the New England cuisine he features both at home and abroad, places a strong emphasis on seafood. And he's the first American I've ever heard admit that Nova Scotia lobsters are better than Maine's: "Everybody knows Nova Scotia has the best lobsters. Maine lobsters are soft-shelled. I pay the premium price of $6 (per pound) for Nova Scotia lobsters, even when I can get Maine's for $2.50," he told me while I watched him opening littleneck clams for an appetizer of white clam pizza. His cod cake recipe is from his cookbook *Jasper White's Cooking from New England.*

1 pound (500 g) boneless salt cod (see note)
2 pounds (1 kg) potatoes, peeled and cut in half
1/4 cup (50 ml) finely chopped onion
4 tablespoons (60 ml) unsalted butter
1 teaspoon (5 ml) dry mustard
Worcestershire sauce
1 egg
3 egg yolks
Freshly ground black pepper
All-purpose flour for dusting
For serving:
1/2 pound (250 g) slab smoked bacon, cut in strips, 1/4 inch
    (6 mm) thick
Garnish: parsley, lemon wedges

Note: Salt cod must be soaked in water before cooking. Jasper starts by rinsing the fish under cold running water for 10 to 15 minutes, then soaks fillets for between 16 to 24 hours, depending on thickness of fish. For whole fish he recommends between 36 and 48 hours for soaking. For either type, it is important to change the water at least four times during the soaking process.

Soak cod according to instructions above.

Remove from soaking liquid, place in a flat pot, and cover with cold water. Bring to a simmer. Simmer 5 minutes and remove. Drain well. Break salt cod into flakes and keep warm.

Boil peeled potatoes in salted water until done (about 30 minutes). Drain thoroughly in a colander. It is important for potatoes to be as dry as possible. Cook onion in butter until limp.

Purée or mash potatoes while still warm. Add melted butter and onion, flaked fish, dry mustard and a few dashes of Worcestershire sauce. Add egg and egg yolks. Mix very thoroughly with a fork. Season with pepper. Form into small cakes and chill in refrigerator. This may all be done up to four hours in advance.

When ready to serve, dust fish cakes with flour. Panfry bacon until browned but not too crisp; remove from pan and keep warm. Fry fish cakes in bacon fat in the same pan, about 2 minutes on each side. Serve with small slices of bacon, parsley and lemon wedges. Tartar sauce can be served on the side.

beef

A lthough much had been said about the fat and cholesterol content of meat, results of a late-1980s study at the University of Guelph showed that commercially trimmed Canadian beef had much lower fat values than was commonly believed. Then came 1990 and we heard this: Canadian beef is lean and mean. Canadian pork belongs on your fork. And, if it's a celebration, look to Nova Scotia lamb—it's "lambtastic."

It was then that promoters of the red meat industry, tired of taking kicks in the rump, staked a claim on the nutritional value of their products: "Lean red meats make an important contribution to the nutritional and sensory quality of the diet," said Dr. Jean Henderson Sabry, professor emeritus in the Department of Family and Consumer Studies, University of Guelph. While red meat contributes only modestly to energy intake, she said it's a major source of dietary protein and an important source of several minerals and vitamins. She pointed especially to iron, thiamine, niacin, and riboflavin. "Inclusion of red meat in the diet has been shown to be associated with superior iron status in women," she said.

As national communications manager for Beef Information Centre (BIC), Marg Thibeault, of Mississauga, Ontario, has long kept me abreast of what was happening in the world of beef. It sometimes amazed me how she was always right on the mark as she chose subjects and recipes for whatever was current. I don't remember her ordering beef when we lunched at Bish World Cuisine with Janet Bryson, of BIC's Atlantic office. "Not in Atlantic Canada, where seafood is fresh and available!" was Marg's defense.

Swimmer Mark Tewksbury, Canada's 1992 Summer Olympics gold medallist, visited Halifax in 1992 and gave his personal reasons for favouring meat. Having once dropped red meat from his diet, in preference to granola, skinless chicken, a lot of pasta, and vegetables, he thought he was eating all the right things. "But my iron level dropped so low and I was tired all the time," he told me in an interview, adding that blood work eventually showed an iron deficiency. In fact, he was border-line anaemic. He tried iron supplements, but they didn't work. "I literally had to eat red meat to get iron back into my system. I came to realize that the key is balance, and that covers (among other things) chicken, vegetables, AND beef." While iron is an essential component of haemoglobin, responsible for the transport of oxygen to all body cells to release energy from the food we eat, not all iron is created equally. High quality heme iron found in meat sources is more easily utilized by the body than non-heme iron from vegetables, nuts, and grains.

Mark Tewksbury's Fantastic Beef Fajitas

1 lime, grated peel and juice
2 tablespoons (30 ml) orange juice
2 teaspoons (10 ml) minced garlic
2 tablespoons (30 ml) steak sauce (fruit-flavoured)
1/2 teaspoon (2 ml) cumin
1 pound (500 g) inside round or sirloin tip steak
8 flour tortillas (6-inch/15 cm diameter)
1 cup (250 ml) shredded cheddar cheese
1/2 cup (125 ml) guacamole (purchased ready-to-serve or prepared from packaged seasoning mix and avocados)

In shallow dish, prepare marinade by combining peel, juices, garlic, steak sauce and cumin. Slice steak across grain into thin (quarter-inch/5 mm) strips and toss with marinade. Cover and leave for 15 minutes.

Wrap tortillas in foil and place in a non-stick frypan, over medium heat, for 5 minutes, turning once. Remove from pan and turn heat to high.

Drain beef strips; sear on both sides in preheated frypan 2 to 3 minutes. Top warmed tortillas with beef strips, cheese and guacamole. Fold one end up about 1-inch (2.5 cm) over beef mixture. Fold left and right sides over to form a neat package. Makes 6 servings.

Roast Beef with Yorkshire Pudding

This recipe was a World Culinary Olympics medal-winner, prepared by world-renowned chefs who were judged for their culinary excellence in international competition.

8-pound rib roast of beef with bone

Insert meat thermometer in thickest part of meat, being sure it reaches centre of roast without touching any bone. Place roast, fat side up, directly on bottom of roasting pan, and place pan in centre of a 450F (230C) oven for 20 minutes.

Reduce heat to 325F (160C) and continue cooking without basting until done (see following table). Season the roast with salt and pepper half way through the cooking. Remove from oven and let stand for 15 minutes before serving.

Meanwhile, prepare Yorkshire pudding. Serve meat with cooking juices, horseradish, and Yorkshire pudding. Makes 6 to 8 servings.

Roasting table:
Rare: about 12 minutes per pound (500 g) or 140F (60C) on meat thermometer
Medium: about 15 minutes per pound (500 g) or 160F (70C) on meat thermometer
Well done: about 20 minutes per pound (500 g) or 170F (75C) on meat thermometer

Yorkshire Pudding

1 cup (250 ml) all-purpose flour
1/2 teaspoon (2 ml) salt
2 eggs
1 cup (250 ml) milk
2 tablespoons (30 ml) cooking fat from roast or lard

Combine flour and salt. Place eggs in small mixing bowl and beat until thick (8 to 10 minutes). Stir in milk. Make a well in centre of flour and pour in egg mixture. Beat at low speed until smooth, about 2 minutes. Chill about 1 hour if desired; beat lightly before using.

Put 2 tablespoons (30 ml) of cooking fat in roasting pan or 13x9-inch (33x23 cm) baking dish. Heat in oven until fat almost smokes. Pour batter over sizzling fat and bake immediately at 450F (230C) about 20 minutes or until pudding has puffed up and is golden brown. Reduce temperature to 350F (180C) and cook 15 minutes longer. Serve immediately with roast beef.

Note: The Yorkshire pudding can be cooked in individual pans. Divide fat in 12 muffin pans. Heat pans as directed and pour in batter. Bake in a 450F (230C) oven about 15 minutes. Reduce heat to 350F (180C) and bake 10 minutes longer.

Pepper Beef

In February, 1985, King's Palace, Quinpool Road, prepared an authentic eight-course Chinese meal for a Chinese New Year feature in The Chronicle-Herald and The Mail-Star. Eight of us enjoyed the meal and at least two of the recipes, Palace Pork and Pepper Beef, proved to be favourites with Herald readers.

8 ounces (250 g) flank steak
2 teaspoons (10 ml) vegetable oil
1 teaspoon (5 ml) cornstarch
1/4 teaspoon (1 ml) salt
1 green pepper
1 red pepper
1/2 carrot
1/2 jumbo Spanish onion
Vegetable oil
1 teaspoon (5 ml) salt
1 teaspoon (5 ml) chili oil
1/4 cup (50 ml) chicken stock
1 teaspoon (5 ml) soy sauce
1 teaspoon (5 ml) cornstarch
1/4 cup (50 ml) water
1/2 teaspoon (2 ml) sesame seeds

Cut beef against the grain into thin slices. Make a marinade of the 2 teaspoons (10 ml) vegetable oil, 1 teaspoon (5 ml) cornstarch and 1/4 teaspoon (1 ml) salt. Stir in meat and set aside to marinate for 15 minutes.

Cut into bite-size pieces the red and green peppers and Spanish onion. Cut carrot into thin slices. Heat 1/4 cup (50 ml) vegetable oil in wok and bring to a boil. Add beef and stir-fry for 10 seconds; remove.

In 4 teaspoons (20 ml) hot vegetable oil, stir-fry peppers, onion and carrot. Add salt, chili oil, chicken stock, and soy sauce; stir-fry over high heat for 30 seconds. Make a smooth paste of cornstarch and water, add to mixture in wok and blend thoroughly. Add beef and cook another 15 seconds. Remove and serve, sprinkled with sesame seeds. Makes 4 servings.

Curried Pot Roast

3 pounds (1.5 kg) boneless cross-rib, blade, or shoulder roast
1 tablespoon (15 ml) canola oil
2 onions, thickly sliced
2 apples, peeled, cored, and coarsely chopped
1 tablespoon (15 ml) curry powder
1 tablespoon (15 ml) flour
1 cup (250 m) chicken bouillon
2 garlic cloves, crushed
generous pinch ground cinnamon
generous pinch of ground ginger
1/2 cup (125 ml) raisins (optional)

In a heavy saucepan, heat oil; brown roast in oil on all sides; remove from saucepan. Reduce heat; add onions and apples, sprinkle with curry powder, and cook until onions are soft; push to one side of pan. Blend in flour and cook, stirring, for a minute or two to remove raw taste of flour. Stir in bouillon, garlic, cinnamon and ginger. Cook until slightly thickened.

Return meat to pot; cover and simmer over low heat for 2 hours, or until tender. Add raisins, if using, during the last 30 minutes of cooking. Makes 8 to 10 servings.

Bonnie Conrad

■ Bonnie Conrad of Portuguese Cove, Nova Scotia, is one of those people who takes her work home with her. As a registered dietitian and public health nutritionist with Capital Health, Halifax, nutrition is a way of life and her life's work. Bonnie contributed her Slow Cooker Beef Stew recipe to *Great Food Fast*, a cookbook produced by Dietitians of Canada and co-authored by Toronto-based dietitians Bev Callaghan and Lynn Roblin.

To help busy cooks get the evening meal on the table with little effort and less stress, Bonnie recommends a weekly meal plan and as much advance preparation as possible: "I always keep basics on hand, such as beans, pasta, and frozen vegetables, and I keep a grocery list on the go," she said. "A meal plan is a security blanket, but I'm flexible. If I don't like the look of an ingredient when I'm shopping, I switch to something else."

Slow Cooker Beef Stew

1 pound (500 g) lean stewing beef, cut into 1-inch (2.5 cm) cubes and patted dry
1 tablespoon (15 ml) all-purpose flour
2 teaspoons (10 ml) canola oil
2 cups (500 ml) cubed turnips
2 cups (500 ml) cubed carrots
1 cup (250 ml) sliced onions
1 1/2 cups (375 ml) boiling water
2 beef bouillon cubes or sachets
3 tablespoons (45 ml) red wine vinegar
3 tablespoons (45 ml) ketchup
4 teaspoons (20 ml) prepared mustard
1 teaspoon (5 ml) Worcestershire sauce
2 tablespoons (30 ml) all-purpose flour
3 tablespoons (45 ml) cold water

In a large bowl, toss beef cubes with flour; set aside. In a large non-stick skillet, heat oil over medium-high heat. Add beef and cook for 4 to 5 minutes or until browned on all sides. Place in slow cooker. Add turnips, carrots and onions.

In a medium bowl, blend together water, bouillon, vinegar, ketchup, mustard and Worcestershire sauce. Add to slow cooker; stir gently. Cook, covered, on low heat setting for 9 hours.

In a measuring cup, whisk together flour and water. Add flour mixture to stew; stir gently to blend. Increase slow cooker heat setting to high; cook, covered, for 15 minutes or until thickened. Makes 4 servings.

Anne Lindsay

■ My kitchen gained stature in April 1994, when Anne Lindsay stood in front of my stove, albeit not to cook, but to be photographed with her latest cookbook. She's one of my heroes because her cookbooks have done more for the health of Canadians than anything I know. Lighthearted was just a frivolous word before Anne applied it to the titles of two of her books, which feature recipes for healthy heart cooking. By 1994, her three books had sold over a million copies, and she's had two more books published since. Family Favourite Shepherd's Pie is from Anne's *The Lighthearted Cookbook*.

Family Favourite Shepherd's Pie

1 pound (500 g) lean ground beef or pork or lamb, or a combination of these
2 onions, chopped
2 cloves garlic, minced
1 carrot, minced (optional)
1/3 cup (75 ml) tomato paste
2/3 cup (150 ml) water
1 tsp (5 ml) dried thyme
2 tsp (10 ml) Worcestershire sauce
freshly ground pepper
paprika
2 cups (500 ml) mashed potatoes

In skillet over medium heat, cook beef, stirring to break up meat, until brown; pour off fat. Add onions, garlic and carrot, if using; cook until tender. Add tomato paste, water, thyme, Worcestershire sauce, and pepper to taste. Simmer for 5 minutes, stirring up any brown bits on bottom of pan.

Spoon meat mixture into 8-cup (2 L) baking or microwave-safe dish; spread mashed potatoes evenly on top. Sprinkle with paprika to taste. Bake in 375F (190C) oven for 35 minutes or until heated through, or microwave at high (100 per cent) power for 9 minutes. Makes 5 servings.

Carol Ferguson in a field of canola in Saskatoon

■ Do we side with nutritionists and opt for a diet that will benefit our health? Or do we take our chances and go for taste?

Carol Ferguson has made deciding easier. We've come to know and trust this proud-to-be-Prairie-born home economist through her cookbooks and magazine articles, her ten-year stint as food editor of *Canadian Living*, editor of *FOOD* magazine, and later, food and nutrition director for *Homemakers* magazine.

Her cookbook, *A Century of Canadian Home Cooking—1900s through the '90s*, was co-authored with Margaret Fraser, and is a classic that should be in every Canadian household. The same can be said of *The New Canadian Basics Cookbook*, which Carol co-authored with Murray McMillan, food editor for *The Vancouver Sun*.

Easy "Cabbage Roll" Casserole

1 1/2 pounds (750 g) ground beef
2 onions, chopped
2 cloves garlic, minced
1 teaspoon (5 ml) salt
1/4 teaspoon (1 ml) pepper
1 can (14 ounce/398 ml) tomato sauce
1 cup (250 ml) water
1/2 cup (125 ml) rice (uncooked)
4 cups (1 L) shredded cabbage (shredded in food processor or with knife)

In non-stick skillet, brown beef, stirring to break it up. Stir in onions, garlic, salt, pepper, tomato sauce and water; bring to boil. Stir in rice; cover and simmer for 10 minutes or until rice is partially cooked. Place half of shredded cabbage in greased 11x7-inch (28x18 cm) or 9-inch (23 cm) square baking dish. Cover with half of beef mixture. Repeat layers. Do not stir. Cover and bake in 350F (180C) oven for 1 hour or until rice is tender. Makes about 6 servings.

Margaret Fraser

■ You know Margaret Fraser through her many food articles in *Canadian Living* and other magazines. She became a home economist and settled in Toronto and has also travelled across Canada doing research for *A Century of Canadian Home Cooking*, the wonderful book she co-authored with Carol Ferguson. She fondly remembers the fresh apple cider she enjoyed in the Annapolis Valley, the unmatched melt-in-your-mouth oatcakes from Cape Breton, and values among her favourite cookbooks, a well-worn copy of Lunenburg's *Dutch Oven*.

Cleopatra's Chili

Rumour has it that Elizabeth Taylor is so fond of this chili that she had it shipped to her from Chasen's in Los Angeles during the filming of Cleopatra in Egypt.

1/2 pound (250 g) pinto beans
5 cups (1.25 L) canned or fresh tomatoes
1 pound (500 g) green or red peppers, chopped
1 1/2 tablespoons (22 ml) salad oil
1 1/2 pounds (750 g) chopped onions
2 crushed garlic cloves
1/2 cup (125 ml) chopped fresh parsley
2 1/2 pounds (1.2 kg) coarse-ground chuck beef
1 pound (500 g) lean ground pork
2 tablespoons (30 ml) salt
1/3 cup (75 ml) chili powder
1 1/2 teaspoons (7 ml) black pepper
1 1/2 teaspoons (7 ml) cumin

Wash beans and soak overnight; simmer in soaking water until tender. Add tomatoes and simmer for 5 minutes. Sauté green peppers in salad oil for 5 minutes. Add onion and cook until tender, stirring often. Add garlic and parsley.

Sauté beef and pork in butter. Add meat to onions, tomato and green pepper, stir in chili powder and cook for 10 minutes. Add beans and spices and simmer, covered, for 1 1/2 hours. Uncover pot and simmer for another 30 minutes. Skim grease from top. Makes 8 servings.

One-Pot Sauerkraut Dinner

When you run out of months to which promoters can attach a special food, you start using weeks. One of those already allotted, in the United States, at least, is National Kraut and Frankfurter Week—a week with ten days! They must have heard about the famous sauerkraut produced on Nova Scotia's South Shore.

1 corned brisket of beef, about 2 1/4 pounds (1 kg)
6 peppercorns
1 bay leaf
6 medium-size carrots, pared
6 medium-size potatoes, pared
3 small onions, halved
2 cups (500 ml) cubed pared rutabaga (turnip)
5 cups (1.25 L) sauerkraut

Place meat in a Dutch oven or deep saucepot; cover with cold water. Add peppercorns and bay leaf. Cover and heat to boiling. Reduce heat and simmer, covered, 1 1/2 hours.

Remove meat to plate and pour off liquid, reserving 1 1/2 cups (375 ml). Remove and discard peppercorns and bay leaf. Add 1 cup (250 ml) liquid to pot, reserving remaining 1/2 cup (125 ml). Add carrots, potatoes, onions and rutabaga. Spread sauerkraut over all. Place meat on top. Cover and heat to boiling. Reduce heat and simmer about 25 minutes, or until potatoes are tender, adding reserved liquid if needed. Makes 6 servings.

Stuffed Peppers

4 large sweet red or green peppers
1 tablespoon (15 ml) canola oil
1 medium onion, minced
1 large clove garlic, minced
3/4 pound (375 g) lean ground beef
1/2 cup (125 ml) uncooked bulgur or cracked wheat
1 1/2 cups (375 ml) tomato or spaghetti sauce
1 tablespoon (15 ml) Worcestershire sauce
1 teaspoon (5 ml) salt (or less)
1/8 teaspoon (0.5 ml) red pepper flakes
1 tablespoon (15 ml) water

Slice stem ends off peppers. Remove cores and seeds; set aside. Mix oil, onion, garlic and beef in microwave-safe 2-quart (2 L) casserole dish big enough to hold peppers upright with 1/2 inch (1 cm) between them. Push meat mixture into doughnut shape around edge of casserole.

Cover with wax paper and microwave on high 7 to 8 minutes, stirring at half time to break up beef, and cook until no longer pink.

Mix in bulgur, 1 cup (250 ml) tomato sauce, Worcestershire, salt and red pepper flakes. Cover with vented plastic wrap and microwave on high 5 minutes. Stir, cover and microwave on medium 4 1/2 to 5 minutes until bulgur is tender-firm. Let stand, covered, 10 minutes.

Fill peppers with meat mixture and arrange 1/2 inch (1 cm) apart in same casserole. Add water and cover casserole with lid or vented plastic wrap. Microwave on high 7 to 8 minutes until peppers are barely tender, rotating casserole 180 degrees at half time. Let stand, covered, 3 minutes.

Lift peppers to heated serving plates. Discard casserole liquid and pour in remaining 1/2 cup (125 ml) tomato sauce. Cover, and microwave on high 2 minutes until uniformly hot. Spoon sauce over each pepper. Makes 4 servings.

pork

It was June 1984, and we were traveling through what seemed to be miles of Quebec's sugar bush. While most of the sucreries had closed operation until the next run of the sap, some eighty newspaper food editors (mostly American) had set their course for an old sugar shack comfortably nestled among the tall maples that surround Rigaud. Here, at Sucrerie de la Montagne, we knew we could experience the delectable taste of nature's oldest sweetener, in a setting reminiscent of earlier times. Once we left our modern mode of transportation, we would step back into history.

Though the outside temperature was registering 32 degrees Celsius, we tried to imagine sun-drenched woods sweltering under a heavy coat of slowly melting snow, and by night a maple moon that witnessed an abrupt drop in temperature. All of this, in combination, would start the spring flow in the age-old maples. Full-bearded and dressed in Habitant costume, our host, Pierre Faucher, was the epitome of hospitality. His wife Sandy and son Stefan, also dressed in period costume, busied themselves in seeing that we were soon sipping on a cooling yet heart-warming beverage.

Then lunch. A lunch of many courses, all of which were traditional French-Canadian fare. The now-famous pea soup was simmered to perfection—and it seemed only natural that one of the ingredients was maple syrup. Orielles de Crisse, billed as "a Sugar Shack delight," were slices of salt pork, freshened in boiling water and milk, and fried in hot oil until crisp. "Our Omelet Souffle" was another taste treat, accompanied by huge platters of sliced ham baked in maple syrup, baked beans, and tourtiere. Then there was the bread—great round loaves freshly baked over a wood fire. None of us could resist, any more than we could resist the maple sugar pie. Even now, the memory is sweet.

Home economist Marg Routledge, of Fredericton, who co-authored with Donna Young *New Maritimes Seasonal Cooking*, values the whisk she's using here—it was given to her by Madame Jehane Benoit, a long-time hero and role model.

Country Maple Ham (Glazed)
A la Sucrerie de la Montagne

1 lean, boneless, precooked ham
1 bottle beer
2 cups (500 ml) molasses
1/2 cup (125 ml) red wine
2 cups (500 ml) grated maple sugar or 1 cup (250 ml) maple syrup

Put ham in a large pot or saucepan, half-cover with water, add beer and molasses and bring to a boil. Reduce heat and simmer slowly for about 20 minutes per pound, being careful not to overcook.

Place ham in a pan; pour wine over and top with the maple sugar or maple syrup. Place in a 325F (160C) oven for about 15 to 20 minutes, until glaze is set.

Pork with Peppers and Cashews

■ In November 1984, the Department of Agriculture presented Food Fest in Scotia Square and we were there to taste some of the newest dishes concocted by the home economists and food consultants representing the various Nova Scotia producer associations. It was impressive. Such tempting treats to please the eye and appease the appetite. Jill Harris, then with the Nova Scotia Pork Producers, came up with Pork with Peppers and Cashews—a great dish, most appropriate for entertaining.

1 pound (500 g) pork steaks, cut in three-quarter-inch (2 cm) cubes
1 tablespoon (15 ml) soy sauce
1/2 teaspoon (2 ml) granulated sugar
2 tablespoons (30 ml) canola oil
1 large green pepper, cut in three-quarter-inch (2 cm) cubes
1 large red pepper, cut in three-quarter inch (2 cm) cubes
1 onion, chopped
1 tablespoon (15 ml) cornstarch
1/2 cup (125 ml) cold water or chicken broth
4 ounces (125 g) cashews
Cooked rice

Combine pork, soy sauce, and sugar; set aside. Prepare vegetables. Heat oil in wok, add pork mixture and stir-fry for 4 to 5 minutes. Remove pork from wok. Stir-fry onion for 1 to 2 minutes. Add peppers and stir-fry 2 to 3 minutes. Return pork to wok and add combined cornstarch and water, which has been stirred into a smooth paste. Heat and stir gently until sauce is thickened and clear. Add cashews and allow them to heat through. Serve at once with rice. Makes 4 servings.

■ Just when it seems there's nothing new under the sun that shines on Kermesse, somebody comes up with a new idea to bolster the coffers of the annual IWK Children's Hospital fair. In 1993, it was *The Coffee Shop Cookbook*. The coil-bound book, with just under three hundred "tried and true" recipes was a project of the former Coffee Shop Committee. The Coffee Shop, located in the hospital for twenty-two years, was operated by the IWK Children's Hospital Auxiliary. Difficulties in keeping it staffed by volunteers forced it to close. Cherry Pork Roast was contributed to the project by Debbie Matheson.

Cherry Pork Roast

5—6 pounds (2.5 kg) boneless rolled pork loin roast
Salt and pepper
1 (12-ounce/341 ml) jar cherry jam
1/4 cup (50 ml) red wine vinegar
2 tablespoons (30 ml) corn syrup
1/4 teaspoon (1 ml) ground cinnamon
1/4 teaspoon (1 ml) grated nutmeg
1/4 cup (50 ml) slivered almonds, toasted

Rub pork with salt and pepper and place in roasting pan. Roast, uncovered, in a 350F (180C) oven for 2 hours and 30 minutes.

Prepare sauce during second hour of roasting. In saucepan, combine jam, vinegar, corn syrup, cinnamon, nutmeg, and a pinch of salt, if desired. Heat slowly, stirring, until mixture boils. Reduce heat and simmer for 5 minutes. Add almonds. Keep sauce warm.

After 2 hours and 30 minutes, remove roast from oven and spoon small amount of sauce over pork. Return to oven; bake for 30 minutes more. Watch that sauce doesn't burn. To serve, spoon sauce over carved meat.

Pork Chops with Apple Cider

Apple cider differs from apple juice, not only in a richer, more intense flavour, but apple juice is heated for pasteurization—cider is the pure juice. Always available over the Christmas holidays, apple cider can be frozen for future use. Just remove a cup or so from the container to allow for expansion, recap, and freeze.

2 pork loin chops
1 cup (250 ml) apple cider
1 apple, cored and sliced
1 onion, cut in quarters
1/2 clove garlic, crushed
Pinch of ground cinnamon
Salt and pepper, to taste
1 tablespoon (15 ml) cornstarch
1/4 cup (50 ml) cold water

Place pork chops in a baking dish just large enough to hold them. Pour apple cider over pork. Top with apples slices, onion, garlic, salt and pepper. Cover and bake in a 375F (190C) oven for 1 hour or until pork is tender. Remove chops, apple and onions.

Make a sauce by pouring pan juices into a saucepan and bring to a boil. Combine cornstarch and water, stirring until a smooth paste is formed. Gradually stir cornstarch mixture into boiling juice. Cook, stirring constantly, until thickened. Makes 2 servings.

■ Chinese New Year came early for eight of us who, in mid-February 1985, were at Kings Palace to try selections from an authentic Chinese menu. Host chef was the restaurant's manager, Ken Yee, who chose and prepared the menu that would see us through three hours of happy eating.

A delicious Sai Wu Egg Drop Soup was followed by an appetizer of Peking Duck Skins and julienned vegetables served up in pancake wrappers—it had us licking our fingers and smacking our lips. Then following a digesting period, the serious eating began. The entrees, which arrived singly or in pairs, with "rest periods" in between, consisted of Crystal Shrimp, Sizzling Chicken, Palace Pork, Steamed Fish, Peking Duck with Vegetables, and Pepper Beef. We were grateful to Ken and Kings Palace for sharing the recipes.

Palace Pork

1 pound (500 g) pork tenderloin
1 egg
1/4 teaspoon (1 ml) salt
Cornstarch
2 tablespoons (30 ml) diced pineapple
1 small piece garlic, chopped
1/2 sweet green pepper, cut up
1/2 sweet red pepper, cut up
1 tomato, cut into sections
4 teaspoons (20 ml) granulated sugar
4 teaspoons (20 ml) white vinegar
1/2 cup (125 ml) tomato ketchup
1 teaspoon (5 ml) cornstarch paste
Canola oil

Cut pork into 2-inch (5 cm) slices. Beat egg; add salt and 4 teaspoons (20 ml) cornstarch. Dip pork in egg mixture and then in dry cornstarch until well coated. Deep-fry over medium heat until golden brown and crispy, about 6 minutes.

Boil together the sugar, vinegar and ketchup, stirring until well blended. Remove from heat.

Heat a wok with 2 teaspoons (10 ml) canola oil to boiling. Add pineapple, garlic, green and red peppers, and tomato. Then add 1 teaspoon (5 ml) cornstarch paste and bring to a boil. Finally add pork pieces to wok, stir-fry for 30 seconds, just until pork is heated. Serve immediately. Makes 4 servings.

Pork Chops with Rhubarb Sauce

4 loin or butt pork chops
Canola oil
1 cup (250 ml) stewed rhubarb
1/2 cup (125 ml) tomato ketchup
1/4 cup (50 ml) vinegar
1 to 2 tablespoons (15—30 ml) brown sugar, to taste
1 tablespoon (15 ml) soy sauce
1/2 teaspoon (2 ml) salt

In a large frying pan, brown pork chops in hot oil. In a small bowl, combine rhubarb, ketchup, vinegar, brown sugar, soy sauce and salt. Drain excess fat from frying pan. Cover chops with rhubarb sauce and simmer over low heat until tender, about 1 hour. Thin sauce with a little water, if necessary. Makes 4 servings.

Note: To stew, cut 1 pound (500 g) of rhubarb into 1-inch (2.5 cm) pieces and combine with 1/3 cup (75 ml) granulated sugar in a medium-size saucepan. Sprinkle with 1 tablespoon (15 ml) water and bring to boiling, stirring frequently. Reduce heat and simmer until tender, about 15 minutes.

Pork Chop Suey

2 tablespoons (30 ml) canola oil
1 pound (500 g) pork, cut in 1/2 inch (1 cm) strips.
1 medium onion, chopped
1 1/2 cups (375 ml) diagonally sliced celery
8 ounces (250 g) mushrooms, quartered
1 cup (250 ml) chicken stock
1/2 tablespoon (7 ml) cornstarch
3 tablespoons (45 ml) soy sauce
Salt and pepper
2 cups (500 ml) bean sprouts

In wok, heat oil. Stir-fry pork for 2 to 3 minutes. Add onion, celery and mushrooms. Stir-fry 2 to 3 minutes. Combine stock, cornstarch, soy sauce, salt and pepper; add to wok. Add bean sprouts and bring to boil. Cook until sauce has thickened and vegetables are well heated. Serve immediately. Makes 8 servings.

Stephen Bell, Colin Conrad, and Nancy McCombs

■ It was to be fifteen years before we had the opportunity to enjoy another feast of deliciousness, such as we were treated to at Kings Palace in 1985. This time, it was six Dartmouth-area friends who got together and cooked up a Chinese dinner of fried wontons, wonton soup, egg rolls, ginger beef, lemon chicken, Szechuan chicken, pork chop suey, stir-fried vegetables, fried rice and Chinese fortune cookies. The cooks were Nancy McCombs, Stephen Bell and Colin Conrod, ably assisted by Mary Conrod, Trish Bell and Allison Lund. Margaret Mitchell and I did nothing but watch and eat. We were guests.

Julia Aitken

■ In June 2002, cookbook author and food editor Julia Aitken was in Halifax on a cross-country tour to discuss the food supply in Canada. She was enthusiastic about what the tour revealed: "I was impressed by the confidence Canadians have with the food supply in this country," she said, crediting the government's regulatory system and Canada's food marketing boards for instilling confidence in the consumer. "These food marketing boards are unique to Canada. The system matches what the farmers produce with what consumers need and want," she said. Using the egg marketing agency as an example, she explained that the system ensures Canadians have a stable supply of reasonably priced eggs by managing supply and avoiding the market volatility that could result in shortages and high prices. The recipe for Maple-Mustard Glazed Pork Tenderloins is from Julia Aitken's *Easy Entertaining Cookbook*.

Maple-Mustard Glazed Pork Tenderloins

Marinade:
1/2 cup (125 ml) Worcestershire sauce
1 teaspoon (5 ml) hot pepper sauce
1 clove garlic, minced
2 large pork tenderloins (each about 1-pound/500 g), trimmed of fat
Maple-Mustard Glaze:
1 cup (250 ml) chicken stock
2 tablespoons (30 ml) maple syrup
2 tablespoons (30 ml) Dijon mustard
Salt and pepper
Garnish: watercress or fresh sage sprigs

Marinade: In large shallow non-reactive baking dish, whisk together Worcestershire sauce, hot pepper sauce and garlic. Add tenderloins, turning to coat well. Marinate an hour at room temperature, turning meat once, or cover and refrigerate for up to 24 hours, turning meat occasionally.

Remove tenderloins from marinade, shaking off excess; reserve marinade. Heat a large heavy ovenproof skillet or lightly oiled shallow flameproof casserole, over medium-high heat. Add tenderloins and cook, turning often, 2 to 3 minutes, or until browned on all sides.

Transfer skillet to oven; cook 18 to 20 minutes or until meat thermometer inserted into thickest part of tenderloins registers 155F (68C).

Wearing oven mitts, remove skillet from oven. Remove tenderloins to a cutting board; tent loosely with foil and let rest in a warm place for 5 minutes.

Glaze: Meanwhile, in 2-cup (500 ml) liquid measure, whisk together stock, maple syrup, mustard, salt, pepper and 2 tablespoons (30 ml) of reserved marinade; add to skillet. Bring to boil over high heat, stirring to scrape up any brown bits from bottom of skillet. Boil 5 to 7 minutes or until stock mixture is reduced to about 3/4 cup (175 ml) and has thickened slightly. Add any juices that have accumulated under pork on cutting board. If desired, season to taste with more salt and pepper.

Cut each tenderloin diagonally into half-inch (1 cm) slices. Arrange on a warm platter; drizzle with glaze. Serve garnished with watercress or fresh sage sprigs. Makes 4 to 6 servings.

Note: Pork should not be overcooked; at 155F (68C) it should still be slightly pink inside.

■ Honey Garlic Ribs were high on the popularity list at the Royal Canadian Legion, Scotia Branch Number 25, when I visited the kitchen and dining room in June 1986. Eileen Beaver was cook and Doris McKay, president of the Ladies' Auxiliary, was in charge of the kitchen.

Honey Garlic Ribs

4 pounds (2 kg) side spare ribs, cut into 2-inch (5 cm) pieces
1/2 cup (125 ml) soy sauce
1 teaspoon (5 ml) garlic powder
2 tablespoons (30 ml) cornstarch
1/4 cup (50 ml) liquid honey
1 (350 ml) jar dry spare rib garlic sauce
Cooked rice

Place ribs in pan; half cover with water. Add soy sauce and garlic powder. Cover, bring to a boil, reduce heat and simmer for about 20 minutes, until ribs are tender. Drain half the water. Make a paste with cornstarch and a little water. Push ribs to side; add honey, garlic sauce and the cornstarch mixture. Cook, stirring about 1 minute, until the sauce is thick enough to coat ribs. Serve with rice. Makes 6 to 8 servings.

Apple-Kraut and Bratwurst Dinner

Bratwurst, the German word for a frying sausage, is generally a fresh, raw sausage that must be fried or grilled before eating. However, some of the 150 different varieties come fully cooked. Oktoberfest-Bratwurst, one of the most popular sausages, is a fully cooked white bratwurst made of beef and pork.

1 pound (500 g) bratwurst
2 teaspoons (10 ml) canola oil
1 tart apple, cored
1 medium onion, sliced
1 pound (500 g) sauerkraut, drained
1/4 cup (50 ml) apple juice
Freshly ground black pepper

In a large nonstick skillet over medium-low heat, cook bratwurst in oil until browned, about 10 minutes. Remove from skillet.

Cut apple into 12 wedges. Add apple and onion to skillet and cook, stirring, over medium heat for 5 minutes, or until lightly browned. Stir in sauerkraut and apple juice. Season with pepper to taste.

Add bratwurst and bring to a boil. Reduce heat, cover and simmer for 20 minutes or until bratwurst is cooked through and juices run clear. Makes 4 servings.

lamb

When Tom Harvey, well-known actor of stage, film, and television, visited Halifax in 1983, he took full advantage of the availability of fresh seafood, although the purpose of his visit was to promote lamb. "When I come to Nova Scotia, I eat fish," he said. But as consumer spokesperson for the New Zealand Lamb Information Centre (NZLIC), he also ate a lot of lamb.

It's not that he felt pressed to do so by his commitment to the job—his taste for this tender alternative to beef and pork was established long before he was approached by the New Zealand organization. Having seen a publicity shot of Harvey cooking in his kitchen, the NZLIC called and asked, "Are you really what you are in the picture?" "Yes, I am," replied Tom, and he accepted the contract with the proviso that the lamb promotion be worked around his acting career.

Referring to the Canadian disregard for his favourite meat (Canadians, at that time, ate only a pound-and-a-half (750 g) of lamb per capita per year, compared to 90 pounds of beef and 60 pounds of pork), Harvey said: "I feel people are missing a good thing…not only good nutritious eating, but also in terms of economical meals." Harvey meant what he said. He had been a lamb enthusiast since he was a struggling young radio an-

A lot of trust is generated from the *Canadian Living* test kitchen, where home economist Heather Howe is manager. Canadians are fortunate to have such an excellent source of recipes, as well as qualified people at the helm to develop, test, and retest them "until perfect." It's a tall order that Heather fills proficiently for *Canadian Living* magazine and for all of us who read it.

nouncer in St. Louis, Missouri. And when he invited Johnny Wayne, Frank Shuster, John Byner, and forty other friends over for a barbecue, it was lamb that received top billing. Tom handled the barbecuing with all the flourish of a professional chef, though he modestly called his efforts "just a little better than average."

Tom Harvey's Lamb Chops

| 8 lamb chops, thawed
Marinade:
1/4 cup (50 ml) canola oil
2 tablespoons (30 ml) lemon juice
1 onion, chopped
1 garlic clove, minced
2 drops Tabasco pepper sauce
1/2 teaspoon (2 ml) Worcestershire sauce
1/4 teaspoon (1 ml) dry mustard
1 bay leaf
1/4 teaspoon (1 ml) freshly ground pepper

Combine marinade ingredients and pour over lamb chops. Marinate 1 to 2 hours at room temperature, or overnight in the refrigerator.

Scrape off marinade. Barbecue or broil chops 4 inches (10 cm) from heat source (4 to 5 minutes a side for rare). Makes 4 servings.

Orange-glazed Leg of Spring Lamb

| 1 5-lb (2.5 kg) spring lamb leg
Whole cloves
1/3 cup (75 ml) orange marmalade
2 tablespoons (30 ml) soy sauce
2 tablespoons (30 ml) fresh lemon juice
1/2 teaspoon (2 ml) powdered ginger
Garnish: orange slices and fresh mint or parsley leaves

With a very sharp knife and without cutting deeply, score the outer layer of fat diagonally in both directions to make 1-inch (2.5 cm) diamonds. Stick a whole clove at corners of the diamonds. Place on rack in shallow roasting pan and roast, uncovered, for 10 minutes in a 450F (230C) oven. Reduce heat to 325F (160C) and continue roasting about 1 hour and 25 minutes longer for rare, or until a meat thermometer registers an internal temperature of 150F (65C). Allow more time (10 to 20 minutes) for medium (160F/70C) or well done (170F/75C).

Starting about 20 minutes before roast is done, stir together marmalade, soy sauce, lemon juice and ginger and drizzle some of the mixture over the lamb. Repeat every few minutes until marmalade is used and meat is a dark shiny brown. If you wish a darker glaze, increase oven temperature to 400F (200C) for a few minutes at the end of roasting time.

Let rest 15 to 20 minutes before carving. Garnish platter with orange slices and fresh mint. Makes 6 to 8 servings.

Lamb Chops in Beer

1 can (12 ounce/341 ml) beer
1/3 cup (75 ml) canola oil
1 clove garlic, minced
1 tablespoon (15 ml) lemon juice
1 tablespoon (15 ml) granulated sugar
3/4 teaspoon (3.5 ml) salt
Dash pepper
4 shoulder lamb chops

In shallow dish, combine beer, oil, garlic, lemon juice, sugar, salt and pepper. Add lamb chops. Cover and refrigerate overnight. Remove chops from dish; drain. Broil 4 to 5 minutes on each side for rare. Makes 2 to 4 servings.

Stuffed Lamb Breast

There was a time when lambs would be born in January to be slaughtered in early spring, usually (but not always) in time for the Easter market. Lamb lovers could indulge them-selves for a few weeks, and then the pleasure would be over, until spring rolled around again. New farming technologies, along with a highly specialized nutrition plan, has made fresh lamb available year round.

1/2 pound (250 g) sausage meat
1/2 cup (125 ml) breadcrumbs
2 onions, finely chopped
1 clove garlic, finely chopped
2 tablespoons (30 ml) tomato paste
Salt and pepper to taste
Pinch cloves
2-4 pounds (1-2 kg) boneless lamb breast

Brown sausage and stir in breadcrumbs, onions, garlic, tomato paste, salt, pepper and cloves. Stuff lamb with the meat mixture, roll up and tie. Roast in a 325F (160C) oven for 2 hours. Makes 4 to 6 servings.

Chef Christophe Luzeux

■ Starting his Canadian career at the Digby Pines Resort, Christophe Luzeux moved on to the World Trade and Convention Centre in Halifax, where he has been executive chef since 1992. In culinary competitions he has won several medals, has served as captain of Team Nova Scotia, and was named "Chef of the Year" by the Nova Scotia Association of Chefs and Cooks. He has also achieved his Certified Chef de Cuisine (C.C.C.) status, and was appointed a member of Culinary Team Canada, which represents the Canadian Federation of Chefs and Cooks until 2005.

When asked about future culinary trends, he predicted that Maritimers will replace the vanishing fish supply with specialized meats like lamb, and restaurants will cater to tourists looking for new presentations of fine foods, an eventuality he is prepared for with his Tian of Lamb Provencal.

Tian of Lamb Provencal, Piperade and Red Wine Risotto

3 tablespoons (45 ml) olive oil
half each of red, green, orange and yellow pepper, diced
4 tomatoes, peeled, seeded, juiced, diced
1 clove garlic, peeled, puréed
1 1/2 teaspoons (7 ml) chopped fresh basil
1 1/2 teaspoons (7 ml) chopped fresh oregano
Salt and pepper, to taste
2 medium zucchinis
1 cup (250 ml) chicken stock
2 cups (500 ml) red wine
2 tablespoons (30 ml) olive oil
1 medium onion, peeled, diced
1 cup (250 ml) arborio rice
1 radicchio, shredded
1/4 cup (50 ml) butter
1/4 cup (50 ml) grated parmesan cheese
4 racks of lamb

Piperade: Sauté diced peppers in oil over low heat for 5 to 6 minutes, until tender. Add diced tomato and garlic, cover for 5 minutes. Raise heat, remove cover, and toss vegetables for several minutes over high heat to evaporate liquid. Add herbs, salt and pepper. Set aside.

Cut a thin slice lengthwise from zucchini to make it sit solidly on the counter. Cut crosswise (without peeling) into 1/8 inch (3 mm) thick slices. Dip slices in boiling water for 1 minute, then refresh immediately in ice water. Remove from water, place on a towel to dry. Set aside.

Risotto: In a small saucepan, bring chicken stock and wine to a boil.

In a large saucepan, sauté diced onion in olive oil. Stir in rice. Add chicken stock and wine, a bit at a time, stirring constantly over medium heat until liquid is absorbed, adding more as you go. Rice is done when it's al dente (a slight bit of crunch remains). Toss in the radicchio, butter, parmesan, salt and pepper, if needed. Set aside.

Lamb: Trim lamb racks of excess fat and silver skin, also called fell. Remove filets from two of the racks; cut other two racks into chops.

Make jus by roasting bones in oven with a little white wine, onions and thyme. Remove juices to pan; reduce until about 1/3 cup (75 ml) remains.

Sear filets and chops until rare or desired doneness; set aside before slicing filets.

To serve: Place a 3-inch (8 cm) stainless steel ring (a cleaned tuna can with top and bottom removed, will do) in centre of each serving plate. Inside the ring, arrange a layer of zucchini in overlapping slices vertically around side. Put a layer of piperade inside the ring. Slice lamb filets and arrange them over piperade.

continued on next page

Carefully remove steel ring. Shape spoonfuls of risotto into ovals and place on plate at 2, 6 and 10 o'clock spots. Lay one lamb chop against each quenelle and pour some jus between each chop. Garnish with fresh herbs. Makes 4 servings.

Banana Lamb Curry

Times have indeed changed since the turn of the century, when Nova Scotia tabulated five sheep for every person in the province. Those were the days when most rural families kept a small flock for their own use.

2 1/2 pounds (1.2 kg) boneless leg of lamb
1/2 cup (125 ml) flour
1/2 teaspoon (2 ml) salt
1/4 teaspoon (1 ml) pepper
1/4 cup (50 ml) canola oil
2 medium onions, peeled and sliced
2 medium red peppers, seeded and cut into strips
2 green peppers, seeded and cut into strips
1 clove garlic, crushed
2 - 3 tablespoons (30 - 45 ml) curry powder (yep! that much)
1 (10-ounce/284 ml) can condensed beef broth
1 cup (250 ml) cream
1 cup (250 ml) flaked coconut
1 cup (250 ml) dark raisins
4 medium bananas, peeled and cut into chunks

Cut meat into 1 1/2-inch (4 cm) cubes. Combine flour, salt and pepper in a plastic bag. Toss meat cubes in seasoned flour until well coated.

In a large skillet heat oil over medium heat; brown floured meat cubes on all sides; remove and set aside.

Sauté onion slices and red and green pepper strips until just tender, about 5 minutes. Add garlic, curry powder, beef broth and cream, stirring until well blended. Return browned meat to sauce. Cook over medium heat until thoroughly heated. Add coconut, raisins, and banana chunks. Heat 2 minutes. Makes 8 servings.

Lamb in Patty Shells

The most popular cuts of fresh Nova Scotia lamb (if it's frozen, it's imported) are legs and loin chops, but the lower-priced shoulder produces a boneless roast, stew meat, and ground meat that can be served in a variety of tasty ways.

2 pounds (1 kg) lamb, trimmed of fat and diced
2 tablespoons (30 ml) canola oil
1 1/2 cups (375 ml) diced onion
1 large clove garlic, minced
1 cup (250 ml) beef or chicken bouillon
1/2 cup (125 ml) white wine
1 cup (250 ml) diced carrots
1 teaspoon (5 ml) dried oregano
1/2 teaspoon (2 ml) dried basil
Salt and pepper to taste
6 frozen patty shells
1/2 cup (125 ml) water
1 tablespoon (15 ml) flour
1 (14-ounce/398 ml) can artichoke hearts, drained
1 cup (250 ml) frozen peas

Over high heat, in heavy saucepan or skillet with tight-fitting cover, brown lamb in oil, stirring constantly. Add onion and garlic. Cook over medium heat until onion is translucent. Add bouillon, wine, carrots, oregano, basil, salt and pepper. Cover and cook over medium-low heat for 30 minutes.

Meanwhile, bake patty shells according to package directions. Blend flour with water. Gradually add to lamb and cook, stirring constantly, until thickened. Add artichoke hearts and peas. Heat through. Spoon lamb into hot patty shells and serve. Makes 6 servings.

poultry

W ho was it that said chicken is to the cook what canvas is to the painter? The words are a constant reminder that there are as many ways to prepare chicken as there are interpretations of a work of art. In Grandma's day, roast chicken was a much enjoyed Sunday dinner. Today, chicken is enjoyed any day, in a number of ways, by everyone—including those concerned with healthy eating.

Although fat is necessary as an energy booster, many Canadians consume too much of it, especially the saturated fat found in animal sources. This is one reason why chicken, especially its naturally lean white meat, is a good meal choice. Since much of the fat in chicken is visible, it can be removed prior to or after cooking. Just removing the skin on chicken can cut fat almost in half.

One concern about chicken, as with all poultry, lies in keeping it free of bacteria, prior to and following cooking. A little care in this direction will ensure the safety factor as well as the nutritional value of this delicious and economical protein choice. My friends at the Chicken Marketing Board offered this sound advice: Cook whole chicken or bone-in parts to an internal temperature of 180F (82C); boneless parts to 160F (71C). Properly cooked chicken is fork tender; comes away easily from the bone; juices

Marie's son Bob Nightingale carves the turkey, Thanksgiving 2000

run clear; and the pink colour will have disappeared. Keep cooked chicken either hot or cold (in the refrigerator). Never keep chicken at room temperature for more than 2 hours. After a meal, do not "cool" leftovers to room temperature before refrigeration. Place any leftovers or cooked chicken to be used for other recipe purposes in the refrigerator to cool.

Lemon-Garlic Roast Chicken

This tasty chicken can be roasted in a little more than an hour. You can serve it hot with gravy, mashed potatoes, and vegetables, or just keep it refrigerated to use in casseroles, sandwiches, or salads.

4-pound (2 kg) roasting chicken
1 medium head garlic
1 lemon, thinly sliced
Garnish: lemon slices, parsley

Remove giblets and neck. (These may be used to make stock.) Rinse chicken and cavity under cold running water. Pat dry with paper towels. Season cavity with salt and pepper. Separate garlic into cloves; peel. Place garlic cloves and lemon slices in chicken cavity. Tie legs down to chicken, tuck tail inside cavity, and bend wings over back.

Place chicken, breast-side-up, on a rack in roasting pan. Roast at 325F (160C) for 1 1/4 to 1 1/2 hours. Chicken is done when internal temperature reaches 180F (82C) or juices run clear and a fork can be inserted in chicken with ease. Remove chicken to a platter and keep warm. Let stand 10 minutes before carving.

To serve: If desired, use roasted garlic cloves to prepare gravy (recipe follows). Discard lemon stuffing. Garnish with lemon slices and parsley.

Slim Chicken Gravy

If desired, make chicken stock by cooking giblets and neck in 1 1/2 cups (375 ml) water seasoned with parsley and onion, for about 30 minutes. Remove meat, cool stock and skim off fat.

Purée roasted garlic cloves removed from chicken cavity. Remove and discard any fat from pan drippings. Combine 1 cup (250 ml) cooled chicken stock with 1 tablespoon (15 ml) cornstarch; pour into roasting pan. Bring to a boil over high heat, stirring to scrape up brown bits from pan. Add puréed garlic; cook, stirring, until thickened and bubbly. Makes 8 servings.

■ A talented Nova Scotia cook has won recognition in her kitchen. Arlene Bennett of Boulardarie Island, Cape Breton, created a unique recipe that captured the hearts and taste buds of a panel of judges in a nationwide chicken recipe contest sponsored by the Canadian Chicken Marketing Agency. Her winning recipe, Roast Chicken with Outside Dressing, is certainly an interesting twist to the all-time favourite Sunday dinner, combining apples and sweet potatoes in the dressing.

Roast Chicken with Outside Dressing

5-pound (2.5 kg) roasting chicken
1/2 teaspoon (2 ml) salt
1/2 teaspoon (2 ml) pepper
1/2 teaspoon (2 ml) dried thyme leaves
2 large sweet potatoes, peeled, cut into chunks
2 firm green cooking apples, cored, quartered
1 tablespoon (15 ml) brown sugar
1/4 teaspoon (1 ml) ground ginger
1/4 teaspoon (1 ml) ground cinnamon
1 tablespoon (15 ml) butter or margarine
1/4 cup (50 ml) apple jelly
1 1/4 cups (300 ml) apple juice
2 to 3 tablespoons (30 to 45 ml) all-purpose flour
1/4 cup (50 ml) water

Remove chicken giblets and neck; use to make stock if desired. Rinse chicken and cavity under cold running water. Pat dry with paper towels. Sprinkle half of salt, pepper and thyme on chicken. Tie legs down to chicken; tuck tail inside cavity; bend wings over back.

Place chicken breast-side-up on a rack in roasting pan. Roast in a 400F (200C) oven for 30 minutes. Reduce heat to 350F (180C); cover chicken loosely with foil and continue roasting for 45 minutes.

In large casserole, combine sweet potatoes, apples, brown sugar, ginger and cinnamon; dot with butter. Cover tightly and place in oven with chicken. Continue cooking for about 45 minutes.

In saucepan, melt apple jelly. During last 20 minutes of chicken roasting time, remove foil and brush chicken with jelly; continue basting chicken with pan juices until nicely glazed and chicken is cooked. Chicken is cooked when internal temperature reaches 180F (82C) or juices run clear and fork can be inserted in chicken with ease. Remove chicken to large serving platter and keep warm.

Meanwhile, remove excess fat from pan juices; stir in remaining salt, pepper, thyme and apple juice. Combine flour and water; add to juice mixture and cook until thickened. Spoon sweet potato-apple mixture around chicken and serve with apple gravy. Makes 8 servings.

Basic Poached Chicken Breasts

6 whole chicken breasts with bones, split
2 tablespoons (30 ml) butter
1 1/2 cups (375 ml) canned chicken broth

Skin chicken breasts, remove as much fat as possible, and rinse well. Put 1 tablespoon (15 ml) butter and half of the chicken broth in a large skillet with lid. (Work 2 skillets at one time, or repeat process.) Bring broth to simmer; add six chicken pieces, flesh side up. Cover skillet, tilting lid slightly to let steam escape. Simmer over low heat (do not boil) for 15 minutes.

Turn off heat; leave chicken in broth 15 minutes more. Cut open one piece of chicken to check if meat is cooked. If pink, turn heat on and simmer 5 minutes. Remove chicken from hot broth, rinse in cool water; cover and refrigerate until next day. Strain broth into a jar and refrigerate for future use. Separate chicken from bones; cut into three-quarter-inch (2 cm) cubes. Makes 6 cups cubed chicken.

Chicken and Mushrooms in Sherried Cream Sauce

This recipe is a good one to prepare ahead and keep in the freezer for entertaining. It can be served over cooked rice. Reheat thawed chicken briefly but thoroughly in a saucepan over low heat. The sauce will look grainy when thawed, but it becomes creamy when reheated. If too thin, remove chicken and vegetables with slotted spoon and let sauce cook down a bit.

4 cups (1 L) chicken broth
2/3 cup (150 ml) butter
4 tablespoons (60 ml) minced shallots or onion
1 pound (500 g) mushrooms, cleaned, trimmed and sliced thin
1/2 cup (125 ml) flour
1 cup (250 ml) light cream or milk
1 cup (250 ml) dry sherry
1/2 cup (125 ml) chopped parsley
Salt, to taste
4 cups (1 L) cooked, cubed chicken (see page 125)

Heat chicken broth in saucepan over medium heat.

Meanwhile, melt 2 tablespoons (30ml) butter in large skillet or Dutch oven over medium heat. Add onions and mushrooms; cook stirring, until onions are soft and mushrooms have given up some of their liquid. With a slotted spoon, remove mushroom mixture; set aside.

Simmer liquid in pan until reduced to about 2 tablespoons. Add remaining butter (about 1/2 cup/125 ml) to skillet and melt. Add flour, cook for a minute or two, stirring constantly. Pour in hot broth all at once, stirring briskly. Bring to a boil, lower heat, and stir until sauce is smooth and thick.

Reduce heat to very low; stir in cream, sherry, parsley, mushroom mixture and a little salt. Cook, stirring 3 minutes; taste, add salt if needed. Add chicken; stir well. Serve hot. Makes 8 servings.

Julian Armstrong

■ Julian Armstrong could scoff at my twenty years as a food writer. She's been at it twice as long, and a good chunk of that time she spent as food editor for the *Montreal Gazette*. But Julian is not that kind of person. Instead, she marvels at my career and graciously calls me a pioneer in the field of researching the traditional foods of Nova Scotia.

I return the compliment many times over: I have always admired the way she can put a story across. Although Quebec is not her native province, Julian loves it and has documented its regional cuisine in her book, *A Taste of Quebec*. After we ran this recipe sometime in 1991, at least one reader considered it the "best way to do chicken," and is still making it today.

Maple-baked Chicken Breasts

Julian says chicken and pork are often baked or braised in maple syrup in Quebec's Beauce region. "This easy recipe can also be used with a whole cut-up broiler-fryer chicken. It's from the collection of Jeanne d'Arc Nadeau, long-time proprietor of Le Danube Bleu reception hall in St. Marie and a cookbook author."

4 single chicken breasts
1/4 cup (50 ml) all-purpose flour
Salt and ground black pepper
2 tablespoons (30 ml) butter
1/2 cup (125 ml) maple syrup
1 teaspoon (5 ml) dried savoury
1/2 teaspoon (2 ml) dried thyme
1/4 teaspoon (1 ml) dried sage
1 onion, sliced
1/2 cup (125 ml) water

Dredge chicken pieces in flour seasoned with salt and pepper to taste. In a heavy, flameproof casserole, heat butter until bubbling and brown chicken pieces quickly on both sides. Pour maple syrup over chicken. Sprinkle with savoury, thyme and sage. Arrange onion slices on top of chicken pieces. Pour water into bottom of casserole. Bake, uncovered, in a 350F (180C) oven for 50 to 60 minutes or until tender, basting chicken occasionally with pan juices. Makes 4 servings.

Microwave method: Arrange chicken breasts, skins removed, in bottom of a large, shallow baking dish. Combine 1/4 cup (50 ml) maple syrup with 1/4 teaspoon (1 ml) dried savoury and a pinch each of dried thyme and sage; season with salt and pepper to taste. Pour over chicken and cover with sliced onion. Microwave, covered with vented plastic wrap, at high (100 per cent) for 12 to 14 minutes or until chicken is tender and juices run clear when meat is pierced. Remove chicken to a serving platter, cover and keep warm. Microwave remaining liquid in dish, uncovered, at high (100 per cent) for 3 to 5 minutes or until reduced. Pour sauce over chicken breasts and serve.

Walnut Chicken with Broccoli

The trick to wok cooking is to have all ingredients prepared and at hand before heating the wok to start stir-frying. Cooking time is short so foods must be cut in similar shapes and sizes so they will cook evenly. Have the wok well heated before adding the oil, then add ingredients in the order called for in the recipe. It's also a good plan to have rice steaming over hot water, plates hot, and table set. And send out the call to dinner as soon as you start stir-frying. It's that quick. And so delicious.

2 whole chicken breasts, skinned and boned
1 egg white
1 tablespoon (15 ml) cornstarch
1/2 teaspoon (2 ml) salt
1/2 teaspoon (2 ml) sugar
1 small bunch broccoli
3 green onions
4 tablespoons (60 ml) canola oil, or more
1/4 cup (50 ml) chicken broth or water
1 cup (250 ml) walnut pieces
2 cloves garlic, crushed
3 thin slices fresh gingerroot
1 tablespoon (15 ml) soy sauce
Hot steamed rice

Cut chicken into 1-inch (2.5 cm) cubes. Place in bowl; add egg white, cornstarch, salt and sugar; toss until mixed.

Peel outer layer of broccoli stalks; cut each stalk crosswise in half. Separate top half into florets; cut lower half into 1/2 inch (1 cm) strips. Cut green onions into 1-inch (2.5 cm) lengths.

Heat wok or large, deep skillet over high heat. Add 2 tablespoons (30 ml) oil; swirl to coat bottom and side of wok or pan. Add broccoli and onions; stir-fry until coated with oil. Add broth or water, cover, and cook 2 minutes or until broccoli is tender-crisp. Remove to bowl.

Reheat pan; add remaining oil (more, if needed). Add walnuts; stir-fry until lightly browned. Remove to paper towel to drain. Add garlic and ginger; cook until lightly browned. Remove, and discard, if desired. Add chicken; stir-fry until golden brown. Stir in vegetables and soy sauce; stir-fry for 1 minute to heat through. Serve over hot steamed rice, sprinkle with walnuts.. Makes 4 servings.

Easy Chicken Cordon Bleu

There's something elegant about classic Chicken Cordon Bleu. And it's still special when prepared this easy way.

8 large chicken breasts, skinned and boned
8 thin slices cooked ham
8 thin slices Swiss cheese
2 envelopes regular coating mix for chicken

Remove filet section from each chicken breast. Place filets between two pieces of wax paper and pound lightly to 1/8 inch (3 mm) thickness. Make a cut down centre of chicken breast (not all the way through the breast). Cut meat slightly on either side of centre cut and open to form a pocket. Place a piece of cheese in centre, and then a piece of ham. Top each breast with filet and press to cover ham completely.

Empty coating mix into a plate. Moisten chicken pieces with water. Shake off excess. Coat chicken breasts evenly with coating mix. Place with seam side up on an ungreased baking sheet. Bake in a 400F (200C) oven for 20 minutes. Makes 8 servings.

Classic Chicken Almond

Chicken is a nutritious and economical stand-by for summertime meals. And don't over-look the wok for hot-day cooking. Chicken is a natural for stir-frying.

3 whole chicken breasts, halved
1 large onion, sliced
1 1/2 teaspoons (7 ml) salt
Dash pepper
Water
2 tablespoons (30 ml) canola oil
1 1/2 cups (375 ml) chopped celery
1 1/4 cups (300 ml) frozen peas
1 (10-ounce/284 ml) can mushroom slices or pieces and stems
2 tablespoons (30 ml) cornstarch
1/2 teaspoon (2 ml) ground ginger
2 tablespoons (30 ml) soy sauce
Toasted slivered almonds

Combine chicken breasts, two slices of onion, salt, pepper, and 1 cup (250 ml) water in a large saucepan. Cover and simmer for 20 minutes.

Remove chicken from broth and cool until easy to handle. Strain broth. Remove breast skin and bones; cut meat into thin strips.

When ready to finish cooking, sauté remaining onion in canola oil in a large frying pan, for 2 to 3 minutes; push to side. Stir in celery and sauté 2 to 3 minutes; push to side. Place peas, mushrooms with liquid, and chicken strips in separate piles in pan; pour in broth. Cover and steam for 10 minutes.

Lift vegetables from pan with slotted spoon; place in serving bowl. Lift out chicken strips and arrange on top.

Blend soy sauce, cornstarch and ginger in a cup, stir in 2 tablespoons (30 ml) water until smooth. Stir into liquid in pan. Cook, stirring constantly, until sauce thickens and boils 3 minutes.

Spoon over chicken and vegetables; sprinkle with almonds. Makes 6 servings.

Chicken Fajitas

A fajita (pronounced fah-HEAT-ah) is a Tex-Mex wrap that started as thinly sliced grilled steak and vegetables rolled up in a warm flour tortilla. Now the filling is whatever the do-it-yourselfer wants it to be.

4 boneless, skinless chicken breast halves
2 teaspoons (10 ml) ground cumin
1 1/2 teaspoons (7 ml) Tabasco pepper sauce
1 teaspoon (5 ml) chili powder
1/2 teaspoon (2 ml) salt
8 flour tortillas
1 tablespoon (15 ml) canola oil
3 large green onions, cut in 2-inch (5 cm) pieces

Spicy Tomato Salsa:
1 large ripe tomato, diced
1 tablespoon (15 ml) chopped parsley
1 tablespoon (15 ml) lime juice
1/4 teaspoon (1 ml) Tabasco pepper sauce
1/4 teaspoon (1 ml) salt

Corn Relish:
1 can (12-ounces/341 ml) kernel corn, drained
1/2 cup (125 ml) diced green pepper
1 tablespoon (15 ml) lime juice
1/4 teaspoon (1 ml) Tabasco pepper sauce
1/4 teaspoon (1 ml) salt

Accompaniments:
1/2 cup (125 ml) shredded cheddar cheese
1/2 cup (125 ml) sliced avocado
1/2 cup (125 ml) sour cream

Cut chicken breasts into 1/2 inch (1 cm) strips. In a large bowl, toss chicken strips with cumin, Tabasco, chili powder and salt.
Prepare salsa: In medium bowl, toss tomato, parsley, lime juice, Tabasco and salt.
Prepare corn relish: In medium bowl, toss corn, green pepper, lime juice, Tabasco and salt.
Wrap tortillas in foil; heat in 350F (180C) oven for 10 minutes or until warm.
Meanwhile, in a large skillet, heat canola oil over medium-high heat. Add chicken

continued on next page

mixture and cook for 4 minutes, stirring frequently. Add green onions; cook 1 minute longer, or until chicken is browned and tender.

To serve, set out warmed tortillas along with chicken, salsa, corn relish, cheddar cheese, avocado, and sour cream.

To eat, place strips of chicken in centre of each tortilla, add salsa, relish and toppings, then fold tortilla to cover filling. Makes 4 servings.

Crispy Oven-Fried Chicken with Pan Gravy

3 1/2 pound (1.5 kg) chicken, cut up
Salt, black pepper and cayenne pepper, to taste
1 cup (250 ml) skim milk
1 cup (250 ml) homemade breadcrumbs

Pan Gravy:
2 tablespoons (30 ml) flour
1 cup (250 ml) defatted chicken broth

■ In 1985, Karen Neal, then with the Nova Scotia Chicken Marketing Board, accomplished a major fat reduction in fried chicken. By removing the skin, eliminating deep-fat frying, switching from whole milk to skim, eliminating the egg for breading, and removing the butter in the gravy, she was able to reduce the fat from 479 grams to 6.12 grams per serving. Crispy Oven-Fried Chicken with Pan Gravy is the result.

Rinse chicken, remove skin and fat. Season one side with salt, pepper and cayenne to taste; let sit for 10 minutes. Turn and season other side and let sit for 10 minutes. Coat each piece with milk and roll in breadcrumbs. Chill chicken for 20 minutes.

Place chicken on an ungreased baking dish in a 300F (150C) oven for 45 minutes, raise temperature to 400F (200C) and bake 20 minutes more.

Meanwhile make gravy: Brown flour in a saucepan over low heat until lightly coloured. Let cool. Shake flour with half the broth until smooth. Return to saucepan, add remaining broth and simmer until thickened. Season with salt, pepper and cayenne to taste. Makes 4 servings.

Best Ever B-B-Q Sauce

1 cup (250 ml) ketchup
Grated zest of 1 lemon
Juice of 2 small lemons
1 teaspoon (5 ml) prepared mustard
10 drops Tabasco pepper sauce
1 tablespoon (15 ml) Worcestershire sauce
2 tablespoons (30 ml) brown sugar
2 tablespoons (30 ml) cider vinegar
1/4 teaspoon (1 ml) salt

Combine all sauce ingredients in a non-aluminum pan and heat gently. Do not allow to simmer. Remove and reserve until ready to use. Sauce will keep, covered and stored in refrigerator.

Chicken and Ribs

This recipe is a rare one: it double-bills the winning combination of chicken and ribs.

2 pounds (1 kg) chicken wings or legs
2 pounds (1 kg) pork side ribs

Heat oven to 350F (180C).

Remove wing end tips. If using legs, choose smaller ones, and separate into thighs and drums. Rib racks can be cut into single ribs after cooking.

Rub cast iron sauté pans or heavy cookie sheets with a scant amount of vegetable oil. Arrange chicken and ribs on top in a single layer, and brush with barbecue sauce. Bake for 1 hour, basting with more sauce three or four times. Run under broiler for final few minutes, if desired.

Perfect Picnic Drumsticks

16 drumsticks
2 cups (500 ml) corn flake crumbs
2 teaspoons (10 ml) salt
2 teaspoons (10 ml) paprika
1/2 teaspoon (2 ml) pepper

Combine crumbs and seasonings in plastic bag. Rinse drumsticks in water; add 2 or 3 pieces at a time to bag and shake to coat. Place drumsticks on foil-lined baking sheet or pan; do not crowd. Bake until tender, about 1 hour at 350F (180C). There's no need to cover or turn chicken while cooking. Chill. Makes 6 to 8 servings.

Variations: Instead of corn flakes, use 2 cups (500 ml) of either fine breadcrumbs, cracker crumbs (plain or cheese flavour), all-purpose flour, or crushed potato chips, decreasing the salt by 1 teaspoonful (5 ml) if using potato chips. Or, prepare curried drumsticks by adding 1 teaspoon (5 ml) curry powder and a dash of cayenne to the coating mix.

Old-Fashioned Chicken Pot Pie

Comfort foods of the 1950s were making a comeback, not only in home kitchens but in some of the family-style restaurants where, in 1988, old-fashioned pot pies were popular menu items. This Chicken Pot Pie with tea biscuit topping was a favourite at Mrs. Murphy's Kitchen, once a popular restaurant on Breton Street, in Halifax.

2 1/2 pounds (2 kg) fresh chicken parts, including chicken thighs
4 cups (1 L) water
2 garlic cloves, peeled and crushed
1/8 teaspoon (0.5 ml) celery seed
8 whole peppercorns or a good turn of pepper
1/2 teaspoon (2 ml) salt
2 carrots, peeled, cut in 1-inch (2.5 cm) chunks
6 small onions, peeled
1/4 cup (50 ml) chopped fresh parsley
3 tablespoons (45 ml) margarine or butter
2 tablespoons (30 ml) flour
1/2 cup (125 ml) milk
1 1/2 cups (375 ml) chicken stock
1/4 teaspoon (1 ml) dried dill
Salt and pepper to taste
1/3 cup (75 ml) frozen peas
Tea biscuit dough
3 tablespoons (45 ml) margarine or butter
1/4 cup (50 ml) chopped fresh parsley

Rinse chicken under running water. In a large saucepan, bring water to a boil. Add chicken, garlic, celery seed, peppercorns, and salt. Cover and simmer over low heat for 30 minutes. Remove chicken from broth and allow to cool. Skim fat from broth. Raise heat. Add carrots, onions, and parsley. Simmer until tender, about 20 minutes. Remove vegetables. Strain broth, reserving 1 1/2 cups (375 ml) for sauce (store remainder in refrigerator or freezer for later use).

In another pot, melt margarine over medium heat. Stir in flour and cook, stirring for 3 minutes. Gradually add milk and stock; add dill, and continue to stir until sauce thickens. Remove from heat and season to taste with salt and pepper.

Skin chicken. Remove meat from the bones and cut into bite-size pieces. Discard skin and bones.

Pour half of the sauce in bottom of a 6-cup (1.5 L) casserole. Add chicken, peas, carrots, and onions. Add remaining sauce.

The pie can be prepared ahead to this point, but should be heated slightly in the oven before topping with the biscuit dough.

Make tea biscuit dough, rolled about 3/4-inch (2 cm) thick and cut in 2-inch (5 cm) rounds. Place on top of filling, dot with butter, and sprinkle with remaining chopped parsley. Bake 30 minutes in a preheated 425F (220C) oven, or until biscuit topping is golden. Makes 4 to 6 servings.

Chicken Curry

This recipe was among those prepared by Jassie Singh at Roti Restaurant (now closed), where she also conducted classes on Indian cooking.

4 ounces (125 g) clarified butter or cooking oil
1 cup (250 ml) finely chopped onion
6 garlic cloves, crushed
1/2 ounce (15 g) ginger, finely chopped
1 to 1 1/2 teaspoons (5 to 7 ml) salt
1/2 teaspoon (2 ml) turmeric
1/2 teaspoon (2 ml) chili powder
1/2 teaspoon (2 ml) black pepper
1 cup (250 ml) finely chopped tomatoes
1 chicken, cut up and skinned
2 tablespoons (30 ml) curry powder
1 cup (250 ml) water
1 ounce (30 g) fresh coriander, finely chopped

In a heavy skillet heat clarified butter or oil, add onion, garlic and ginger; fry until golden brown. Add a little water to make mixture soft. Add salt, turmeric, chili powder, and pepper; simmer for 5 minutes. Add tomatoes.

Put in cut-up chicken and cook, stirring for 5 to 10 minutes. Add 1 cup (250 ml) water and simmer for another 10 minutes. Add coriander and curry powder. Cover and simmer for 5 minutes more. Serve with boiled Basmati rice.

■ On a visit to Franklin, Tennessee, in 1998, I had breakfast with Anne Byrn, cookbook author and food writer for Nashville's daily newspaper, *The Tennessean*. We talked about a traditional southern Christmas. In the deep south, turkey and country ham share the starring role, and Anne said she enjoys the best of both worlds. On Christmas Eve she prepares a turkey dinner with "the works," which she lays out buffet style, "with dressing cooked separately, always green beans, sweet potatoes in some fashion (usually with sugar and pecans), a cranberry sauce and the family favourite, summer squash."

On Christmas morning, the last of the turkey is made into a turkey hash and served with cheese, grits, country ham, biscuits, and sweet rolls. Then for dinner, served between five and six o'clock, there's baked ham or a roast of beef. For her turkey, Anne usually roasts a breast.

Roast Turkey Breast

1 (5—7 pound/2.5—3 kg) turkey breast
Butter, melted
Salt and freshly ground black pepper
1/2 cup (125 ml) white wine

Wash turkey breast and pat dry. Brush well with melted butter on all sides. Sprinkle liberally with salt and pepper. Place on a rack in a roasting pan and roast at 325F (160C) for 20 minutes a pound, or until turkey reaches 165F (74C) in the thickest part. During roasting period add wine to drippings. Baste bird with mixture every 20 minutes. Let cool slightly before slicing. Makes 10 to 12 servings.

Turkey and Rice Skillet

1/2 cup (125 ml) chopped celery
1/2 cup (125 ml) chopped green pepper
2 tablespoons (30 ml) butter or margarine
1/2 teaspoon (2 ml) marjoram leaves, crushed
2 (10-ounce/284 ml) cans mushroom gravy
2 cups (500 ml) cooked rice
1 1/2 cups (375 ml) cubed cooked turkey
1 cup (250 ml) diced tomato
1/2 cup (125 ml) cashews
1/4 cup (50 ml) golden raisins

In frypan, cook celery and green pepper in butter with marjoram until tender. Add remaining ingredients. Heat, stirring occasionally. Makes 4 servings.

Curried Turkey and Green Beans

This recipe is from Kiss the Cook Who Microwaves: One-Dish Meals, the third book in a series prepared by Mary Mouzar, of Halifax, and her niece Joanne Uhlman.

1 tablespoon (15 ml) butter or margarine
1/2 teaspoon (2 ml) curry powder
1/2 cup (125 ml) chopped onion
2 tablespoons (30 ml) flour
1/8 teaspoon (0.5 ml) salt
1/8 teaspoon (0.5 ml) pepper
1/8 teaspoon (0.5 ml) summer savoury
1 1/4 cups (300 ml) milk
2 cups (500 ml) cooked or thawed green beans or mixed vegetables
2 cups (500 ml) cubed cooked turkey
1 tablespoon (15 ml) chopped pimiento
1/4 cup (50 ml) toasted slivered almonds

In a 2-quart (2 L) microwave-safe casserole, heat butter at 100 percent power 25 seconds, or until melted. Add curry and onion. Cover and cook at 100 percent power 1 minute or until tender and translucent. Add flour, salt, pepper and savoury; mix well. Gradually stir in milk. Cook at 100 percent power 3 minutes or until thickened, stirring often. Add beans, turkey and pimiento; mix gently. Cover and cook at 100 percent power 2 minutes or until hot, stirring once or twice. Sprinkle with almonds. Makes 4 servings.

Note: To toast almonds, arrange in microwave-safe pie plate or shallow dish. Heat at 100 percent power 2 minutes or until they begin to change colour.

barbecue

Sure, we know all about the recent poll that placed women as the top barbecuers in this country. But I don't believe it. That isn't the way it is in my family, I can assure you. And when I count noses sniffing up the charcoal fumes, it's the masculine proboscis that gets the nod, hands down.

So, what's on the menu this year? How about that he-man dinner—ribs? Right on! When it comes to ribs, not everybody knows where to begin. All they know is that they like them. But not all ribs are created equal. There are three kinds of pork ribs: back ribs, side ribs (often called spareribs), and country-style ribs. Back ribs are cut from the blade and centre sections of the loin. These are the rib bones left after the boneless pork is removed. The tender back ribs are shorter than side ribs and have a higher ratio of meat to bone. Side ribs contain the long rib bones, and since the breast bone is removed, they're easy to divide into serving portions. These are generally the least expensive of pork ribs because they have the larger amount of bone and fat.

Canada Pork recommends precooking back and side ribs in liquid before grilling. This helps assure the meat will stay moist and tender. Time on the barbecue is also reduced. Precooking can be done earlier in the day, with the ribs refrigerated until barbecuing time.

To precook, place ribs in a large saucepan, cover with water, bring just to a boil, then reduce heat and simmer, covered, about 30 minutes. Drain well before transferring the ribs to the grill. Place on grill over low to medium-low heat and coat with basting sauce, basting and turning frequently for 15 to 20 minutes, until ribs are nicely browned.

Country-style ribs come from the front end of the loin and their cooked yield is similar to pork chops, so you don't have to buy as much. Two pounds will serve up to six people, depending on appetites. To shorten grilling time, country-style ribs can also be precooked in a small amount of liquid on top of the stove or in the microwave. (See Canadian Maple Ribs.)

If you choose to barbecue the ribs without precooking, place them on a well-greased grill, rib ends

There was only one time while he was growing up that my son Frank willingly took up a mixing spoon to try his hand at cooking. That was to earn a badge from his Cub troop. I think it was Carrot Loaf that did the trick. He does somewhat better today, at the barbecue.

down, about six inches above the coals. Barbecue for 1 hour to 1 hour and 30 minutes, turning ribs often to brown evenly. Brush on barbecue sauce frequently but only during the final twenty minutes of cooking.

Canadian Maple Ribs

1 large onion
1 teaspoon (5 ml) chili powder
1/2 teaspoon (2 ml) dry mustard
1/2 teaspoon (2 ml) maple extract
2 pounds (1 kg) country-style pork ribs
Basting sauce:
1/2 cup (125 ml) maple syrup
3 tablespoons (45 ml) tomato paste
1 tablespoon (15 ml) vinegar
1 1/2 teaspoons (7 ml) chili powder
1/2 teaspoon (2 ml) maple extract, optional
1/4 teaspoon (1 ml) hot pepper sauce

Finely chop or purée onion. Blend half of chopped onion with chili, mustard, and maple extract. Spread on meat. Place ribs in shallow microwave-safe casserole; cover loosely. Microwave at defrost (30 per cent power) 35 to 45 minutes, rotating dish occasionally and turning meat over once, until meat is almost cooked but juices are still slightly pink.

To cook on stovetop: Place seasoned ribs in large saucepan; add 1 cup (250 ml) water; simmer 45—60 minutes until meat is almost cooked.

Meanwhile, combine remaining onion with basting sauce ingredients; mix well.

Preheat two-burner gas barbecue on high for 10 minutes. Turn off burner under half of grill; turn second burner to medium, or medium-low heat. Insert meat thermometer to centre of ribs' thickest portion. Place ribs on grill over unlit burner; brush with basting sauce; close barbecue. Baste frequently; barbecue about 30 minutes or until meat thermometer reads 160F (71C), meat juices run clear and ribs are richly browned. Do not overcook. Makes 4 to 6 servings.

Spicy Barbecue Pork Chops

Marinades are used to add flavour and to tenderize meat before it is cooked. Tea can be used as an inexpensive base for body and flavour. Allow a lot of time for marinating. You can start it in the morning for an evening meal, or even let it marinate overnight.

1 medium onion, chopped
2 cloves garlic, chopped
2 tablespoons (30 ml) oil
1/2 cup (125 ml) hot tea
1/4 cup (50 ml) ketchup
2 tablespoons (30 ml) cider vinegar
1 tablespoon (15 ml) molasses
1 tablespoon (15 ml) Worcestershire sauce
1/4 to 1/2 teaspoon (1 to 2 ml) Tabasco sauce
6 pork chops, cut 3/4 inch (2 cm) thick, trimmed of excess fat

Sauté onion and garlic in oil until softened but not browned. Add remaining ingredients, except pork chops. Bring to a boil; reduce heat and simmer, uncovered, for 10 minutes. Set aside to cool.

Score remaining fat on pork chops, so they don't curl during cooking. Fit chops snugly in one layer in a non-metal dish. Pour cooled sauce over and marinate, covered, in the refrigerator, for at least one hour, but preferably longer, 4 to 8 hours.

Preheat barbecue. Just before cooking, brush hot rack with oil. Remove chops from marinade and grill over medium heat, turning and basting often with marinade. This should take about 15 to 20 minutes. To test for doneness, make a small slit in the meat close to the bone; if juices are no longer pink, the chops are done. Makes 6 servings.

Laurie Nightingale 1928–2000

■ It was December 1995 when *Canadian Living*'s food director Elizabeth Baird called to ask me for a recipe to include in an up-coming book. Since she specified a country weekend barbecue feast, I decided that the top of the round steak on which my husband had earned his reputation would be the perfect choice.

There were so many weekend visitors to our cottage on Indian Point, Halifax County (and even after we made it into a year-round home) who raved about "Laurie's steak." They would arrive hoping, if not expecting, to get another taste. If it was good enough for them, I reasoned, it was certainly good enough for the rest of Canada. So I asked Laurie how he did it, and I typed while he dictated over my shoulder.

He said it was far easier to cook it than to tell how, but after an hour or so, we finally had it right and sent the recipe off to Elizabeth. It appeared in *Winning Tastes of Beef*. So for all who miss Laurie's thick barbecued steak, as I certainly do, here it is again.

Country Weekend Barbecue Feast

3 pounds (1.5 kg) inside round steak, 2 1/2-inches (6 cm) thick
1/2 cup (125 ml) Tomato Barbecue Sauce (recipe follows)

Place steak on greased grill over medium-high heat; close lid and cook, turning once, for 20 minutes.

Brush steak with half of the sauce; close lid and cook for 5 minutes. Turn and brush with remaining sauce; cook for about 5 minutes or until meat thermometer registers 140F (60C) for rare, or until desired doneness.

Transfer to cutting board; tent with foil and let stand for 15 minutes before slicing thinly across the grain. Serve with grilled potatoes and onions and, if desired, more sauce for dipping. Makes 8 to 10 servings.

Tomato Barbecue Sauce

1 cup (250 ml) tomato juice
1 cup (250 ml) tomato ketchup
1/2 cup (125 ml) cider vinegar
2 tablespoons (30 ml) liquid honey
1 tablespoon (15 ml) dry mustard
1 small clove garlic, minced
1/2 teaspoon (2 ml) Worcestershire sauce
1/4 teaspoon (1 ml) powdered ginger
1/4 teaspoon (1 ml) Italian herb seasoning

In saucepan, combine tomato juice, ketchup, vinegar, honey, mustard, garlic, Worcestershire, ginger and Italian herb seasoning; bring to boil. Reduce heat and simmer, stirring often, for 15 minutes or until thickened. (Sauce can be refrigerated in airtight container for up to 2 weeks or frozen for up to 6 months.) Makes 2 cups (500 ml).

Steak and Smoked Salmon Roll

Early in 2001, the Beef Information Centre asked me to develop a recipe for a barbecue brochure they were distributing. The recipe was to feature beef with local ingredients. I immediately thought "surf and turf" and proceeded to start testing. This is the recipe that resulted.

1 1/2 pounds (750 g) flank (or inside round) marinating steak, three-quarters inch (2 cm) thick
4 ounces (125 g) light spreadable cream cheese
4 ounces (125 g) thinly sliced smoked salmon
2 green onions, finely chopped
pepper to taste

If possible, have butcher pass the steak through a mechanical tenderizing machine. With a mallet, pound steak to about 1/2 inch (1 cm) thickness. Spread with cream cheese to within 1/4 inch (0.5 cm) of edge. Sprinkle with green onions and pepper. Cover completely with smoked salmon.

Starting with long side, roll up like a jelly roll. Tie tightly in several places with butcher's twine, or hold together with metal skewers. Barbecue over medium-high heat (400F/.200C) for 30 to 40 minutes, turning approximately every 8 minutes to brown all sides.

Insert a meat thermometer into centre of roll and cook until it reads at least 155F (68C). Remove roll from grill; place seam-side down on cutting board and tent with foil for 5 minutes. Remove string and cut into slices. Serve with salad greens or steamed broccoli and new PEI potatoes. Makes 4—6 servings.

Note: Because there is a little more waste on blade and cross rib steaks, allow six to eight ounces per person. For round or flank steak, four to six ounces is usually sufficient.

Sandi Richard

■ You can't be in Sandi Richard's company for long without doing one of two things: either you become exhausted by her energy or you get so fired up by her enthusiasm that you feel that you too can make dreams happen.

This vibrant forty-four-year-old mother of seven determined to change her life with an organized approach to meal-planning. When it worked, she decided to share her plans with others. That's now a full-time job for Sandi and her husband, Ron, who travel the country, promoting her plan, described in her three cookbooks: *Life's on Fire*, *Getting Ya Through the Summer*, and *The Healthy Family*.

BBQ Pizza

2 (12-inch/30 cm) bakery pizza crusts
1 cup (250 ml) pizza sauce
2 teaspoons (10 ml) Italian seasoning
4 - 6 slices deli lean cooked ham (7 ounces or 200 g)
1 small green pepper
1 small onion
6 - 8 mushrooms
2 cups (500 ml) grated part-skim mozzarella cheese

Preheat barbecue to medium-low (about 300F/150C). Spread sauce over crusts as desired with a spoon or spatula. Sprinkle with seasoning.

Chop ham, pepper, onion and mushrooms into small pieces and distribute evenly over crusts. Sprinkle with cheese.

Make foil diffuser by folding a long piece of heavy foil in half, shiny side out. Crumple edges together on all sides. (The final size must be larger than the bottom of the pan you are using.) Use to deflect direct heat from burners to prevent scorching of food.

Place pizzas on foil diffuser on preheated barbecue, cutting them in half, if necessary, to be sure they fit. Close lid. They only take a few minutes. Check often. When bottom crusts are browned, pizzas are ready. Makes 4 to 6 servings.

Teriyaki Steak

Marinade:

1/2 cup (125 ml) orange juice	1 clove garlic, minced
1/4 cup (50 ml) canola oil	1 teaspoon (5 ml) ground ginger
1/4 cup (50 ml) soy sauce	1 tablespoon (15 ml) brown sugar
1/4 cup (50 ml) sherry	

Meat:

1 1/2 pounds (750 g) blade, round or cross rib steak

Combine marinade ingredients, blending well.

Pierce steak with a fork or slash surface diagonally; place in a non-metallic dish and pour marinade over it. Cover, and place in refrigerator to marinate overnight.

Just before barbecuing, drain steak, reserving marinade. Place marinade in a saucepan and bring to a boil. Reduce heat and boil gently for at least 5 minutes.

Barbecue steak about 7 minutes per side, or to desired doneness, brushing with marinade during the last 5 minutes of cooking. Makes 6 servings.

■ I get asked questions about food. Sometimes I have answers, or can find the answers. Like when a colleague asked if I could get the recipe for the hamburgers served at Gentleman Jim's, a restaurant that eight years earlier had a franchise in Halifax. He had tried to capture just the right combination of meat and seasonings, and came close, but each time something was missing.

This man's patience should be rewarded, I decided as I reached for the phone. My first call turned up the name of the man who still (in June, 1991) held the Gentleman Jim franchise. From there the trail led to the head office in Toronto and then to the producers of the patties. Just twenty-four hours after my first call, the recipe came through the fax machine. Well, really, it was the batching formula—200 pounds of ground chuck, 16 pounds of rolled oats, four ounces of salt, three ounces each of pepper, sage and garlic, and 15 pounds of tomato juice. The secret, of course, would lie in the spices. I got stuck on the fourth breakdown as I attempted to divide 3 teaspoons by 3/4. So back to Toronto and the sophisticated computers of Joan Fielden. Now, the question was, would my colleague be elated when he read the Gentleman Jim Patties recipe? Or was it the challenge of the search that sparked his interest?

Gentleman Jim Patties

Note: For safety reasons, all ground meat should be thoroughly cooked. Cook patties until meat is no longer pink and juices show no pink colour.

2 pounds (1 kg) ground chuck
1 cup (250 ml) rolled oats
1/4 teaspoon (1 ml) salt
Dash each of pepper, ground sage and garlic powder
1/4 cup (50 ml) tomato juice

Combine ingredients and form into 6 patties. Grill over medium-hot fire, 4 to 6 inches (10-15 cm) from coals, (8 to 12 minutes for rare to medium-rare). Serve in heated hamburger buns with garnishes of choice.

Barbecued Whole Turkey

1 whole turkey, 10—12 pounds (4.5—5.5 kg)

Preheat barbecue for 10 minutes. Insert meat thermometer in inner thigh. Put unstuffed turkey in pan and place on grill, at medium setting. Close barbecue cover and keep closed. (Basting is not necessary, and opening the cover increases cooking time.) Barbecue about 1 hour and 45 minutes, or until meat thermometer registers 170F (77C). Cover with foil and let stand 20 minutes before carving.

Note: Barbecuing a whole turkey is a simple procedure. Prepare the turkey as you would for the oven, but don't stuff it—the barbecue doesn't give off enough heat to safely cook stuffing.

Beer Barbecued Chicken

 4 boneless, skinless chicken breasts
 1/2 bottle of ice beer
 1 each small carrot, onion, celery rib, all finely diced

Marinate chicken in beer and vegetables for at least 2 hours, preferably overnight. Remove chicken; pat dry. Place marinade in a saucepan and bring to a boil. Reduce heat and boil gently for at least 5 minutes. Lay chicken on preheated grill. Barbecue, turning and basting with marinade for 7 to 9 minutes, or until chicken is cooked through. Makes 4 servings.

Barbecue Cheddar Wursts

 1 1/2 cups (375 ml) shredded cheddar cheese
 3 tablespoons (45 ml) beer
 2 tablespoons (30 ml) mayonnaise or salad dressing
 1/2 teaspoon (2 ml) Worcestershire sauce
 2 tablespoons (30 ml) chopped, hot pickled banana pepper, optional
 2 tablespoons (30 ml) butter
 2 large onions, thinly sliced
 salt and pepper
 6 knockwurst sausages (see note)
 6 hot dog rolls

Combine cheese, beer, mayonnaise and Worcestershire in blender jar. Cover, and blend at medium speed until smooth. Scrape sides of blender jar. Mix in banana pepper, if using, or a few drops of hot pepper sauce. Let stand 1 hour to blend flavours.

Melt butter in large frying pan; add onions. Cook over low heat, stirring frequently, for 20 minutes or until onions are soft and golden. Add salt and pepper to taste. Keep warm.

Grill sausages four inches (10 cm) from heat, turning frequently, for 15 minutes or until golden brown. Place one cooked sausage in each bun. Spoon onions over sausages and top with cheese mixture. Serve with ketchup and relish. Makes 6 servings.

Note: Weiners or any ready-to-serve European-style sausage may be substituted for the knockwurst, and a few drops of hot pepper sauce can replace the pickled pepper.

Heavenly Barbecued Trout

Whole fish or thickly cut fish steaks are your best choices for a fish barbecue and a hinged basket-like metal grill makes turning the fish easy and ensures even cooking on both sides.

4 trout
2 tablespoons (30 ml) flour
salt and freshly ground black pepper
1/2 cup (125 ml) butter, melted
lemon or lime wedges (optional)

Clean trout and wipe with a damp cloth. Toss fish in a plastic bag containing flour seasoned with salt and pepper. Dip floured trout in melted butter.

Set fish in a hinged grill basket (or a well-greased grill with a small grid) and cook over coals about 4 to 5 minutes on each side, basting with melted butter, until skin is crisp and lightly browned and flesh flakes easily when tested with a fork.

Serve immediately with more butter, lemon or lime wedges and freshly ground pepper. Makes 4 servings.

Barbecued Whole Salmon

Every Maritimer has his or her own way of barbecuing a whole salmon. Some like to wrap it completely in foil. Others say that isn't barbecuing, it's steaming. Either way it's delicious. Just be careful not to overcook salmon or the texture will be dry.

2 1/2 to 3 pounds (1 to 1.5 kg) whole salmon, cleaned
salt and freshly ground black pepper
juice of 1 lemon
1 tablespoon (15 ml) olive oil or canola oil
3 sprigs fresh dill
1/4 cup (50 ml) chopped fresh dill
2 tablespoons (30 ml) chopped fresh parsley
3 tablespoons (45 ml) butter, at room temperature

Heat barbecue. Cut two pieces of foil long enough to hold salmon with extra for handles; lay one piece of foil on top of the other; place salmon on foil. Season cavity with salt, pepper, lemon juice, and oil; lay dill sprigs inside. Let salmon stand at room temperature for 1 hour before cooking.

Meanwhile, combine chopped dill and parsley with the butter; season with salt and pepper. Shape into a cylinder, place on a piece of foil and put in freezer to harden.

When barbecue is heated, place salmon on its foil on a rack; grill for 5 to 7 minutes. Using the inside piece of foil, lift the salmon and turn it over, placing it on top of the outside piece of foil. Discard the inner piece. Grill for 5 to 7 minutes.

Place fish on a serving platter or large cutting board. Carefully remove skin from upper side of salmon. Using a metal spatula, pull salmon meat away from backbone. Remove backbone. Remove skin from other side of salmon.

Slice herb butter into eight pieces. Put a slice or two of butter on each helping of salmon. Makes 4 to 6 servings.

vegetables

It seems appropriate to start the vegetable chapter with excerpts from an article published in The Herald's weekend edition, The Novascotian, on Feb. 11, 1984. (Make sure your tongue is in your cheek, as mine was when I wrote it.)

Valentine's Day is coming, and the modern Romeo and Juliet are pondering what each can do to woo the other into amatory submission. Romeo has been thinking of flowers or a box of chocolates. Juliet knows better. Just as Eve in an earlier time did seductively tempt—and win—her Adam, Juliet is already in the kitchen planning the menu. But that's not a cookbook in her hand; it is Ovid, reminiscing about the aphrodisiac foods which had helped him in his pursuit of happiness.

Quickly passing over such things as rhinoceros horns, camel humps, and sparrow brains (when did Sobeys last stock these?), Juliet becomes fascinated by all the powers attributed to simple herbs, such as parsley, once said to be "grown for the wicked, but not for the just." She begins her shopping list. Thyme is described as a "notable herb of Venus." She'll try it. Then there's sage, said to strengthen the sinews. Better get some. Next, basil, chervil, and dill are added to the list. She heads her menu with Cream of Herbs Soup.

Reading on, Juliet learns that greens are a great aid to heightening virility. (And all this time she thought salads were only nutritious.) While lettuce is "moderately stimu-lating," she opts for spinach, described as "the most pro-vocatively gratifying food in the garden." (Well, it helped Popeye win Olive Oyl, didn't it, or was it the other way around?) Juliet, having been duly impressed by the words of Ovid, that great authority on love remedies and sensual pleasures, decides to toss a few sprigs of "shameless" watercress into the salad. Onions, too, must be included. Although chives might be more elegant, they are only mildly stimulating, while the aphrodisiac content of the onion has been lauded throughout the ages.

Choosing the vegetables for this provocative meal, Juliet considers the words of Shaykh Nafzawi in The Perfumed Garden for the Soul's Delectation: "He who boils aspara-gus, and then fries them in fat, and then pours upon them the yolks of eggs with pounded condiments, and eats every day of this dish, will grow strong for coitus, and find in it a stimulant for his amorous desires." Juliet will serve Asparagus with Hollandaise Sauce.

Can it possibly be that the lowly carrot, no longer exotic because of its almost daily appearance on the dinner table, is an aphrodisiac? According to Juan Ruiz, who wrote the Book of Good Love, the carrot is one of the best, having been introduced into Europe by the Arabs. "Well," Juliet reasons, "I can dress them up in a carrot ring." Then, on reading that "mushrooms can equip a man admirably for night duty," she decides to fill the ring with sautéed mushrooms.

If all fails, she may seek a new Romeo.

Juliet's Carrot Ring with Sautéed Mushrooms

5 cups (1.25 L) peeled and grated raw carrots
4 eggs, well-beaten
1 1/2 cups (375 ml) light cream or milk
1 teaspoon (5 ml) salt, or to taste
1/4 teaspoon (1 ml) white pepper
1 teaspoon (5 ml) sugar
1 tablespoon (15 ml) lemon juice
1/2 cup (125 ml) slivered blanched almonds
1/4 cup (50 ml) breadcrumbs

Boil carrots in salted water for 5 minutes. Drain well; put in a bowl. Add beaten eggs, cream, salt, pepper, sugar, lemon juice, almonds and breadcrumbs. Mix together and pour mixture into an oiled 9-inch (23 cm) ring mould, set in a pan of hot water and bake in a 350F (180C) oven for 1 hour, or until mixture starts to shrink from sides of mould.

Let stand for 5 minutes. Turn out on a serving platter. Fill centre of ring with sautéed mushrooms. (The carrot ring is enough for 6 to 8 people, so Romeo and Juliet will have leftovers.)

Sautéed Mushrooms

2 tablespoons (30 ml) butter
1/2 pound (250 g) mushrooms
Lemon juice
Salt and freshly ground pepper to taste

Wipe mushrooms clean with a damp paper towel. Trim stems and slice mushrooms vertically. Melt butter in a heavy skillet over high heat. When it's hot and foaming, add mushrooms. Squeeze on a few drops of lemon juice and sprinkle with salt and pepper. Toss over high heat for 3 minutes. Fill centre of carrot ring and serve.

■ The original point of Marinated Broccoli Stems with Ripe Olives was to rescue and use abandoned broccoli stems, "but it's well worth doing for its own sake," wrote Judy Schultz, of Edmonton, in her delightful cookbook, *From The Garden.* She says this dish keeps well in the refrigerator for three or four days. "Amounts aren't critical. Simply use as many stems as you have."

Marinated Broccoli Stems with Ripe Olives

2 bunches broccoli stems
1/2 cup (125 ml) vinegar
1/2 cup (125 ml) water
1 teaspoon (5 ml) sugar
3 inch (7.5 cm) stick cinnamon
1 teaspoon (5 ml) pickling spice
1 small dried chili
2 tablespoons (30 ml) olive oil
1 cup (250 ml) black olives

Peel broccoli stems and cut into slender wands about 3 inches (7.5 cm) long. Place in flat glass dish.

In a small pot, heat together vinegar, water, sugar, stick cinnamon, pickling spice, chili and olive oil. As soon as it boils, pour mixture over broccoli stems. Let everything marinate for about an hour at room temperature, then add the olives. Chill until ready to serve. Makes 6 servings.

Fresh Orange Cabbage Wedges

1 medium head cabbage, cut in 6 wedges
Boiling water
1/4 cup (50 ml) sliced green onions
2 tablespoons (30 ml) butter
1 teaspoon (5 ml) prepared horseradish
Grated peel of half an orange
1/4 cup (50 ml) orange juice
2 oranges, peeled, cut in half-cartwheel slices
1 to 2 tablespoons (15 to 30 ml) grated parmesan cheese

In a large saucepan, cook cabbage, covered, in 1-inch (2.5 cm) boiling water until tender, 7 to 8 minutes. Drain well. Place cabbage on serving plate and keep warm.

In saucepan, sauté green onion in butter. Stir in horseradish, orange peel and juice. Add oranges; heat. Serve over cabbage. Sprinkle with parmesan. Makes 6 servings.

It was in February 1995 that fifteen members of the Scandinavian Society got together at Miller's Lake to dish out generous portions of the hospitality and camaraderie that mark the sharing of good food in their culture. They had done it before and have done it since, but this time they had invited me to join them. I was impressed.

Working in teams, each member had a hand in the cooking. But before heading to the kitchen, cooks and guests alike warmed up with a cup of coffee and munched on Swedish gingersnaps and Danish Kringle, prepared by the hostess, Lissi Jeppesen. With offerings from each of the five Scandinavian countries—Denmark, Finland, Iceland, Norway, and Sweden—the meal started in the kitchen with steamed fruit juice, a favourite beverage in Finland, and generous portions of Icelandic caviar pie spread on chewy flatbread. Norway's famous Bergen fish soup was the meal starter, followed by a Danish dish, pork chops in casserole with caramelized potatoes, and cucumber salad. Nearly three hours after it began, the delightful Scandinavian meal ended with Swedish apple cake and vanilla sauce.

Danish Brunede Kartofler (Caramelized Potatoes)

24 small new potatoes
1/2 cup (125 ml) sugar
1/2 cup (125 ml) unsalted butter

Put unpeeled potatoes in a large saucepan, cover with boiling water and cook for about 15 minutes, until they offer no resistance when pierced with a fork. Cool slightly and peel.

In a large heavy skillet, melt sugar over low heat. (Sugar liquefies and browns during the melting process.) Stirring constantly with a wooden spoon, and watching carefully so it doesn't burn, continue to cook sugar for 3 to 5 minutes, until it turns a light brown caramel colour.

Melt butter and stir into caramelized sugar. Add as many potatoes as possible without crowding the pan. Shake the pan continually so that potatoes roll around and are coated on all sides.

Put hot, caramelized potatoes in a heated serving dish and set aside. Repeat the process until all potatoes are coated. Makes 8 servings.

Italian Stuffed Artichokes

One of the best ways to enjoy the delights of an artichoke is to steam or boil it, and serve it hot, warm, or chilled with a dipping sauce. This is one time when fingers must be used. Just pull off a leaf, dip it into the sauce, and draw the meaty part of the leaf through the teeth, scraping off the delectable flesh as it moves through. When the centre is reached, discard the fibrous leaves and cut out the fuzzy choke. Then, cut the base into bite-size pieces, dipping the chunks into the sauce. It's a good idea to have paper napkins handy and a bowl for discarding the leaves.

4 large or medium artichokes
1 1/2 cups (375 ml) seasoned breadcrumbs
1/2 cup (125 ml) grated parmesan cheese
1 large tomato, stemmed, seeded, chopped
2 tablespoons (30 ml) chopped parsley
Olive oil
Salt and pepper to taste
Optional: finely chopped garlic, almonds, ham
Lemon juice

Prepare artichokes for cooking, removing small leaves at base and cutting off stem. Mix ingredients using olive oil to moisten bread and parmesan.

continued on next page

Jean Hoare

■ "Our potatoes were great favourites and time and time again we were asked what we did to make them so good," said Jean Hoare, who for twenty years ran the famous Flying N restaurant in Claresholm, Alberta. "The answer was simple," she said, as she recounted the procedure, as described in The Secret Flying N Potatoes. She found she could reheat potatoes cooked this way by adding them to fresh water and cooking just until piping hot. "The waxy texture of real new potatoes will take two or three such reappearances without disintegrating into soup," she said. After selling the restaurant, Jean decided on her seventieth birthday to turn to writing about food. Her first book, *Jean Hoare's Best Little Cookbook in the West*, was followed by *Jean's Beans* and *More Easy Beans*. Later, she hosted a television show. Jean Hoare is gone now, but she left her imprint on Canadian cooking. And, she was a nice person to know.

Stuff filling between leaves of artichokes working from outside to centre until leaves are tightly packed. Place artichokes in pot with 1/2 inch (1 cm) water so that they touch. Pour olive oil and lemon juice over artichokes.

Bring water to boil; reduce to simmer and cover. Cook 1 hour or until leaves are easy to pull away from artichoke. Makes 4 servings.

The Secret Flying N Potatoes

New potatoes, no bigger than a plum
Boiling salted water
Butter
Fresh chives or dill weed, chopped fine

Clean the potatoes. Do not peel. Just cut a strip around the middle. Boil in salted water until just barely tender. Drain. Put in a serving bowl, add butter, chives, or dill weed.

Fiddlehead Stir-Fry

To distinguish fiddleheads from other ferns, look for distinct clumps from small round masses of brown scaly tissue. When they emerge from the soil, they are unopened and curled. They are encased in a brown papery covering which must be cleaned away before eating.

2 and 1/2 cups (625 ml) fiddleheads
1 cup (250 ml) sliced mushrooms
1/2 cup (125 ml) onion rings
1/4 cup (50 ml) shredded carrot
2 tablespoons (30 ml) butter or margarine
1/2 teaspoon (2 ml) lemon juice
1/4 teaspoon (1 ml) basil
1/4 teaspoon (1 ml) salt
Dash pepper
1 clove garlic, crushed

Combine all ingredients and sauté until onion is translucent. Cover and cook until fiddleheads are tender (about 8 minutes). Add water, if necessary. Makes 4 servings (1/2 cup/125 ml each).

Chef Alex Clavel

■ Swiss-born Alex Clavel made a strong impact in the development of fine cuisine in Nova Scotia after his arrival here in 1956. Not only did he design and open several restaurants for the Historic Properties complex in Halifax, but he loved to teach advanced culinary preparation to those who would learn. After thirty years of hard work, Alex finally realized his dream of opening his own restaurant— Chez la Vigne, in Wolfville. Alex is gone now, and is sadly missed in the food industry. It was Alex who first introduced me to a new type of squash when we chanced to meet at a Valley roadside stand. "They're sweet baby dumplings and they're so sweet and tender you can even eat the skin," he told me.

Squash and Apple Sauté

The little squash is the perfect size for two side servings. Or, it can make a full meal for one if stuffed with meat or a grain filling. You can also stuff it with cooked dried fruits or apples, top it with cheese and nuts, and run it under the broiler. And it's just as good when cooked in the microwave. After a thorough scrubbing, halve it and spoon out the seeds. Place halves, cut-side down, on a microwave-safe plate and cook on high for 9 to 11 minutes. When it tests nearly done, cover halves and let stand for 5 to 10 minutes to finish cooking.

2 sweet baby dumpling squash
2 tablespoons (30 ml) butter or margarine
2 large apples, cored and chopped
1 leek, sliced (white part only)
2 tablespoons (30 ml) white wine
1/4 teaspoon (1 ml) ground cinnamon
1/8 teaspoon (.5 ml) ground black pepper
1/8 teaspoon (.5 ml) ground allspice

Halve squashes; cook, covered, in small amount of boiling water 15 minutes. Melt butter in a large skillet. Add apples and leek slices and sauté 5 minutes. Add wine and seasonings; cook 3 minutes more. Carefully scoop out squash and mash; add to skillet and blend with apple mixture. Spoon mixture into squash shells and serve immediately. Makes 4 servings.

Curried Beans and Vegetables

Hey Mom, what's wrong with a meal built around baked beans and brown bread? Like old-time religion, it was good enough for mother and father, and with a little help from a can, it is good enough for us.

2 tablespoons (30 ml) canola oil
2 ribs celery, diced
2 onions, chopped
1 tablespoon (15 ml) curry powder
1/2 teaspoon (2 ml) ground cumin
2 (19-ounce/540 ml) cans baked beans
1 (10-ounce/283 g) package fresh spinach
Optional condiments:
1/2 cup (125 ml) plain, low-fat yogurt
1/3 cup (75 ml) dry-roasted peanuts
1/3 cup (75 ml) coconut
Cooked rice

In a large saucepan, heat oil until hot; add celery and onions. Sauté 3 to 5 minutes. Add curry powder, cumin, and baked beans. Simmer 5 to 10 minutes.

Wash and dry spinach thoroughly. Discard stems and tear leaves into large pieces; stir into beans. Cover and heat about 5 minutes or until spinach is cooked.

Serve yogurt, peanuts and coconut as optional condiments. Serve with rice. Makes 4 to 6 servings.

■ Fresh corn—it's the perfect summer meal. And the best is the corn just picked. Break it from the stalk, run from the garden to the pot of already boiling water, husk it, and call the family to the table. Then, while they're tying their bibs, thrust the pale-gold ears into the water for no more than five minutes. It's a meal many simply can't experience. Few city dwellers have vegetable gardens in their backyards and, even in rural areas, many don't savour corn at its best.

For eating outdoors, nothing could be simpler than grilling corn in the husk. If you've got a good-size tub or bucket, fill it with cold water and allow the corn to soak with husks on for 15 minutes. Then remove the corn, shake off excess water, and lay it, just as it comes, directly on the grill, turning every five minutes as it cooks. Close the cover and cook for 30 minutes.

Don't worry about the husks blackening—the corn inside will be sweet and nicely steamed. When cool enough to handle, peel off the husks and silk and serve.

Harvest Vegetable Stir-Fry

| 2 teaspoons (10 ml) canola oil
| 1 teaspoon (5 ml) herb seasoning
| 2 medium carrots, thinly sliced
| 1 1/2 cups (375 ml) cauliflower florets
| 1 1/2 cups (375 ml) broccoli florets
| 1 red bell pepper, chopped
| 1/4 cup (50 ml) chicken broth

In wok or skillet, heat oil over medium-high heat. Add seasoning and stir-fry 1 minute. Add carrot, cauliflower and broccoli; stir-fry 3 or 4 minutes. Add red bell pepper; stir-fry 1 minute. Add chicken stock. Cover and steam for 2 minutes or until vegetables are tender-crisp. Makes 4 servings.

Snow Peas and Pepper Strips

If we all followed the eating plan laid down for people with diabetes, we might enjoy healthier lives. Snow Peas and Pepper Strips serves six and each serving counts for 1/2 starch choice and 1/2 fruits and vegetables choice.

| 8 ounces (250 g) snow peas, trimmed
| 1 tablespoon (15 ml) olive oil
| 1 medium sweet red pepper, cut into strips
| 1 medium sweet yellow pepper, cut into strips
| 1 small sweet green pepper, cut into strips
| 1/4 teaspoon (1 ml) freshly ground pepper

In saucepan, bring water to boil. Cook snow peas in steamer basket over boiling water for 4 minutes or until barely tender. Refresh in cold water; drain and pat dry.

In large nonstick skillet, heat oil over medium-high heat; cook red, yellow and green peppers for 4 to 5 minutes or until crisp-tender. Add snow peas 2 minutes before peppers are cooked; sprinkle with pepper and serve. Makes 6 servings.

breads and muffins

y father was, in his later years, a student of nutrition. His interest was aroused by the Bible and it grew from there. He had very decided ideas about what one should and should not eat. Unfortunately, several hundred miles separated us, so I couldn't benefit from his studies, but I do remember certain "lessons" he taught me. Perhaps he was considered by some to be a food fanatic. He did not hesitate to express his opinion of the food choices of others. "You wouldn't serve that junk to your son!" he scolded as he "caught" me frying some bacon for my two-year old, Frank.

Although I continued to use bacon (and other pork cuts as well) much of what Dad practised so many years ago began finding a wider audience in the 1980s. I remember one day while visiting my father in Toronto, my stepmother was making bread. She had just come home from her work and wanted to put dough to set before she prepared dinner. (Dad did not trust me to prepare his meals.) As she mixed and kneaded, I noticed she was using two types of flour. Since Dad did not permit white flour in his bread, I questioned her about this. She admitted she wasn't yet used to the distinctive flavour and texture of 100 per cent whole wheat bread, so she "cheated" by adding a little white flour. I think her "little" meant half and half. I've often wondered if Dad ever learned that he was betrayed by the woman who loved him.

Sourdough Starter

On November 4, 1998, my column responded to requests for a sourdough culture with this excerpt and recipes from the makers of Fleischmann's yeast.

2 cups (500 ml) all-purpose flour
1 package (8 g) traditional active dry or quick-rise instant yeast (see note)
2 cups (500 ml) lukewarm water (105F-115F/40C-45C)

In a 2-quart (2 L) or larger plastic container with a tight-fitting lid, combine flour and undissolved yeast. Gradually add water to dry ingredients and beat until smooth. Cover loosely; let stand in a warm place until bubbly and sour-smelling, about 2 to 4 days. Starter may darken, but if it changes to another colour, discard and start over. To store, cover tightly and refrigerate until ready to use.

To keep starter alive: Once a week, stir in 1 tablespoon (15 ml) all-purpose flour and 1 tablespoon (15 ml) lukewarm water. Beat until smooth. Cover loosely and let stand until bubbly, from 12 to 24 hours. Store as above.

To replenish starter: For each 1 1/2 cups (375 ml) of starter used, add 1-and-1/3 cups (325 ml) each of all-purpose flour and lukewarm water. (For each three-quarter cup (175 ml) of starter used, add 2/3 cup (150 ml) each of flour and water. For each 1 1/4 cups (300 ml) of starter used, add 1 cup (250 ml) each of flour and water. Beat until smooth. Cover loosely; let stand until bubbly, 12 to 24 hours. Store as above.

Note: For bread machines, 2 1/4 teaspoons (11 ml) of bread machine yeast may be substituted, if desired.

Sourdough Bread

1 1/2 cups (375 ml) sourdough starter
3 1/2 to 4 1/2 cups (875 to 1125 ml) all-purpose flour
  (see note)
1 package (8 g) traditional active dry yeast or quick-rise instant yeast
1 teaspoon (5 ml) salt
1 cup (250 ml) very warm water (120F-130F/50C-55C)
Cornmeal

Stir sourdough starter before measuring. Measure out 1 1/2 cups (375 ml) sourdough starter and bring to room temperature.

In large bowl, combine 1 1/2 cups (375 ml) flour, undissolved yeast and salt. Gradually add water and starter to dry ingredients; beat 2 minutes at medium speed of electric mixer, scraping bowl occasionally. Beat 2 minutes at high speed.

continued on next page

With spoon, stir in enough remaining flour to make soft dough. Knead on floured surface until smooth, about 8 minutes. Place in greased bowl, turning to grease top. Cover; let rise in warm, draft-free place until doubled in size, 30 to 60 minutes. (With quick-rise instant yeast, cover kneaded dough and let rest on floured surface for 10 minutes. Proceed with recipe.)

Punch dough down. Remove dough to floured surface; divide in half. Roll each half to 12x9-inch (30x23 cm) rectangle. Beginning at long end of each, roll up tightly as for a jelly roll. Pinch seams and ends to seal. Taper ends by gently rolling back and forth. Place, seam sides down, on large greased baking sheet sprinkled with cornmeal. Cover; let rise in warm, draft-free place until doubled in size, about 30 to 45 minutes.

With sharp knife, make 4 or 5 diagonal slashes (1/4 inch/5 mm deep) across top of each loaf. Bake at 400F (200C) for 30 to 35 minutes or until done. For crispy crust, spray loaves with water just before baking and every 5 minutes during the first 10 minutes of baking time. Remove from baking sheet; let cool on wire rack. Makes 2 loaves.

To make round loaves: Divide dough in half. Shape each half into a 5-inch (13 cm) ball. Place on large greased baking sheet sprinkled with cornmeal. Cover; let rise in warm, draft-free place until doubled in size, about 30 to 45 minutes. With sharp knife, make 4 slashes (1/4 inch/5 mm deep) in crisscross fashion on top of each loaf. Spray with water and bake as directed.

Note: The amount of flour needed varies according to consistency of starter.

Nutty Cereal Bread

1-and-three-quarter cups (425 ml) all-purpose flour
1 cup (250 ml) granulated sugar
2 1/2 teaspoons (12 ml) baking powder
1 teaspoon (5 ml) salt
3/4 cup (175 ml) grapenuts
1 cup (250 ml) milk
1 egg, well-beaten
2 tablespoons (30 ml) butter or margarine, melted

Sift flour with sugar, baking powder and salt. Fold in cereal. Combine milk with egg and butter or margarine. Add flour mixture, stirring only enough to dampen flour. Pour into a greased 9x5-inch (23x13 cm) loaf pan and bake in a 350F (180C) oven for 1 hour, or until cake tester inserted in centre comes out clean. Cool in pan for 10 minutes. Remove from pan and finish cooling on a rack.

For easy slicing, store bread overnight, wrapped in waxed paper, plastic wrap, or foil.

Jean Boyd

■ Years ago, when her family was at home, Jean Boyd, of Halifax, was famous for her bread. She baked large batches and always had extra loaves in the freezer to take out when needed. Whole Wheat Bread with Oatmeal was a family favourite.

Whole Wheat Bread with Oatmeal

2 envelopes dry yeast
2 cups (500 ml) lukewarm water
1 tablespoon (15 ml) sugar
1 cup (250 ml) all-purpose flour
1/2 cup (125 ml) processed (not instant) rolled oats

In a large bowl, sprinkle yeast in water. Add the tablespoon (15 ml) of sugar and let mixture sit for 10 minutes, until yeast is activated. Stir 1 cup (250 ml) of the flour into yeast mixture and let stand for half an hour.

In the meantime, cook the rolled oats (the kind that take 5 minutes to cook) in 1 cup (250 ml) boiling water.

Add the following to the large bowl containing the yeast and flour mixture:

1 1/2 cups (375 ml) lukewarm water
1 teaspoon (5 ml) salt
1 cup (250 ml) brown sugar
Cooked rolled oats
1/2 cup (125 ml) shortening
1/2 cup (125 ml) molasses
3 cups (750 ml) all-purpose flour
6 cups (1.5 L) whole-wheat flour

A little more all-purpose flour (about 1/2 cup/125 ml) can be added if the dough is too sticky to handle. Knead for about 10 minutes, until dough loses its stickiness. Put in a large greased bowl, cover with a towel, and let dough rise in an unheated oven for an hour or so, until its bulk has doubled.

Form into oblong or round loaves. Let the loaves rise for one more hour. Bake at 350F (180C) for 1 hour. Brush crust with butter when baked.

Makes three large round free-standing loaves or four smaller round loaves.

Raisin Bread

Back in 1990, when I ran this recipe, June Nauss of Lunenburg had been making her wonderful raisin bread for over forty years.

2 tablespoons (30 ml) dry yeast
1 cup (250 ml) lukewarm water
1 teaspoon (5 ml) granulated sugar
6 cups (1.5 L) all-purpose flour
1 cup (250 ml) granulated sugar
1 tablespoon (15 ml) salt
2 cups (500 ml) raisins
2 tablespoons (30 ml) shortening
1 tablespoon (15 ml) margarine
1 tablespoon (15 ml) lemon extract

Dissolve yeast in lukewarm water in which 1 teaspoon (5 ml) sugar has been dissolved. Let stand 10 minutes.

In large bowl, combine flour, 1 cup (250 ml) sugar, salt, raisins, shortening, margarine, and lemon extract. Add yeast, mix with hand. If dough feels too stiff add 1/4 cup (50 ml) warm water or more to make desired stiffness.

Cover and let rise in a warm place until double in size. Divide into four equal portions. Knead down and put in bread pans or large juice cans which have been sprayed with vegetable cooking spray. Set in a warm place and let rise again until double in size. Bake at 350F (180C) for 50 to 60 minutes.

Variation: For festive occasions, you may substitute 2 cups (500 ml) mixed fruit for part or all of the raisins.

Basic Bagel Dough

Bagel dough is very difficult to knead unless you have a mixer with dough hooks, Freda Perlin, of Halifax told us. This was her recipe.

1 package yeast
1 teaspoon (5 ml) sugar
1/4 cup (50 ml) lukewarm water
6 cups (1.5 L) all-purpose flour
1/4 cup (50 ml) sugar
1 tablespoon (15 ml) salt
1/4 cup (50 ml) oil
4 eggs (at room temperature)
1 cup (250 ml) lukewarm water (approximate)

Dissolve yeast with 1 teaspoon (5 ml) sugar in 1/4 cup (50 ml) lukewarm water. Let stand until it bubbles, about 10 minutes.

Combine flour, sugar and salt. Make a well, add yeast, oil and eggs. Mix. Add enough water to make a medium-soft dough. Knead for about 10 minutes. Put in a greased bowl, brush with oil, and cover. Let rise until double in size. Punch down, cover, and let rise a second time in refrigerator overnight or on counter for about an hour.

Heat oven to 500F (260C). Put ungreased baking sheet in oven to heat.

For each bagel, roll about 3 ounces (90 g) of dough into a rope. Join ends well so they don't separate. Let rise for 30 to 45 minutes until double in size.

Half-fill a wide pot with water, add 1 tablespoon (15 ml) sugar, and bring to a boil. Drop in 6 bagels at a time and bring water back to a boil. Boil bagels 30 seconds to 1 minute. Use a spatula to carefully remove bagels and place them on a cookie sheet or tray to dry. Sprinkle with sesame or poppy seeds. Lightly grease heated baking sheet; transfer bagels. Bake in centre of oven for about 3 minutes, then turn bagels and bake 2 to 5 minutes longer, until golden. Watch carefully to prevent burning. Makes about 24 medium bagels.

Chef Yvonne LeVert

■ Yvonne LeVert was brought up in Margaree Forks, Cape Breton, where she developed a love of cooking under her mother's excellent tutelage. As a graduate home economist, she later received the grand diplome from the Academie du Cordon Bleu de Paris. When we asked about her favourite recipes in the *Cape Breton Pictorial Cookbook*, which she and photographer Warren Gordon produced in 1993, she recommended Four Cent Cake, the traditional bread made by the Mi'kmaq of Eskasoni, saying: "It's absolutely wonderful. It smells like pizza when it's cooking and almost tastes like pizza crust. You simply must try it."

tip *A pumpkin will peel more easily if you put it in a 300F (150C) oven for 5 minutes.*

Mi'kmaq Four Cent Cake

2 cups (500 ml) flour
3 teaspoons (15 ml) baking powder
1 teaspoon (5 ml) salt
1 cup (250 ml) cold water
Cooking oil

Mix flour, baking powder, salt and water together. Form mixture into a ball and knead on floured board 2 to 3 minutes. Divide dough into two pieces and with your hands flatten each into a circle about 1/2 inch (1 cm) thick and about six inches (15 cm) in diameter.

Heat 2 tablespoons (30 ml) oil in a large skillet. Fry cakes 5 minutes on each side. When cooked, cut in wedges and serve as a bread. Makes 8 to 12 wedges.

Pumpkin Cornbread

Here's a good way to use some of that nutritious pumpkin pulp.

1 cup (250 ml) all-purpose flour
1 cup (250 ml) cornmeal
1 tablespoon (15 ml) baking powder
3/4 teaspoon (3 ml) ground cinnamon
1/4 teaspoon (1 ml) ground ginger
1/4 teaspoon (1 ml) salt
3/4 cup (175 ml) drained pumpkin pulp
1/2 cup (125 ml) skim milk
1/4 cup (50 ml) canola oil
3 tablespoons (45 ml) liquid honey
2 egg whites

Combine flour, cornmeal, baking powder, cinnamon, ginger and salt.

In a large bowl, combine pumpkin, milk, oil, honey and egg whites. Add flour mixture and stir until well blended. Pour into an oiled 8-inch (20 cm) square pan. Bake at 375F (190C) for 25 minutes or until a cake tester inserted in centre comes out clean. Cut into squares and serve hot or warm.

Potato Bannock

1 cup (250 ml) hot mashed potatoes
1/4 cup (50 ml) butter or margarine
2 cups (500 ml) all-purpose flour
1 tablespoon (15 ml) baking powder
1 teaspoon (5 ml) baking soda
1/4 teaspoon (1 ml) salt
1 tablespoon (15 ml) granulated sugar
1/2 cup (125 ml) milk
Melted butter or margarine

Mix potato and butter in a large bowl. Combine flour, baking powder, baking soda, salt and sugar. Add dry ingredients to potatoes. Stir in milk and mix well to form a soft biscuit-type dough.

Place in a greased deep 10-inch (25 cm) pie plate and pat down evenly. Brush with melted butter. Bake in a 425F (220C) oven for 20 to 25 minutes or until top is golden. Cool slightly and cut into wedges. Serve warm with butter or molasses. Makes about 12 servings.

Cathy Slaunwhite's Cheese Tea Biscuits

■ Back in the 1980s, Cathy Slaunwhite was hired to make sandwiches at Mrs. Murphy's Kitchen, a popular little restaurant on Brenton Street in Halifax (now closed). It wasn't long before her talents as a baker were recognized and she was moved into that position. Encouraged by Mrs. Murphy, Cathy entered some of her baked goods into competition at the Atlantic Winter Fair. The result was that she carried away eight prizes out of the nine categories she entered. Her cheese tea biscuits were among her first place winners.

4 cups (1 L) all-purpose flour
2 tablespoons (30 ml) granulated sugar
8 teaspoons (40 ml) baking powder
1 teaspoon (5 ml) salt
1/2 cup (125 ml) margarine
2 cups (500 ml) grated cheddar cheese
2 eggs
1 and 1/3 cups (325 ml) milk

In a bowl, combine flour, sugar, baking powder and salt. With a pastry blender or two knives, cut in margarine until mixture resembles coarse meal. Add grated cheese and stir to distribute evenly.

In a separate bowl, combine eggs and milk, beating until frothy. Add to dry mixture, mixing lightly with a fork. Turn out on a board and knead lightly until all flour has been incorporated. Roll out on a lightly floured board. Do not use a back and forth motion, but roll in short strokes from the centre out, to desired thickness. (Cathy rolls to 1-inch (2.5 cm) thickness, but for a smaller biscuit, 1/2 inch/1 cm is average).

continued on next page

Cut with a floured biscuit cutter, using a straight down and up motion—do not twist the cutter. Place on an ungreased cookie sheet about 2 inches (5 cm) apart. Bake in a 450F (230C) oven for 12 to 15 minutes. Makes about 16 large biscuits.

Note: For the festive season Cathy adds 1 cup (250 ml) mixed glazed fruit to the dough before rolling out.

Rhubarb-Walnut Muffins

Although it doesn't top the list of nutrient-rich foods, rhubarb does contain good amounts of vitamin C and potassium, as well as vitamin A, thiamin, riboflavin, niacin, and phosphorus. When cooked and sweetened, it has as much fibre as an unpeeled apple.

1/2 cup plus 2 tablespoons (125 ml plus 30 ml) brown sugar, packed
1/4 cup (50 ml) melted butter
1 egg
1 teaspoon (5 ml) vanilla
1/2 cup (125 ml) buttermilk
3/4 cup (175 ml) diced rhubarb
1/2 cup (125 ml) coarsely chopped walnuts
1 1/4 cups (300 ml) all-purpose flour
1/2 teaspoon (2 ml) baking soda
1/2 teaspoon (2 ml) baking powder
1/4 teaspoon (1 ml) salt
1 tablespoon (15 ml) melted butter
1/4 cup (50 ml) granulated sugar
3/4 teaspoon (3 ml) ground cinnamon

Combine brown sugar, 1/4 cup (50 ml) melted butter, egg, vanilla and buttermilk in a large bowl, beating until blended. Stir in rhubarb and nuts.

In a separate bowl, combine flour, baking soda, baking powder and salt. Stir into rhubarb mixture just until moistened. Spoon batter into greased muffin cups, filling about 2/3 full. Set aside.

In a small bowl, combine 1 tablespoon (15 ml) melted butter, granulated sugar and cinnamon. Sprinkle mixture over tops of muffins, pressing lightly into batter with fingers. Bake in a 400F (200C) oven about 20 minutes, or until muffins spring back when lightly pressed. Serve warm. Makes 10 to 12 muffins.

In May, 1990, a story about a prize-winning muffin recipe appeared in *The Chronicle-Herald*. It had been written by a talented reporter in the Bridgewater bureau. It was a good story. The only problem was that she didn't know the computers used at that time would not accept fractions. Imagine the turmoil caused when 1/4 cup of butter became 1 1/2 cups, and 1/2 cup of sugar tripled in volume, as did the baking soda.

It wasn't my story. It wasn't my recipe. But, with smoke filling their kitchens as the over-stimulated batter foamed up, spilled over, and coated the oven floor in its effort to push through the chamber's confines, harried cooks called me for help. It was a difficult time as I sympathized with those put through this unpleasant experience. In particular, I sympathized with June Christian of Bridgewater, who had created the recipe that won the $5,000 first prize in a recipe contest staged by Kraft. Imagine the complaints she must have received!

I tested the corrected recipe, and ran it in my "Food For Thought" column the following week, with a postscript reminding readers that all the world's great chefs have had catastrophes.

June Christian's Cheddar Cheese Muffins

2 cups (500 ml) all-purpose flour
1/2 cup (125 ml) granulated sugar
1 tablespoon (15 ml) baking powder
1 teaspoon (5 ml) salt
1/2 teaspoon (2 ml) baking soda
1 1/2 cups (375 ml) shredded medium cheddar cheese
1 cup (250 ml) plain yogurt
1/4 cup (50 ml) melted butter or margarine
2 eggs, beaten

Mix flour, sugar, baking powder, salt and baking soda together and stir in grated cheese. Thoroughly combine yogurt, butter and eggs; add all at once to dry ingredients. Stir until moistened. Divide batter into 12 large muffin cups. Bake at 400F (200C) for 18 to 20 minutes. Serve warm with Apple Butter.

Apple Butter: Cream 1/2 cup (125 ml) soft butter with 1/2 cup (125 ml) apple jelly and 1/4 teaspoon ground cinnamon. Makes about 1 cup (250 ml).

Chef Howard Selig at a cooking demo at the Harvest Food Festival in Middleton, Nova Scotia, with Margaret Jansen

■ Flax is back—after an absence of several thousand years. And an Annapolis Valley couple has built a successful cottage industry based on the grain's food value. A registered dietitian and chef, Howard Selig, and his wife Wendy Rodda, of Middleton, started milling flax seeds into flour in 1997. "Not only does flax flour contain high-quality vegetable protein, fibre and omega-3 fatty acids, it also contains lignan, a precursor to phytoestrogen," Selig said, adding that this phytochemical provides protection against prostate, breast, and ovarian cancer tumours in humans as effectively as chemotherapy. "Using flax flour regularly can help to improve heart health by reducing LDL cholesterol and serum triglycerides," he added. For further information visit his website www.flaxflour.com

Banana Flax Muffins

1 egg
1 cup (250 ml) 1 percent milk
1/4 cup (50 ml) canola oil
1/2 cup (125 ml) granulated sugar
3 ripe bananas, mashed
1 teaspoon (5 ml) vanilla extract
1 cup (250 ml) flax flour
1 cup (250 ml) all-purpose flour
1 cup (250 ml) whole wheat flour
1 teaspoon (5 ml) baking soda
1 tablespoon (15 ml) baking powder

In a bowl, combine egg, milk, oil, sugar, bananas and vanilla. In another bowl, combine flours, baking soda and baking powder.

Mix the wet and dry ingredients together just until blended. Scoop batter into 12 nonstick or paper-lined muffin cups, filling each cup full. Bake in a 400F (200C) oven for 20 to 25 minutes, or until firm to the touch. Makes 12 large muffins.

Spur-of-the-Moment Muffins

2 cups (500 ml) all-bran cereal
1 1/2 cups (375 ml) buttermilk or sour milk
3 eggs
1 (19-ounce/540 ml) can crushed pineapple, undrained
1/2 cup (125 ml) canola oil
1 1/2 cups (375 ml) all-purpose flour
1 cup (250 ml) whole wheat flour
3/4 cup (175 ml) packed brown sugar
1 teaspoon (5 ml) salt
1 tablespoon plus 1 teaspoon (15 ml plus 5 ml) baking soda
1 cup (250 ml) raisins
1/2 cup (125 ml) chopped toasted almonds

In a large bowl, combine cereal and buttermilk; let stand 5 minutes. Stir in eggs, undrained pineapple and oil.

In separate bowl, combine flours, brown sugar, salt, soda, raisins and almonds. Fold liquid ingredients into dry ingredients, mixing just until moistened. Batter will not be smooth. Spoon into paper-lined or sprayed muffin cups and bake at 375F (190C) for 20 to 25 minutes. Makes 24 muffins.

High-Fibre Prune Muffins

1/2 cup (125 ml) bran
1/2 cup (125 ml) prune juice
1/2 cup (125 ml) milk
1/4 cup (50 ml) packed brown sugar
2 eggs, lightly beaten
1 1/2 cups (375 ml) all-purpose flour
2 teaspoons (10 ml) baking powder
1 teaspoon (5 ml) grated nutmeg
1/2 teaspoon (2 ml) salt
1/4 cup (50 ml) melted butter or margarine
1 cup (about 6 ounces) (250 ml/170 g) pitted prunes, coarsely chopped
1/2 cup (125 ml) chopped walnuts

In a large bowl mix bran, prune juice, milk and sugar; set aside for 10 minutes. Stir in eggs. Add combined flour, baking powder, nutmeg and salt and blend thoroughly. Add butter and combine well. Stir in prunes and walnuts.

Spoon, equally divided, into 12 greased or paper-lined medium muffin cups. Sprinkle with additional bran, if desired. Bake in a 425F (220C) oven for 15 to 20 minutes or until lightly browned and springy to the touch. Turn out on a rack to cool. Makes 1 dozen muffins. Can be frozen.

cookies

On December 12, 1990, my column featured a cookie exchange, hosted by Marion Gordon, then of Halifax (now deceased). Marion, who was known as a great cook, invited three of her friends to come, socialize, and swap cookies in order to have a variety for the up-coming holiday season. Each guest was asked to bake two kinds of cookies and bring three dozen of each to swap. Marion made four varieties herself, so there were ten types of cookies nicely arranged on plates, trays, and in baskets to tempt all palates and set a festive mood. After each guest had made her choices of six dozen cookies, Marion served tea along with—what else?—cookies. Everyone left with a good feeling, each knowing that the holiday cookies were baked, and there was a good variety with very little effort. Whether you're planning to organize a cookie exchange, or just bake up a batch or two for yourself, the following tips may help make your cookie-baking easy.

Scissors dipped in hot water cut gumdrops and dried fruit easily.

Shiny baking pans should be used, since dark surfaces absorb heat more quickly and cookies tend to overbrown on bottom.

Grease pans lightly—when the recipe calls for it. Soft cookie dough spreads further on a greased cookie sheet than an ungreased one.

Soft doughs are best pre-chilled a bit before dropping, rolling, or moulding.

Space dough on cookie sheets. Allow 3 inches (8 cm) for cookies which spread a lot, and 2 inches (5 cm) for those that don't.

When slicing refrigerator cookies, do it quickly with a thin-bladed slicing knife. Dough softens quickly and gets harder to slice.

Do not crowd oven—hot air must circulate. One cookie sheet at a time is best.

Know your oven and adjust temperatures as required. Most cookies should be taken from the oven while still a little soft.

Store crispy and soft cookies separately in airtight containers—never together.

Unbaked dough may be dropped onto cookie sheets and frozen; then removed, packaged and stored in the freezer until needed. Allow a little extra time for baking frozen dough.

Marion Gordon's Christmas Fruit Drops

8 ounces (250 g) candied cherries
8 ounces (250 g) candied pineapple
8 ounces (250 g) blanched almonds
8 ounces (250 g) brazil nuts
8 ounces (250 g) dates
1 cup (250 g) butter, softened
1 1/2 cups (375 ml) granulated sugar
2 eggs
1 teaspoon (5 ml) vanilla extract
2 1/2 cups (625 ml) all-purpose flour
1 teaspoon (5 ml) baking soda
2 teaspoons (10 ml) ground cinnamon
1 teaspoon (5 ml) salt

Chop fruit and nuts; set aside.

Thoroughly cream butter and sugar; add eggs and vanilla, blending well. Combine dry ingredients and add to creamed mixture. Stir in fruits and nuts. Form into small balls, place 2 inches (5 cm) apart on ungreased cookie sheet. Bake in a 350F (180C) oven for 10 minutes or until lightly browned. Makes about 6 dozen.

Vivian Fleming's Thimble Cookies

Cookie makers Vivian Fleming, Ev Bauld, and Marian MacFadden

1/2 cup (125 ml) butter
1/4 cup (50 ml) granulated sugar
1 egg, separated
1 teaspoon (5 ml) vanilla or almond extract (or 1/2 teaspoon/2 ml) each
1 cup (250 ml) all-purpose flour
3/4 cup (175 ml) finely chopped walnuts or almonds
Red jelly (red currant, strawberry, or apple)

Cream butter; gradually add sugar, mixing well. Blend in well-beaten egg yolk and flavouring. Stir in flour. Shape into 1-inch (2.5 cm) balls. Dip in unbeaten egg white, then into finely chopped nuts.

With thimble (or your thumb) make an indentation in centre. Place on greased baking sheet and bake at 350F (180C) for 5 minutes. Indent again. Bake 12 to 15 minutes. Fill with jelly while still hot. Makes about 2 dozen.

Ev Bauld's Million Dollar Cookies

1 1/2 cups (375 ml) butter, softened
2 cups (500 ml) granulated sugar
1 teaspoon (5 ml) vanilla
2-and-three-quarter cups (675 ml) all-purpose flour
1 teaspoon (5 ml) baking powder
1 teaspoon (5 ml) baking soda
1 cup (250 ml) desiccated coconut
1 cup (250 ml) sunflower seeds

Cream butter, add sugar, blending thoroughly. Add vanilla. Stir in combined dry ingredients, coconut and sunflower seeds; mix well. Shape into 1-inch (2.5 cm) balls, place on greased baking sheets and flatten with a fork. Bake in a 350F (180C) oven for 12 to 15 minutes. Makes about 7 dozen.

Marian MacFadden's Santa's Whiskers

1 cup (250 ml) butter or margarine, softened
1 cup (250 ml) granulated sugar
2 tablespoons (30 ml) milk
1 teaspoon (5 ml) vanilla extract
2 1/2 cups (625 ml) all-purpose flour
3/4 cup (175 ml) finely chopped red or green glazed cherries
1/2 cup (125 ml) finely chopped pecans
3/4 cup (175 ml) flaked coconut

In mixing bowl, cream together butter or margarine and sugar. Blend in milk and vanilla. Stir in flour, cherries and pecans. Form dough into two 8-inch (20 cm) rolls. Roll in coconut to coat outside. Wrap in waxed paper or clear plastic wrap; chill thoroughly. Cut into 1/4 inch (5 mm) slices. Place on ungreased cookie sheet. Bake in a 375F (190C) oven until edges are golden, about 12 minutes. Makes about 5 dozen.

Elizabeth Baird

■ Before she became food editor for *Canadian Living* magazine, Elizabeth Baird wrote cookbooks, a regular food column for the *Toronto Star*, and food articles for *Canadian Living*. She also taught Canadian cooking and preserving in Toronto. Before that she was a French teacher. Her passion for researching traditional Canadian cooking led to the publication of *Elizabeth Baird's Favourites*. Included is a recipe for aulets, which are cookie "dolls" traditionally given to Acadian children by their godparents at Christmas time. It was a ritual among the children to see who had the largest aulet.

Aulets

1/2 cup (125 ml) lard
1/2 cup (125 ml) butter
1 cup (250 ml) granulated sugar
1 teaspoon (5 ml) vanilla
1 egg
4 teaspoons (20 ml) white vinegar
2 1/2 cups (625 ml) all-purpose flour
1 teaspoon (5 ml) baking soda
1/2 teaspoon (2 ml) freshly grated nutmeg
1/4 teaspoon (1 ml) salt
Garnish: raisins, small candies or coarse granulated sugar

Lightly grease 2 baking sheets; set aside.

In a large bowl, cream together the lard, butter, sugar and vanilla until light and fluffy. Beat in egg and vinegar.

Mix together flour, soda, nutmeg and salt; blend into batter. Form the dough into 3 smooth balls. (Cover and chill if not rolling out immediately. Bring dough back to room temperature before proceeding.)

On a lightly floured counter or pastry cloth, roll out each portion of dough to slightly less than 1/4 inch (5 mm) thickness and cut into shapes. Use a ginger-bread cutter for authentic aulet, (but Elizabeth says the cookies taste just as good in other seasonal shapes, even circles). Decorate with raisins or candies or sprinkle with sugar. Transfer carefully to baking sheets.

Bake at 375F (190C) for 8 to 10 minutes or until golden underneath. Pay careful attention while cookies are baking, turning baking sheets around on racks and switching top to bottom so cookies brown evenly without burning.

Makes about 36 aulets or 48 2-inch (5 cm) cookies.

■ Maria Kulcher of St. Stephen, New Brunswick, credits her career to the Chocolate Fest. In the early eighties she was asked to prepare a chocolate dessert buffet as one of the festival events. She later opened her own catering business: "I like to do things that are quite often out of the ordinary, such as a nice dinner for twenty-four," she said in an interview. Included here is Maria's adaptation of a very old Nova Scotia recipe. "The addition of the pecans and chocolate make it extra special," she said.

Maria's Scratch-me-Backs

1 cup (250 ml) shortening
1 cup (250 ml) brown sugar
1 egg
1 cup (250 ml) all-purpose flour
1/2 teaspoon (2 ml) baking soda
1/2 teaspoon (2 ml) baking powder
1/2 teaspoon (2 ml) salt
2 cups (500 ml) large flake rolled oats
1 cup (250 ml) coconut
1 cup (250 ml) pecan pieces
1 cup (250 ml) miniature chocolate chips

Cream shortening and sugar until well blended. Add egg and beat well. Stir in combined flour, baking soda, baking powder, and salt. Add remaining ingredients, mixing well.

Drop by teaspoonfuls onto a lightly greased cookie sheet; press down with a fork. Bake in a 325F (160C) oven for 10 to 15 minutes, until lightly browned around the edge.

■ Chester Soling, owner of a luxury inn in Williamstown, Massachusetts, was determined to find the best chocolate chip cookie to serve to his guests as a bedtime snack. In partnership with *Chocolatier* magazine, he launched the Chocolate-Chip Cookie Bake-Off, which resulted in 2,600 entries. For weeks, the pastry chefs at The Orchards were busy testing more than three hundred recipes, and in the process used 60 dozen eggs, 110 pounds of sugar, 400 pounds of flour, and 150 pounds of butter. Eleven recipes were chosen as finalists, and the judges named Laura Clontz, of Las Vegas, the winner. Apart from the prestige of having the best chocolate chip cookie to her credit, her prize was an all-expense trip for two to Williamstown, with four nights at The Orchards. Chocolate-Chocolate Chip Cookies has been my own favourite cookie recipe ever since.

Chocolate-Chocolate Chip Cookies

1 3/4 cups (425 ml) all-purpose flour
1/4 teaspoon (1 ml) baking soda
1 cup (250 ml) butter or margarine
1 teaspoon (5 ml) vanilla extract
1 cup (250 ml) granulated sugar
1/2 cup (125 ml) packed dark brown sugar
1 egg
1/3 cup (75 ml) unsweetened cocoa powder
2 tablespoons (30 ml) milk
1 cup (250 ml) chopped pecans or walnuts
6 ounces (175 g) semi-sweet chocolate chips

Stir together flour and baking soda; set aside.

Using an electric mixer, cream butter. Add vanilla and sugars and beat until fluffy. Beat in egg. At low speed, beat in cocoa, then milk. With a wooden spoon, mix in flour just until blended. Stir in nuts and chocolate chips.

Drop by rounded teaspoonfuls onto non-stick or foil-lined cookie sheets. Bake in preheated 350F (180C) oven for 12 to 13 minutes. Remove from oven and cool slightly before removing from cookie sheet. Makes 3 dozen cookies.

Killer Peanut Butter Fudge Cookies

If you can't decide between peanut butter and chocolate, make this most delicious choice: Have both.

1 cup (250 ml) peanut butter
6 tablespoons (90 ml) canola oil
1 cup (250 ml) granulated sugar
1 cup (250 ml) lightly packed brown sugar
2 eggs
1 tablespoon (15 ml) vanilla extract
2/3 cup (150 ml) cocoa powder
1 cup (250 ml) all-purpose flour
1 teaspoon (5 ml) baking soda
1/2 teaspoon (2 ml) salt

Cream together peanut butter, oil and sugars. Add eggs and vanilla; mix well. Combine cocoa, flour, soda and salt; stir to mix. Add to creamed mixture, kneading with back of wooden spoon to moisten dry ingredients. Dough will be stiff and somewhat crumbly.

Form dough into balls and place 3 inches (8 cm) apart on cookie sheet lined with bakers' parchment or foil. Flatten to make thick, round disc shapes. Bake at 350F (180C) for 8 to 9 minutes, or until set. Let cool a few minutes before removing to racks to cool completely. Makes about 2 dozen cookies.

Elaine Elliot

Virginia Lee

■ Elaine Elliot, of Kentville, Nova Scotia, and her sister Virginia Lee, who now spends her summers in Lower Cunard, had a cookbook in mind when they started visiting inns and restaurants across the Maritimes. Using their charms to pry recipes from chefs and cooks, they had soon compiled *The Nova Scotia Inns and Restaurants Cookbook*. That was back in 1988; it was the first of eighteen cookbooks to be authored by the sisters.

Even after Virginia moved with her family to Tennessee, the sisters weren't ready to get out of the kitchen. They have penned nine more titles, including establishments not only from the Atlantic region but from across Canada. The duo also updated a fifth edition of *Maritime Flavours Guidebook and Cookbook* in 2002.

On a personal note, I have always given high marks to a restaurant that includes oatcakes in its bread baskets. The Palliser, in Truro is one of these. The recipe is included in *Maritime Flavours*.

Nova Scotia Oatcakes

1 1/2 cups (375 ml) all-purpose flour
1/4 teaspoon (1 ml) baking soda
1/4 teaspoon (1 ml) baking powder
Generous dash of salt
1 1/2 cups (375 ml) rolled oats
1/2 cup (125 ml) packed brown sugar
1/2 cup (125 ml) shortening
1/2 cup (125 ml) butter or margarine
2 1/2 tablespoons (37 ml) water
1/4 teaspoon (1 ml) vanilla extract

Mix dry ingredients in large bowl. Cut in shortening and butter with pastry blender. Add water and vanilla. Roll out on floured surface to 1/4 inch (.5 cm) thickness. Cut in squares and place on greased cookie sheet. Bake at 375F (190C) for 10 to 12 minutes, or until golden brown. Makes 12 to 16 oatcakes.

Mincemeat Oatmeal Cookies

One year I tested four kinds of mincemeat, including old fashioned (with meat), green tomato, pear, and my favourite, Tangy Apple Cranberry Mincemeat (see page 240). With so much mincemeat at hand, I had to find ways of using it all. These cookies proved to be popular with my family, including those who claimed they didn't like mincemeat.

1/2 cup (125 ml) butter
1 cup (250 ml) granulated sugar
1 egg
1/2 teaspoon (2 ml) vanilla extract
1 cup (250 ml) mincemeat
1 cup (250 ml) all-purpose flour
2 cups (500 ml) rolled oats
1 teaspoon (5 ml) baking powder
1/2 teaspoon (2 ml) ground allspice
1/4 teaspoon (1 ml) salt
1/4 teaspoon (1 ml) ground cloves

Cream butter and sugar. Beat in egg and vanilla. Add mincemeat. Combine flour, oats, baking powder, allspice, salt and cloves. Add to butter mixture and mix well. Drop by tablespoonfuls onto greased baking sheets. Flatten with floured fork. Bake at 350F (180C) until lightly browned, about 15 minutes. Makes about 5 dozen cookies.

Gingerbread People

2 cups (500 ml) sifted all-purpose flour
1/2 teaspoon (2 ml) salt
1/2 teaspoon (2 ml) baking soda
1/2 teaspoon (2 ml) baking powder
1 teaspoon (5 ml) ground ginger
1 teaspoon (5 ml) ground cloves
1 1/2 teaspoons (7 ml) ground cinnamon
1/2 teaspoon (2 ml) grated nutmeg
1/2 cup (125 ml) soft shortening
1/2 cup (125 ml) granulated sugar
1/2 cup (125 ml) molasses
1 egg yolk

Sift together flour, salt, baking soda, baking powder, ginger, cloves, cinnamon, and nutmeg. Blend together shortening, sugar and molasses until creamy. Add egg yolk; beat well. Blend in flour mixture.

On lightly floured surface, roll out dough about 1/4 inch (.05 cm) thick. With floured cutters, cut out gingerbread people; place on ungreased cookie sheets 1/2 inch (1 cm) apart. Bake in a 350F (180C) oven for 8 to 10 minutes, or until done. Cool. Then, with ornamental cookie frosting in paper cone or cake decorator, decorate cookies as desired.

Pistachio White Chocolate Chip Cookies

3/4 cup (175 ml) butter or margarine, softened
1-and 1/4 cups (300 ml) light brown sugar
1 egg
1 teaspoon (5 ml) vanilla
1-and-1/3 cups (325 ml) all-purpose flour
1/2 teaspoon (2 ml) baking soda
1/2 teaspoon (2 ml) baking powder
1/3 cup (75 ml) rolled oats
1-and-1/3 cups (325 ml) white chocolate chips
3/4 cup (175 ml) natural pistachios

In a large bowl, cream butter with sugar. Beat in egg and vanilla. In separate bowl, combine flour, baking soda, baking powder and oats. Gradually add to butter mixture, stirring until thoroughly combined. Stir in chocolate chips and 1/2 cup (125 ml) pistachios.

Place heaping teaspoonfuls of dough on ungreased baking sheets, allowing room for spreading. Press some of remaining pistachios into top of each unbaked cookie. Bake in a 350F (180C) oven for 8 to 10 minutes or until light golden brown. For chewy cookies, do not overbake. Makes 3 dozen cookies.

Monster Cookies

Here's one to make for your Hallowe'en callers. There'll be no tricks with this treat.

1 cup (250 ml) peanut butter
3/4 cup (175 ml) canola oil
1 cup (250 ml) lightly packed brown sugar
1 cup (250 ml) white sugar
2 eggs
1 teaspoon (5 ml) vanilla
1 1/4 cups (300 ml) quick-cooking rolled oats
3/4 cup (175 ml) all-purpose flour
1 teaspoon (5 ml) baking soda
1 cup (250 ml) peanuts
1 (6-ounce/175 g) package chocolate chips
1/2 cup (125 ml) raisins

In a large bowl beat together peanut butter, oil, brown and white sugars, eggs and vanilla. In a second bowl, combine rolled oats, flour, baking soda, peanuts, chocolate chips, and raisins. Stir dry ingredients into large bowl and mix well. Drop by large spoonfuls onto greased cookie sheet. Bake in a 350F (180C) oven for 10 to 12 minutes. Makes 3 and 1/2 dozen large (3-inch/8 cm) cookies.

squares and such

I'm a fan of California walnuts. They're so much better than the dark, often rancid imports from China that you usually find in supermarkets. Although not harmful, rancid walnuts have a bitter flavour and rubbery texture, and smell a bit like paint. Hardly the type of ingredient to add flavour to food, but because the imports are cheaper, they're brought in by bulk and packaged in Canada for generic brands—the only choice in some stores.

I talked about walnuts with cookbook author and home economist Anne Lindsay. She said she had stopped buying them until she located some California walnuts at Costco. "I substituted pecans and almonds whenever nuts were called for, because I didn't like the taste of what were obviously rancid walnuts," she said. Another well-known cookbook author, Elizabeth Baird, didn't hesitate to tell her readers (and me), "If it isn't a California walnut, don't buy it."

In-shell walnuts will remain fresh for several months when stored in a cool, dry place and shelled just before using. Shelled walnuts can be stored, tightly sealed, in the refrigerator for up to six months or in the freezer for up to a year. Toasting them before you toss them into salads, stir-fries, or pasta dishes further heightens the flavour.

Nutritionally, California walnuts provide protein (4.6 g in 1/4 cup or 50 ml), magnesium, vitamin E, thiamine, niacin, vitamin B6, folacin, iron and zinc. Like all nuts, walnuts have a high concentration of calories (196) and fat (19.5 g, in 1/4 cup/50 ml), but the fats are mostly mono- or polyunsaturates. They are also rich in essential linoleic and linolenic fatty acids, which are parent compounds of the heart-healthy omega-6 and omega-3 fatty acids.

Research has shown positive relationship between nut consumption, improved blood lipid profiles, and decreased coronary heart mortality. Some studies have shown that incorporating walnuts into a cholesterol-lowering diet, while not increasing overall caloric intake, has resulted in decreased levels of harmful cholesterol and reduced risk of heart disease. There's no scientific standard for walnut consumption and health benefit, but "a handful a day" is recommended and fits into the meats and alternatives food group of Canada's Food Guide.

I first met Dorothy Duncan, of Willowdale, Ontario, in 1993, at a banquet reenacting the Order of the Good Cheer for the first Northern Bounty conference in Stratford, Ontario. I thought she was sweet, but I subsequently learned that there's far more to her than a good demeanor. She's an author, an educator, a food writer, and editor, and perhaps most significant of all, she's a historian and researcher, especially of early Canadian foodways. She writes a regular column in *Century Home* magazine, and has recently put together in book form some of her favourite columns. The title is fitting: *Nothing More Comforting, Canada's Heritage Food.*

California Walnut Turtle Squares

2 cups (500 ml) all-purpose flour
1/2 cup (125 ml) granulated sugar
3/4 cup (175 ml) butter, softened
2 1/2 cups (625 ml) California walnut halves
25 caramels
1 tablespoon (15 ml) light cream
3/4 cup (175 ml) semi-sweet chocolate chips

In medium bowl, mix together flour and sugar; blend in butter until crumbly. Press into an ungreased 13x9-inch (33x23 cm) pan, lined with heavy-duty foil. Spread walnuts in one layer over dough. Bake in a 350F (180C) oven for 20 to 25 minutes, or until walnuts are lightly toasted, and the base is lightly browned on edges. Remove from oven and set aside.

In medium saucepan, combine unwrapped caramels and cream. Warm over medium-low heat, stirring constantly, until caramels melt. Immediately drizzle caramel mixture over nuts. Scatter chocolate chips over top; let stand 2 to 3 minutes. Swirl through chocolate with knife; cool before cutting into 54 squares.

Apricot Hazelnut Bars

1 cup (250 ml) dried apricots
1/2 cup (125 ml) butter, softened
1/4 cup (50 ml) granulated sugar
1-and-1/3 cups (325 ml) all-purpose flour
2 eggs
1 cup (250 ml) lightly packed brown sugar
1/2 teaspoon (2 ml) baking powder
1/4 teaspoon (1 ml) salt
1/2 teaspoon (2 ml) vanilla extract
1/2 cup (125 ml) chopped hazelnuts

Rinse apricots and cover with water in a small saucepan; bring to boil and simmer for 10 minutes; drain, cool and chop.

In small mixer bowl, cream butter; blend in granulated sugar and 1 cup (250 ml) of the flour. Press into a 9-inch (23 cm) square pan and bake in a 325F (160C) oven for 20 minutes.

In another bowl, beat eggs thoroughly. Add brown sugar; beat well. Combine remaining flour, baking powder and salt; add to egg mixture. Stir in vanilla, chopped nuts and apricots. Spread over baked layer and return to oven until set, about 30 minutes. Cool before cutting. Makes 36 squares.

■ After the recipe for Butter Tart Squares appeared in *The Chronicle-Herald* and *The Mail-Star*, I had a call from a reader who reported a disaster. She said the recipe sounded so good when she read it that she went immediately to her kitchen and made the squares. But when she took them out of the oven and sampled one, it was horrible. It turned out there had been a misprint in the amount of baking powder. Instead of 3/4 of a teaspoon, the amount was given as six teaspoons. Having already discovered the error, I asked the reader how much baking powder she had used. "I don't know," she said, "but it was an awful lot." Indeed! That's two tablespoons (30 ml). I doubt that she ever made the squares again. But don't be intimidated—the recipe is now error-free.

Butter Tart Squares

Crust:
1 1/4 cups (300 ml) all-purpose flour
1/3 cup (75 ml) lightly packed brown sugar
Pinch salt
1/2 cup (125 ml) butter or margarine

Filling:
2 eggs
1 cup (250 ml) lightly packed brown sugar
1/4 cup (50 ml) all-purpose flour
3/4 teaspoon (3 ml) baking powder
1/4 teaspoon (1 ml) salt
1-and 1/2 cups (375 ml) raisins
1/2 cup (125 ml) chopped walnuts

To make crust: In a bowl, combine flour, brown sugar and salt. Cut in butter until crumbly. Press mixture into an ungreased 9-inch (23 cm) square pan. Bake in a 350F (180C) oven for 10 minutes.

To make filling: Beat eggs; gradually add sugar and beat until light in colour. Combine flour, baking powder and salt; add to egg mixture. Stir in raisins and walnuts. Spread over crust in pan and bake at 350F (180C) for 30 minutes, or until centre is almost firm. Cool before cutting into 36 squares.

Chef Diane Clement

■ Diane Clement, of Vancouver, has been called a Julia Child in running shoes; a galloping gourmet if ever there was one. And never perhaps has the shoe fit as well. Both shoes. I have great admiration for Diane, the former Olympic sprinter, who grew up as Diane Matheson in Moncton, New Brunswick. Her long career as chef, restaurateur, and cookbook author brought her to my Herald column on several occasions. But it was our first meeting, in October 1984, that stands out in my mind. She was in Halifax on a publicity tour for her second cookbook, *More Chef on the Run*, and I met her at a coffee party given in her honour. It was there that I first tasted her B-52 Balls, a confection she had invented, as she put it, "to keep you smiling all day or to put you beautifully to sleep at night." After sampling the first one, and then a second, I wondered if I could manage a third and still drive home. I made it safely, but today my motto would be: Don't eat B-52 Balls and drive.

Diane Clement's B-52 Balls

2 cups (500 ml) finely crushed vanilla wafers
1 cup (250 ml) icing sugar
1/4 cup (50 ml) almond paste, at room temperature
2 1/2 tablespoons (37 ml) Kahlua
2 1/2 tablespoons (37 ml) Grand Marnier
2 1/2 tablespoons (37 ml) Bailey's Irish Cream
2 tablespoons (30 ml) white corn syrup
10—12 ounces (300 to 350 g) semi-sweet chocolate
2 cups (approximately) (500 ml) very finely crushed toasted almonds

In a bowl, mix the wafers, sugar, almond paste, liqueurs and corn syrup. Make sure the almond paste is well blended with other ingredients. Press mixture into shallow pie plate and refrigerate until firm enough to form into balls. This should take 20 minutes or so.

Melt chocolate in double boiler over gently simmering water.

Roll mixture into small balls, impale each on a toothpick, and dip into the melted chocolate, coating evenly. Roll gently in toasted almonds, then place on trays to harden. Store in airtight containers in refrigerator. Bring to room temperature before serving. Makes 3 dozen.

■ In her delightful book *Having Tea*, Tricia Foley has done a good sleuthing job in turning up about fifty traditional recipes that accompany the afternoon brew to the English tea table. With the inclusion of Park Pies, she might even have solved the long-standing mystery about how Cape Breton Pork Pies got their name. Little pastry shells, filled with a mixture of dates, brown sugar and lemon were served in a tiny tea room on Clapham Common. Could it be that a Cape Bretoner visited London, brought home the recipe, and simply made a change in the pastry? And could the Cape Breton accent be responsible for turning "park" into "pork"? Or did someone's written "a" look like an "o," as mine does? It's something to ponder over a cup of tea.

Park Pies

Filling:
1 cup (250 ml) chopped pitted dates
2 tablespoons (30 ml) water
2 tablespoons (30 ml) dark brown sugar
Juice of 1 lemon
Grated rind of 2 lemons

Pastry:
1 cup (250 ml) all-purpose flour
1 teaspoon (5 ml) baking soda
1 cup (250 ml) rolled oats
3/4 cup (175 ml) plus 2 tablespoons (30 ml) dark brown sugar
3/4 cup (175 ml) butter, melted
Juice of 1 lemon

To make filling: In a saucepan, combine dates, water, brown sugar, lemon juice and rind. Bring to a boil and simmer gently, uncovered, until thick and smooth but not dry. Stir occasionally. Remove from heat and cool.

To make pastry: Mix together flour, baking soda, rolled oats and sugar. Add melted butter and lemon juice. Blend together using a fork or floured hands. Roll dough out about 1/4 inch (.5 cm) thick on a floured board, and divide into three portions.

Cut 2/3 of dough into sixteen 3-inch (8 cm) circles and pat them into greased regular-size muffin cups. Cut remaining dough into sixteen 1 1/2 inch (4 cm) circles.

Put 1-2 teaspoonfuls (5 to 10 ml) of date mixture into each pastry shell and place smaller circle on top, pressing edges together. Bake in a 375F (190C) oven for 35 minutes, or until lightly browned. Remove from oven, cool in tins, then finish cooling on wire rack. Makes 16 little pies.

San Francisco Foggies

In 1986, Chocolatier *magazine announced the winners of their Great Chocolate Challenge recipe contest. The winner of the Grand Coco Award for the best overall recipe went to Barbara Feldman of San Francisco, for these fudge foggies.*

1 pound (500 g) bittersweet chocolate, finely chopped
1 cup (250 ml) unsalted butter, cut into tablespoons
1/3 cup (75 ml) strong brewed coffee
4 large eggs, at room temperature
1 1/2 cups (375 ml) granulated sugar
1/2 cup (125 ml) all-purpose flour
8 ounces (250 g) walnut halves, coarsely chopped (about 2 cups)

Line a 13x9-inch (33x23 cm) pan with a double thickness of aluminum foil, extending foil 2 inches (5 cm) beyond sides of pan. Butter bottom and sides of foil-lined pan.

In top of double boiler over hot, not simmering water, melt chocolate, butter and dissolved coffee, stirring frequently, until smooth. Remove pan from heat. Cool mixture, stirring occasionally for 10 minutes.

In large bowl, using a hand-held electric mixer at high speed, beat eggs for 30 seconds, or until foamy. Gradually add sugar and continue to beat for 2 minutes, or until mixture is light and fluffy. Reduce speed to low and gradually beat in chocolate mixture until just blended. Using a wooden spoon, stir in flour. Stir in walnuts. Do not overbeat.

Pour into prepared pan. Bake on centre rack of a 375F (190C) oven for 28 to 30 minutes, or until just set around the edges. They will remain moist in centre.

Cool foggies in pan on a wire rack for 30 minutes. Cover pan tightly with foil and refrigerate overnight or for at least 6 hours. Remove top foil and run a sharp knife around edge of foggies. Using two ends of the foil as handles, invert foggies onto a large tray and peel off foil. Invert them again onto a smooth surface and cut into 16 bars.

Monda Rosenberg

■ I think it was 1993 when I first met Monda Rosenberg of Toronto. We were autographing our latest cookbooks at the first Northern Bounty conference, in Stratford. My book was *Marie Nightingale's Favourite Recipes* and hers was *The New Chatelaine Cookbook*. Since there was no mad rush for either book, we fell into conversation. We met again in Montreal in 2000, when she was jury chair of the Canadian Grand Prix New Products Award and I was one of the seventeen jury members who tested, tasted, and rated the products. Hard work, I remember, but there was a lot of camaraderie and a couple of very good meals to keep us interested. Monda, who has been food editor for *Chatelaine* since 1975, is recognized as a top Canadian authority on good food and nutrition, and has received many awards for her writing.

Decadent Nanaimo Bars

3/4 cup (175 ml) butter
1/4 cup (50 ml) granulated sugar
1/3 cup (75 ml) cocoa
1 egg, slightly beaten
1 teaspoon (5 ml) vanilla
1 1/2 cups (375 ml) graham cracker crumbs
1 cup (250 ml) finely shredded coconut
1/2 cup (125 ml) finely chopped walnuts
1/2 cup (125 ml) mix of finely chopped red and green candied cherries (optional)
2 tablespoons (30 ml) finely chopped crystallized ginger (optional)
1/4 cup (50 ml) butter, at room temperature
3 tablespoons (45 ml) milk
2 tablespoons (30 ml) vanilla custard powder
2 1/2 cups (625 ml) sifted icing sugar
4 (1-ounce//28 g) squares semisweet chocolate

Lightly grease a 9-inch (23 cm) square pan; set aside. Melt 3/4 cup (175 ml) butter in a heavy-bottomed saucepan; turn into a bowl. Stir in sugar and cocoa until blended. Cool to room temperature. Whisk in egg and vanilla until smooth. Add graham cracker crumbs, coconut, walnuts, cherries and ginger, if using. Press into bottom of prepared pan in an even layer.

Combine 1/4 cup (50 ml) butter, 1/4 cup (50 ml), milk, custard powder and 2 cups (500 ml) icing sugar in a small bowl; stir until creamy. Spread over crumb base. Place in freezer to set slightly, about 15 minutes.

Meanwhile, melt chocolate in top of a double boiler set over simmering water or in a microwave. Spread chocolate in a thin even layer over cooled custard; refrigerate until firm, about 1 hour.

Prepare a glaze by stirring together 1/2 cup (125 ml) sifted icing sugar with 2 teaspoons (10 ml) water. Drizzle over chilled mixture. Cut into bars or squares and store in a tightly covered container in refrigerator.

Low-fat Fudgy Brownies

As scientists continue to search for miracle synthetic fats, food technologists at the California Prune Board have found that substituting a prune purée for butter, margarine, or oil in all tested baked goods reduces fat content by 75 to 90 percent, and cholesterol to zero. To make 1 cup (250 ml) of prune purée, combine 8 ounces (250 g) or 1-and 1/3 cups (325 ml) of pitted prunes with 6 tablespoons (90 ml) of water in a food processor, and pulse until prunes are finely chopped. Refrigerate leftovers.

4 ounces (4 squares) unsweetened chocolate
1/2 cup (125 ml) prune purée
3 large egg whites
1 cup (250 ml) granulated sugar
1 teaspoon (5 ml) salt
1 teaspoon (5 ml) vanilla extract
1/2 cup (125 ml) all-purpose flour
1/4 cup (50 ml) chopped walnuts

Coat 8-inch (20 cm) square baking pan with vegetable cooking spray; set aside. Cut chocolate into 1-inch (2.5 cm) pieces; place in heat-proof bowl. Set over low heat in small skillet containing 1/2 inch (1 cm) simmering water. Stir occasionally just until chocolate is melted. Remove from heat; set aside.

In mixer bowl, combine all ingredients except flour and walnuts; beat to blend thoroughly. Mix in flour. Spread batter in prepared pan; sprinkle with walnuts. Bake in a 350F (180C) oven about 30 minutes until springy to the touch about 2 inches (5 cm) around edges. Cool on rack. Cut into 1 1/2 inch (4 cm) squares. Makes 3 dozen.

Per square: 58 calories; 2 g fat; 30 per cent of calories from fat, 10 g carbohydrate; 0 cholesterol, 70 mg sodium, 0.4 g fibre.

Mincemeat Squares

If you make the Tangy Apple Cranberry Mincemeat on page 240, be sure to save some for this recipe. You can cut the squares small for a tray of sweets, or larger for an easy-to-make dessert that doubles for mincemeat pie. If serving as a dessert, it is best served warm.

Base:
3/4 cup (175 ml) cup butter, softened
3 tablespoons (45 ml) icing sugar
1 1/2 cups (375 ml) all-purpose flour

Filling:
1/3 cup (75 ml) butter, softened
1/2 cup (125 ml) lightly packed brown sugar
2 eggs, beaten
1 1/2 cups (375 ml) mincemeat
3/4 cup (175 ml) coconut
1/3 cup (75 ml) chopped walnuts

Make base: Combine 3/4 cup (175 ml) butter, icing sugar and flour in a bowl; mix well. Pat into greased 13x9-inch (33x23 cm) baking pan. Bake in a 350F (180C) oven for 10 minutes. Cool.

Make filling: In a mixer bowl, cream 1/3 cup (75 ml) butter and brown sugar until light and fluffy. Add eggs; mix well. Add mincemeat, coconut and walnuts; mix well. Spread over baked pastry layer. Bake at 350F (180C) for 20 to 25 minutes. Cool. Cut into squares. Makes 54 small squares.

Butter Crunch Squares

Visions of sugar plums have a habit of dancing through young heads, regardless of whether or not they belong to a family where baking time is at a premium. The following recipe, a no-bake creation of Kellogg's combining two of their corn cereals, is ready to eat after chilling for 45 minutes.

1/3 cup (75 ml) butter or margarine
3/4 cup (175 ml) firmly-packed brown sugar
1/2 cup (125 ml) corn syrup
1/2 cup (125 ml) smooth peanut butter
1 teaspoon (5 ml) vanilla extract
3 cups (750 ml) corn flakes cereal
1 1/2 cups (375 ml) corn pops cereal
3/4 cup (175 ml) peanuts

In large, heavy saucepan over low heat, melt butter. Stir in sugar and corn syrup. Cook over medium heat, stirring constantly, until sugar is dissolved and mixture is bubbly. Remove from heat.

Blend in peanut butter and vanilla. Add cereals and peanuts, stirring until thoroughly coated.

Press firmly and evenly into a buttered 9-inch (23 cm) square pan. Chill until set, about 45 minutes. Cut into 25 squares. Store covered at room temperature.

Apples 'n Raisins Squares

I egg
1/4 cup (50 ml) canola oil
1/2 cup (125 ml) low-fat plain yogurt
3/4 cup (175 ml) lightly packed brown sugar
I cup (250 ml) applesauce
I teaspoon (5 ml) grated lemon rind
1/2 cup (125 ml) raisins
I cup (250 ml) whole-wheat flour
1/2 cup (125 ml) natural bran
I teaspoon (5 ml) baking powder
2 teaspoons (10 ml) ground cinnamon
I teaspoon (5 ml) ground ginger
1/4 teaspoon (1 ml) grated nutmeg
1/3 cup (75 ml) sliced almonds

In large mixing bowl, beat egg; add canola oil, yogurt, brown sugar, applesauce, vanilla and lemon rind; mix well.

In another bowl, stir together raisins, flour, bran, baking powder, cinnamon, ginger and nutmeg; add to wet ingredients and mix only until combined.

Turn into a lightly greased 8-inch (20 cm) square cake pan. Lightly press almonds into top of batter. Bake in a 350F (180C) oven for 45 minutes or until pick inserted in centre comes out clean. Cool and cut into 25 squares.

cakes

For many generations, a traditional part of holiday baking has been the pound cake, one that could be served with pride if the texture was just right or covered with a sauce and relegated to family consumption if it wasn't. Today, even loyal family members might forego nibbling on the original four-pounder, which got its name because it called for a pound each of butter, sugar, eggs, and flour. When topped with a pound of almond paste, it was that much heavier.

With some old recipes calling for the batter to be beaten for an hour, just think of the elbow grease needed to make such a cake. But the creaming was necessary to trap air in the butter, which, along with the eggs, provided the only leavening. Then along came the electric mixer and a revised "pound" cake. To make one loaf cake, one cup (250 ml) of butter was "worked" until creamy, then 1-and-2/3 cups (400 ml) of sugar was beaten in, maybe 1/2 cup (125 ml) at a time, five eggs were added, one at a time, and 2 cups (500 ml) of flour were gradually folded in with a spoon. The cake was baked in a buttered and floured "bread" pan at 300F (150C) for 90 minutes. This "modern" pound cake might more properly be called a half-pound cake. And sometimes it was.

Certain basic rules still hold in the making of a somewhat lighter but still dense pound cake. All ingredients should be at room temperature. That means the butter should be soft enough to leave an indentation when pressed with a finger. A minute or two of creaming, either with a wooden spoon or an electric beater, will ready the butter to receive the sugar, which is added, a little at a

At a Beta Sigma Phi convention in Halifax, in 1991, Marie and June Taylor, of Halifax, enjoy a conversation in the hospitality suite. But what are those little cakes on the plate?

time, and beaten well after each addition. Where butter was once used exclusively, today the fat is often a combination of butter or margarine and shortening (half of each or two parts butter or margarine and one part shortening). Those wishing to cut back on saturated fats may want to try two parts butter or margarine and one part canola or vegetable oil.

Considering the effort that went into the original pound cakes, it's a wonder that the tradition survived at all. But with modifications almost as numerous as there are cooks, pound cake continues to hold its place as a seasonal offering, to be served with pride when the texture is right.

Pat Farmer's Pound Cake

1 cup (250 ml) margarine, at room temperature
2 3/4 cups (675 ml) granulated sugar
6 eggs, at room temperature
1/2 teaspoon (2 ml) lemon extract
1/2 teaspoon (2 ml) orange extract
1/2 teaspoon (2 ml) almond extract
3 cups (750 ml) all-purpose flour
1/2 teaspoon (2 ml) salt
1/4 teaspoon (1 ml) baking soda
1 cup (250 ml) sour cream

In large mixer bowl, beat margarine until light and fluffy. Gradually add sugar; beat well. Add eggs, one at a time, beating well after each addition and scraping sides frequently. Add extracts; beat well.

In separate bowl, sift together flour, salt and baking soda. Add to creamed mixture alternately with sour cream. Turn batter into a greased and floured 10-inch (25 cm) tube pan; bake at 350F (180C) for 1 hour and 15 minutes. Cool pan on wire rack for 15 minutes, remove cake from pan; cool completely and ice with the following frosting.

Almond Buttercream Frosting

1/2 cup (125 ml) margarine, softened
1/2 cup (125 ml) shortening
5 cups (1.25 L) sifted icing sugar
1/4 cup (50 ml) milk
1 teaspoon (5 ml) almond extract

Blend margarine and shortening until creamy. Add icing sugar; blend well. Add milk and almond extract; beat on low setting of mixer until light and fluffy. Spread over top and sides of pound cake. Decorate as desired.

Pat Farmer

■ Pat Farmer, of Bedford, must have made hundreds of pound cakes in her cake-baking lifetime. It's her traditional birthday cake, and whether you're family or friend, if Pat knows the date of your birth, there's a strong possibility you'll get a cake, decorated according to your personality or preferences. "I customize each cake to suit the occasion," she says.

There have even been days when she's had to double her output. "After baking one and decorating it for my eighty-nine-year-old aunt, I had to hurry home and bake another for someone else." But she has no intention of going into the baking business, much to the disappointment of those who've asked. With a husband, three grown children, two grandchildren, and many friends, she says her oven gets enough use.

Lavinia Parrish-Zwicker

■ Lavinia Parrish-Zwicker, of Lochartville, Nova Scotia, built a successful business on her grandmother's recipe for plum pudding. "My grandmother, Lavinia Parsons-Atwell, brought her English heritage, family traditions, and the Olde English Pudding recipe with her when she arrived in Nova Scotia at the turn of the century," Lavinia said. The tradition of pudding-making was carried on by Lavinia's mother, who ceremoniously passed the recipe on to her daughter, along with a pudding pot and cloth bag, when she became of age. "Caught up in the magic and excitement of a nearly forgotten and seldom practiced cooking art, I created a business, born out of a love and appreciation for a wonderful heritage, and a desire to share such a classic dessert," she said. Lavinia's Olde English Delights, established in 1982, soon expanded into fruitcakes, mincemeat and sauces, which she sells at retail shows. Declining to reveal the secrets of her pudding recipe she graciously offered her "favourite Christmas cake" as a consolation.

Lavinia's Christmas Cherry Pound Cake

1 3/4 cups (425 ml) butter
2 1/4 cups (550 ml) granulated sugar
3 cups (750 ml) all-purpose flour
1 teaspoon (5 ml) baking powder
7 eggs, separated
1 1/2 teaspoons (7 ml) lemon extract or pure vanilla
Salt, if necessary
1 1/2 cups (375 ml) glazed cherries

Cream butter until almost white in colour. Gradually add sugar, beating well after each addition. Remove 1/4 cup (50 ml) of the flour to dust cherries. Combine remaining flour and baking powder. In a separate bowl, beat egg yolks until light. Add a little of the flour mixture to the creamed mixture, followed by a little of the egg yolk. Do this about seven times each, beating after each addition, on low speed, just enough to combine. Add lemon or vanilla.

In another bowl, beat egg whites until light but not dry. Again, add a little of the flour to the batter, followed by a little of the egg whites, making about four additions of each, and mixing until whites are incorporated. (Always begin and end with flour.) Fold in glazed cherries.

Spray a 10-inch (25 cm) spring-form pan with vegetable cooking spray or grease well, and dust with flour. Pour in batter and bake in a 300F (150C) oven for 2 hours. Watch carefully after the first hour and if cake appears to be getting brown, reduce heat to 275F (140C). Cake is done when a tester inserted in centre comes out dry.

After cake has cooled completely (leave on the counter, covered with a towel for several hours), place in an airtight container for 6 days. Wrap and store in freezer. (Lavinia says this is a very rich, dense cake that should be aged for 4 to 6 days before using or storing.) Before serving, ice with a butter icing and decorate with cherries, if desired.

Why am I so protective of Nova Scotia's Gravenstein apple? Even a mispronunciation brings out the mother in me, and I correct the user. "That's Grav-en-steen, not Grah-ven-styne," I admonish. Believed to have originated in Germany, the Gravenstein was brought to Nova Scotia by Charles Prescott, a highly successful banker and businessman of eighteenth-century Halifax. It might have been a stroke of good fortune that failing health forced Prescott to retire while still a young man of forty. Leaving the city, he built a large brick house at Starr's Point, Kings County, and turned his interests to horticulture. Although some are still grown in Germany and Washington state, it's in Nova Scotia that the majority, the best and the juiciest Gravensteins are grown.

Fruit grower Hal Stirling of Wolfville, who harvests 1.9 million Gravensteins in an average year, says the apple's optimum time is from September 1 until Halloween. "With all our fancy storage, you can't maintain that fall flavour. You can keep the firmness, but not the flavour," he says, adding that in its prime the Gravenstein is probably the most preferred variety in Nova Scotia kitchens.

Gravenstein Apple Cake with Buttermilk Sauce

3 cups (750 ml) sifted all-purpose flour
1 teaspoon (5 ml) baking soda
1 teaspoon (5 ml) ground cinnamon
2 cups (500 ml) granulated sugar
3 eggs
1 1/4 cups (300 ml) canola oil
1 teaspoon (5 ml) vanilla extract
1/4 cup (50 ml) orange juice
2 cups (500 ml) grated, unpared Gravenstein apples
1 cup (250 ml) chopped walnuts
1 cup (250 ml) flaked coconut
Buttermilk Sauce (recipe follows)

Generously grease a 10-inch (25 cm) tube pan, dust with flour, and set aside. In a bowl, sift together flour, baking soda, and cinnamon: set aside.

In large mixer bowl, combine sugar, eggs, canola oil, vanilla and orange juice. Beat with electric mixer until well blended. Stir in flour mixture until well mixed. Fold in grated apple, walnuts and coconut. Spoon into prepared tube pan. Bake in preheated 325F (160C) oven for 1 1/2 hours, or until top springs back when lightly pressed with fingertip. Cool in pan on wire rack for 15 minutes.

Remove cake onto serving plate with raised edge. Puncture top of cake all over with a skewer. Spoon hot Buttermilk Sauce over warm cake several times until cake absorbs most of it. Let stand at least an hour before serving. Makes 16 servings.

Buttermilk Sauce

1 cup (250 ml) granulated sugar
1/2 cup (125 ml) butter
1/2 teaspoon (2 ml) baking soda
1/2 cup (125 ml) buttermilk

Combine ingredients in saucepan. Cook, stirring constantly, over medium heat, until mixture comes to a boil. Remove from heat.

Note: If you can't use the whole container of buttermilk within seven days of purchase, you can freeze the leftovers. Although thawed buttermilk will separate, all it needs is a good shake to bring it back to a workable consistency.

Fresh Ginger Cake

7 tablespoons (90 ml) canola oil
1/2 cup (125 ml) apple juice
1/2 cup (125 ml) packed brown sugar
1/4 cup (50 ml) molasses
1/4 cup (50 ml) corn syrup
1 egg
3 tablespoons (45 ml) grated fresh ginger
1 1/2 cups (375 ml) all-purpose flour
1 teaspoon (5 ml) baking soda
1/4 teaspoon (1 ml) salt

In a mixing bowl, combine oil and apple juice; beat in sugar, molasses and corn syrup. Add egg, beating well. Combine dry ingredients and ginger; stir into batter until well blended. Pour batter into a greased, floured 9-inch (23 cm) square pan. Bake in a 350F (180C) oven for 30 to 35 minutes, or until cake tests done.

Cool in pan on rack for 5 minutes; cut into squares and serve warm with Ginger Whipped Cream or Sweet Ginger Sauce (recipes follow).

Ginger Whipped Cream: Whip 1 cup (250 ml) whipping cream until soft peaks form. Add 1 to 2 tablespoons (15-30 ml) sugar, or to taste; whip until stiff. Fold in 4 teaspoons (20 ml) chopped candied ginger.

Sweet Ginger Sauce

1/2 cup (125 ml) fresh ginger, peeled and cut into small pieces
1/2 cup (125 ml) dark brown sugar
1/2 cup (125 ml) water
1/2 cup (125 ml) corn syrup
1/4 cup (125 ml) light cream

In a saucepan placed over medium-high heat, bring ginger, sugar and water to boil, stirring to dissolve sugar. Reduce heat and simmer for 20 minutes, until ginger is soft. Discard ginger pieces. Add corn syrup; stir over medium heat 2 to 3 minutes. Add cream; remove from heat. Cool; store in an airtight container in refrigerator. Makes about 1 cup (250 ml).

Chocolate Sour Cream Cake

1 cup (250 ml) butter, softened
1 cup (250 ml) granulated sugar
2 eggs
1 cup (250 ml) cocoa powder, sifted
1 1/2 teaspoons (7 ml) vanilla extract
1 1/2 cups (375 ml) sifted cake and pastry flour (see note)
1/2 teaspoon (2 ml) baking powder
1/2 teaspoon (2 ml) baking soda
1/2 teaspoon (2 ml) salt
3/4 cup (175 ml) sour cream

Grease and flour two 8-inch (20 cm) round layer cake pans; line bottoms with wax paper.

In large mixing bowl, cream butter; add sugar and beat until light and fluffy. Add eggs, one at a time, beating well after each addition. Stir in cocoa and vanilla.

In a separate bowl, sift together flour, baking powder, baking soda and salt; add to chocolate mixture, alternately with sour cream, combining lightly after each addition.

Spread batter evenly into prepared pans. Bake at 350F (180C) for 25 to 30 minutes, until cake tester inserted in centre comes out clean and centre springs back when lightly pressed.

Cool in pans on wire racks for 10 minutes. Remove from pans; peel off paper, and frost with the following:

Chocolate Cream Frosting

1/2 cup (125 ml) sugar
3 tablespoons (45 ml) cocoa powder
2 tablespoons (30 ml) butter
2 tablespoons (30 ml) hot water
1 cup (250 ml) whipping cream

In a small saucepan, combine sugar, cocoa, butter and water. Heat, stirring until smooth; cool. Whip cream until it starts to thicken; add chocolate mixture and whip until stiff. Spread between layers and on top of cake. Dust with cocoa powder or garnish with chocolate curls.

Note: All-purpose flour may be substituted for cake flour by removing 2 tablespoons (30 ml) for each cup called for in the recipe. In this case, remove 3 level tablespoons (45 ml) from the 1 1/2 cups (375 ml) of measured all purpose flour.

Sauerkraut Cake

1/2 cup (125 ml) butter or margarine
1 1/2 cups (375 ml) granulated sugar
3 eggs
1 teaspoon (5 ml) vanilla extract
2 cups (500 ml) all-purpose flour
1/2 cup (125 ml) cocoa powder
1 teaspoon (5 ml) baking powder
1 teaspoon (5 ml) baking soda
1/4 teaspoon (1 ml) salt
3/4 cup plus 2 tablespoons (175 ml plus 30 ml) apple juice
3/4 cup (175 ml) sauerkraut, rinsed, drained, chopped

Line bottom of two greased 8-inch (20 cm) round cake pans with greased wax paper. Cream butter or margarine and sugar until fluffy. Beat in eggs one at a time, beating well after each addition. Add vanilla.

Combine dry ingredients and add alternately with apple juice. Stir in sauerkraut. Divide batter evenly between the two prepared pans. Bake at 350F (180C) for 40 to 50 minutes, or until skewer inserted in centre comes out clean. Cool and frost with Chocolate Icing, if desired, or sprinkle with sifted icing sugar.

Chocolate Icing

1/2 cup (125 ml) butter, softened
1 teaspoon (5 ml) vanilla
Dash salt
1/3 cup (75 ml) cocoa powder
4 cups (1 L) sifted icing sugar
1/3 to 1/2 cup (75 to 125 ml) milk

Cream together butter, vanilla and salt. Add cocoa powder and 1 cup (250 ml) of the icing sugar. Beat until smooth and fluffy. Gradually beat in remaining icing sugar alternately with enough milk to make proper spreading consistency. Use to fill and frost a two-layer cake.

Blueberry Orange Cake

Long respected for its high vitamin C and fibre content, the blueberry has more recently found a new place in the sun. It tops the list of fruits, juices, and vegetables containing anthocyanin, a natural antioxidant that researchers have linked to better eyesight, improved circulation, and other health benefits.

3/4 cup (175 ml) butter or margarine, softened
1 1/2 cups (375 ml) granulated sugar
3 eggs
1 teaspoon (5 ml) vanilla extract
Peel of 2 oranges, finely chopped (do not include white pith of skin)
2 cups (500 ml) all-purpose flour
1/2 teaspoon (2 ml) baking powder
3/4 cup (175 ml) milk
2 cups (500 ml) blueberries (fresh or frozen)

Glaze:
3 tablespoons (45 ml) orange juice concentrate
1 cup (250 ml) sifted icing sugar

Cream butter, gradually add sugar and beat until creamy. Add eggs, one at a time, beating well after each addition. Stir in vanilla and orange peel. Remove 2 tablespoons (30 ml) of the flour to dust blueberries. Stir baking powder into remaining flour and add to batter alternately with milk, mixing just until flour is blended.

Fold dusted blueberries into batter; do not over-mix. Pour batter into a greased large tube pan or 13x9x2 (33x23x5 cm) pan, and bake in a 350F (180C) oven for 50 to 55 minutes. Let stand on a rack for 10 minutes before removing from pan. (If using a 13x9-inch/33x23 cm) pan, cake can be cut and served from the pan.)

Glaze while hot, or ice with Cream Cheese Icing when cold.

To glaze: Combine orange juice concentrate and icing sugar, stirring until smooth. Spread evenly over top, allowing it to dribble down the sides.

Cream Cheese Icing

4 ounces (125 g) package cream cheese, softened
1/4 cup (50 ml) butter or margarine, softened
2 cups (500 ml) icing sugar, sifted
1 teaspoon (5 ml) vanilla extract

Beat together well, adding a little milk if mixture is too thick.

Pineapple Rightside-Up Cake

1 cup (250 ml) canola oil
2 cups (500 ml) granulated sugar
3 eggs, beaten
3 cups (750 ml) all-purpose flour
1 teaspoon (5 ml) baking soda
1 teaspoon (5 ml) salt
1 (19 ounce/540 ml) can crushed pineapple with juice

Praline Topping:
6 tablespoons (90 ml) butter
3/4 cup (175 ml) light brown sugar
3/4 cup (175 ml) granulated sugar
1/3 cup (75 ml) evaporated milk
1 teaspoon (5 ml) vanilla extract
1 cup (250 ml) chopped pecans or walnuts (optional)

In large mixer bowl, combine oil and sugar; add beaten eggs. Sift flour with soda and salt; add to egg mixture. Stir in pineapple with juice. Pour into two greased 9-inch (23 cm) square baking pans. Baked at 325F (160F) for 35 to 45 minutes, or until tester comes out dry.

As soon as cake comes out of oven, combine frosting ingredients, except vanilla and nuts, in a saucepan. Bring to a boil over medium-low heat; stir constantly for 2 minutes. Remove from heat, add vanilla, and beat until smooth and slightly thickened. Add nuts, if desired. Pour hot icing over hot cakes in pans. Cool. Makes two (9-inch/23 cm) cakes.

Fresh Apple Coffee Cake

Topping:
1/2 cup (125 ml) chopped almonds
1/4 cup (50 ml) lightly packed brown sugar
1/2 teaspoon (2 ml) ground cinnamon
2 cups (500 ml) peeled, coarsely chopped apples

Batter:
2 cups (500 ml) all-purpose flour
2 teaspoons (10 ml) baking powder
1-and-1/3 cups (325 ml) granulated sugar
2 eggs
2/3 cup (150 ml) milk
1/2 cup (125 ml) butter, melted
2 teaspoons (10 ml) grated orange rind

Combine almonds, brown sugar and cinnamon; set aside. Prepare apples: set aside.

Combine flour, baking powder and sugar. Beat eggs well; stir in milk, melted butter and orange rind. Make a well in the dry ingredients and add liquid all at once, mixing lightly until just combined. Do not overmix.

Spread mixture evenly in a greased 9-inch (23 cm) square pan. Bake in a 350F (180C) oven for 15 minutes, then top with apples, sprinkle with topping, and continue baking 30 to 35 minutes more. Cut into squares and serve warm. Makes 9 servings.

Luscious Raspberry Cake

2 cups (500 ml) frozen raspberries
2 teaspoons (10 ml) unflavoured gelatin
1/2 cup (125 ml) water
juice from thawed raspberries, with water to make 1 cup (250 ml)
1 cup (250 ml) heavy cream, whipped
1 angel food cake

Thaw berries; drain well, reserving juice. Soften gelatin in water. Heat raspberry juice and in it dissolve the gelatin. Chill until partially set. Beat until fluffy. Fold in whipped cream. Add berries. Chill until nearly set.

Cut cake horizontally in three layers. Spread raspberry mixture between layers and on top and sides. Chill until set. Makes 10 to 12 servings.

Easy Zucchini Cake

2 cups (500 ml) all-purpose flour
2 teaspoons (10 ml) baking soda
1 teaspoon (5 ml) salt
1/4 teaspoon (1 ml) baking powder
3 teaspoons (15 ml) ground cinnamon
3 eggs
1 cup (250 ml) canola oil
1 1/2 cups (375 ml) lightly packed brown sugar
2 medium zucchini, grated
2 teaspoons (10 ml) vanilla extract
1 cup (250 ml) raisins
1 cup (250 ml) chopped walnuts

Sift together flour, baking soda, salt, baking powder, and cinnamon. In a separate bowl, combine eggs, oil, sugar, zucchini and vanilla, mixing well. Add dry ingredients and stir to combine. Stir in raisins and nuts. Pour batter into an oiled 13x9-inch (32x23 cm) pan. Bake in a 350F (180C) oven for about 40 minutes. Cool. Dust with icing sugar. Makes 12 (3-inch/8 cm) squares.

Angelic Frangelico Cake

Another of my favourite special-event desserts based on angel food cake, this recipe is impressive but easy to make, especially if you start with a cake mix. Whipped cream is delicately flavoured with Frangelico liqueur, and the hazelnut praline, which is fun to make, can be prepared days ahead.

1/2 cup (125 ml) whole hazelnuts
1/2 cup (125 ml) granulated sugar
3 tablespoons (45 ml) water
1 large angel food cake
1/2 cup plus 2 tablespoons (125 ml plus 30 ml) Frangelico liqueur
2 tablespoons plus 2 cups (30 ml plus 500 ml) whipping cream
2 tablespoons (30 ml) icing sugar

Spread nuts in a single layer on a rimmed baking sheet; toast about 5 minutes in a 350F (180C) oven. Turn out onto a clean tea towel and rub gently to remove skins. Lightly grease baking sheet; return nuts in single layer, close together.

In a small, heavy-bottomed saucepan, combine sugar and water; set over medium heat until sugar dissolves. Increase heat to medium-high and boil, without stirring, for 5 to 8 minutes or until it turns caramel colour. Remove from heat; immediately pour over nuts. Cool completely. Break into pieces and chop in food processor. (Can be stored, covered, in refrigerator, up to a week; in freezer for a longer period.)

Cut cake evenly into two layers. Place each layer on separate plates. Combine 1/2 cup (125 ml) Frangelico and 2 tablespoons (30 ml) cream. Prick cake layers all over with a skewer. Drizzle Frangelico mixture over cakes. Cover each with plastic wrap and chill in refrigerator for several hours.

Two hours before serving, whip 2 cups (500 ml) cream. Fold in 2 tablespoons (30 ml) of liqueur and sifted icing sugar. Spread cream on bottom cake layer; put top layer in place. Cover top and sides with whipped cream. Sprinkle hazelnut praline over sides and top of cake. Chill before serving. Makes 12 to 14 servings.

■ I once decided to do a column on cakes made from mixes. After making seven different varieties, I had to borrow refrigerator space from my neighbours Jan Heighton, Lillian Lynch, and Margaret McNaughton to keep the cakes fresh until the Herald's Peter Parsons could arrive for a photo shoot. I also needed an enthusiastic model to look infatuated and hungry, so I shanghaied my nineteen-year-old grandson into doing the job. Since his price was all the cake he could eat, Craig agreed that the results were pretty good. His favourite was Angel Mandarin Cake.

Angel Mandarin Cake

1 package angel food cake mix
1 can (10 ounce/284 ml) mandarin oranges, drained
1/2 cup (125 ml) maraschino cherries, drained, halved
1 package (3 ounce/85 g) strawberry gelatin powder
1 cup (250 ml) boiling water
3/4 cup (175 ml) cold water
1 cup (250 ml) whipping cream

Prepare angel food cake according to package directions. Invert pan and cool one hour. Remove cake from pan. Wash pan thoroughly. Arrange mandarins and cherries in a decorative pattern on bottom of clean pan. Carefully set cake back into pan on top of fruit. With a sharp knife, make several slits in cake. Place cake pan on a plate to catch any dripping.

Dissolve gelatin powder in boiling water; stir in cold water. Slowly pour mixture over cake, into the slits and down the sides, allowing time for it to be absorbed before continuing. Refrigerate several hours.

Just before serving, immerse pan in hot water for a second or two to loosen. Turn pan upside down onto a serving plate. Ice sides with whipped cream, leaving fruit exposed to decorate top. Makes 6 to 8 servings.

■ Back in November 1989, when there was a Hilton Hotel in Halifax and Daniel Lamy was the chef, the baking of the Black Cake was an event that brought the West Indies to our city. The cake was served that year at all of the Hilton's Christmas buffets, including the traditional Dickens English Christmas buffet. Daniel worked with his mother-in-law's recipe until he got it just the way he wanted it—heavy with rum-soaked fruit. His secret weapons proved to be the length of soaking time (at least two weeks, but several months made it better) and the type of rum used. To make the cake we munched on with coffee in the Hilton's kitchen, Daniel had gone into the hotel's liquor stores and opened several bottles, sniffing each one until he found just the right aroma of molasses as well as the colour he wanted. The "perfect" choice happened to be Screech, a blend of Jamaican and Newfoundland rums. He said it's the long, slow cooking that caramelizes the sugar and gives the cake its dark colour and flavour.

Daniel Lamy's Black Cake

1 cup (250 ml) dark rum
1 1/2 pounds (700 g) sultanas
1 1/2 pounds (700 g) currants
3/4 pound (350 g) prunes, pitted
8 ounces (250 g) mixed fruit
4 ounces (125 g) mixed peel
8 ounces (250 g) walnut pieces
1 1/2 bottles Guinness stout
3/4 pound (350 g) unsalted butter
1 1/2 cups (375 ml) granulated sugar
2 cups (500 ml) all-purpose flour
6 large eggs

Coarsely chop fruit and soak in rum for at least one week (longer is better).

In mixer, combine walnuts, stout, butter, sugar, flour and eggs; beat until smooth. Add marinated fruit along with any rum not absorbed by fruit.

Grease and flour two 9x5-inch (23x13 cm) loaf pans; pour batter into them. Bake in preheated 275F (140C) oven for 4 hours.

To store, wrap in a rum-soaked cloth, cover tightly with plastic wrap and store in refrigerator or cool place until ready to use.

Black Cake can be covered with almond paste and icing, if desired, or served with an English Cream Sauce.

Note: Since Daniel Lamy's Crème Anglaise is very rich (14 ounces of whipping cream), I chose to go with a lighter alternative.

Vanilla Custard Sauce

1 1/2 cups (375 ml) milk
2 tablespoons (30 ml) granulated sugar
1/2 teaspoon (2 ml) vanilla extract
3 egg yolks

Put milk in pan with sugar and beat until dissolved. In bowl, beat egg yolks until light in colour; gradually stir in heated milk. Return to pan and stir with wooden spoon over gentle heat. When custard coats back of a metal spoon and looks creamy, strain back into bowl. Add vanilla. Sprinkle with a little sugar and cool. (This coating of sugar melts and helps to prevent a skim from forming.)

Note: If custard gets too hot and starts to curdle, pour it at once into the bowl without straining and whisk briskly for 10 seconds.

pies and pastry

What do you mean you can't make pastry? Of course you can! All you have to do is get rid of that mental block, read the rules, and go to it. If your first effort isn't the best, that's okay—it will be better than not doing it at all, and it can be considered a step toward perfection. Remember, practice makes perfect. You want your pie crust to be tender enough to cut easily with a fork, yet not be too crumbly. The colour should be a nice golden brown.

The simple rules of pastry making are: measure accurately, handle lightly, use a good vegetable shortening or lard (never butter or margarine), use just enough water to bind the mixture, never overmix, roll fairly thin, and bake at the right temperature. Shortening should be cut into the flour with a pastry blender or two knives, until mixture is in particles about the size of small peas. If you cut these pieces too small, you'll have a tender crust, but it won't be flaky. If the particles are too large, the result will be a flaky but not tender crust. When adding the water, distribute it evenly, tossing the flour up lightly from the bottom with a fork. The dough should barely hold when pressed together. Not enough water makes the dough dry and hard to manage, while too much water makes the crust shrink while baking.

Pastry should be rolled on a flat surface, preferably on a pastry cloth with the rolling pin covered in a pastry stocking. This prevents the overuse of flour to avoid sticking. Roll from the centre out, applying light, even pressure. Do not use a back and forth motion, and never stretch the pastry, since this will cause it to shrink during baking. Care should also be taken not to stretch the pastry when it is being fitted into the pan.

Remember to work with chilled ingredients and utensils. Fat particles should not melt during the mixing. Some cooks work with cold hands when handling the dough, and others even chill the pie before placing it in the oven. (Care should be taken, however, not to have the plate so cold that it will crack upon being placed in the hot oven.) If all this doesn't provide the courage needed by the timid cook to make pastry, try the recipe for No Fail Pie Crust.

No Fail Pie Crust

> 4 cups (1 L) all-purpose flour
> 1 1/2 teaspoons (7 ml) salt
> Pinch of baking powder
> 1 1/2 cups (375 ml) vegetable shortening (cold)
> 1/3 cup (75 ml) ice water
> 1 egg
> 1 tablespoon (15 ml) vinegar

Mix flour, salt and baking powder together in a large bowl. Put in half of the shortening and cut into flour with a pastry blender using a short cutting motion, or use two knives cutting in opposite directions, until particles are the size of small peas. Cut in remaining shortening until the particles are the size of dry beans.

Beat egg and vinegar into ice water and sprinkle liquid over the flour mixture, drop by drop, tossing flour up from the bottom with a fork, and working around the bowl. As lumps get wet, push aside and continue working until all has been dampened. Press together into a ball. Wrap dough and chill about an hour before rolling out.

Flatten and round one corner of the dough, and place on a lightly floured surface. Roll from the centre out with a light even pressure until circle measures one inch (2.5 cm) larger than the pie plate (dough should be rolled to about one-16th of an inch [1.5 mm] thick). Fold in half and lift gently into pie plate; unfold and fit loosely in place, being careful not to stretch the dough. Be careful that no air is trapped between the dough and the plate. Trim off excess, leaving up to half-an-inch (1 cm) extra all around. Fold under and make a decorative border.

For a single shell, prick pastry well with a fork. Place in centre of a 450F (230C) oven for 10 to 12 minutes.

For a single shell with filling, bake on lower oven shelf for 10 to 15 minutes at 450F (230C), then lower heat to 325F (160C) and continue baking for 20 to 30 minutes longer.

For double crust pies, bake on lower oven shelf for 10 minutes at 450F (230C), then at 325F (160C) for 25 to 30 minutes.

Chef Roland Glauser

■ A delectable Swiss Apple Raisin Pie from Nova Scotia was one point away from being the grand winner in *Yankee Magazine*'s apple pie bake-off in Boston, in October 1989. The pie, baked by Roland Glauser who, at the time, was chef at Inn On The Lake, Waverley, was judged the best pie in Nova Scotia and came second to the overall winning entry from an inn in Maine.

Open to the public, the bake-off attracted hundreds of people, who were treated to a taste of Nova Scotia, Chef Glauser said. He was presented with a silver tray to commemorate the occasion. For the past eight years, Roland and his wife Kathleen have operated their own restaurant and gift shop, Charlotte Lane Café and Crafts, in Shelburne. In 1999, it was named the Taste of Nova Scotia Restaurant of the Year.

Roland Glauser's Swiss Apple Raisin Pie

Pastry (for 2 10-inch (25 cm) pies:
8 cups (2 L) flour
1 pound (454 g) Crisco shortening
1 teaspoon (5 ml) salt
1-and-2/3 cups (400 ml) milk

Blend flour, salt and shortening until it resembles small peas. Gradually add milk and mix until dough leaves the sides of bowl. Shape into a ball. Divide into quarters and roll each quarter into a crust. Line pie plates with bottom crusts.

Filling:
12 cups (3 L) peeled and sliced McIntosh apples
3/4 cup (175 ml) roasted slivered almonds
3/4 cup (175 ml) raisins
3 cups (750 ml) whipping cream
6 eggs
1/2 cup (125 ml) granulated sugar
Grated rind of 2 lemons
1/2 teaspoon (2 ml cinnamon)
1/4 cup (5o ml) apricot jam
Garnish: roasted slivered almonds

In lined pie plates, layer sliced apples with almonds and raisins. Combine cream, eggs, sugar, grated lemon rind and cinnamon, and pour over apple mixture in crusts, dividing equally between the two pie plates. Place top crusts on, trim pastry, seal and crimp edges. Bake at 325F (160C) for 45 minutes.

Apply glaze: Heat apricot jam, strain, and brush on top of warm pie. Sprinkle edges with slivered almonds. Makes 2 pies, to serve 12.

Blueberry Pie

Pastry for a double-crust 9-inch (23 cm) pie
4 cups (1 L) blueberries
1 cup (250 ml) granulated sugar
2 tablespoons (30 ml) flour or cornstarch
1/4 teaspoon (1 ml) salt
1/4 teaspoon (1 ml) ground cinnamon
Pinch of grated nutmeg
1 teaspoon (5 ml) lemon juice
2 tablespoons (30 ml) butter

Line pie plate with pastry. Place blueberries in pastry-lined plate. Combine sugar, flour, salt and spices and spoon evenly over berries. Dot top with butter. Roll out top crust and set in place, crimping edges to seal. Cut vents in crust. Bake in a 425F (220C) oven for 40 minutes, or until golden brown and fruit is bubbling. Makes 6 servings.

Note: If you'd like blueberry pie to be a year-round treat, you can make up the filling for freezing. To make six pie fillings, mix 3 quarts (3 L) of fresh, rinsed and drained blueberries with 6 cups (1.5 L) of sugar, 1/2 teaspoon (2 ml) salt, 2 cups (500 ml) all-purpose flour, and 3/4 cup (175 ml) lemon juice, blending well. Line 8-inch (20 cm) pie plates with large pieces of foil, then fill the plates with blueberry mixture. Turn foil over filling and seal. Freeze until hard. Remove filling from pie plates and stack in freezer until needed. When ready to use, line a 9-inch (23 cm) pie plate with pastry. Unwrap block of filling and place frozen block into lined pie plate. Cover with crust and seal edges as usual. Bake as for blueberry pie, allowing 10 extra minutes in baking.

Fresh Strawberry Pie

1 baked pie shell, cooled
1 cup (250 ml) granulated sugar
6 teaspoons (30 ml) cornstarch
1 cup (250 ml) hot water
4 tablespoons (60 ml) strawberry gelatin powder
3 cups (750 ml) strawberries
Whipped cream

In a saucepan, combine sugar and cornstarch. Add hot water and bring to a boil. Cook until thick. Remove from heat and stir in gelatin powder. Cool. Arrange strawberries, stem end down in pie shell. Pour cooled gelatin mixture over berries. Cover with whipped cream. Makes 6 servings.

Strawberry Rhubarb Pie

3 cups (750 ml) fresh strawberries, halved
2 cups (500 ml) sliced fresh rhubarb (2 to 3 medium stalks)
1 1/2 cups (375 ml) granulated sugar
6 tablespoons (90 ml) quick-cooking tapioca
Unbaked pastry for double crust 9-inch (23 cm) pie

Mix strawberries and rhubarb with sugar and tapioca; let stand while making pastry. Divide pastry in half. On lightly floured surface roll out one portion 1 1/2 inches (4 cm) larger than inverted 9-inch (23 cm) pie plate. Fit into plate and trim crust even with edge. Fill with fruit mixture.

Roll out remaining pastry; lift onto pie. Trim crust 1/2 inch (1 cm) beyond edge of pie plate. Fold top crust under bottom crust; seal together to make a standing rim and flute edge. Cut vents in top crust. Brush with milk and sprinkle with sugar. Bake in a 400F (200C) oven for 60 to 70 minutes, or until filling bubbles in the centre. After 30 minutes of baking, check pie occasionally and cover edges with foil, if necessary, to prevent browning. If pie begins to bubble over, place foil beneath pie plate. Cool thoroughly before cutting. Makes 1 pie.

Peach Cream Pie

1 can peaches (halves) or fresh peaches
1 cup (250 ml) granulated sugar
2 tablespoons (30 ml) all-purpose flour
2 tablespoons (30 ml) butter (melted)
2 eggs, well beaten

Line a 9-inch (23 cm) pie plate with pastry. Cover with peaches, cut side up. Combine sugar and flour; add butter and beaten eggs. Beat well. Pour over peaches, making sure all are covered. Bake in a 400F (200C) oven for 15 minutes. Reduce heat to 325F (160C) and bake 30 minutes more. Makes 1 (9-inch/23 cm) pie, to serve 6.

■ If we were to look through some of the long established cookbook collections in metro Halifax-Dartmouth, there's a good chance we would find a copy of a little white-bound volume put out by the Evangeline Chapter, IODE. There were five of these popular little cookbooks, which served as fund-raisers for the chapter. The first was published in 1924 and the last in 1952. Marion Crowell, of Halifax, remembers her mother's Peach Cream Pie that appeared in the last of the cookbooks. She says it's still a family favourite.

Old Fashioned Cranberry Pie

Pastry for a double crust 9-inch (23 cm) pie

Filling:
2 cups (500 ml) cranberries
1 cup (250 ml) granulated sugar
1/2 cup (125 ml) water
2 tablespoons (30 ml) flour
1 teaspoon (5 ml) vanilla extract

Line pie plate with pastry; set aside.

Combine all ingredients in a saucepan and cook for 10 minutes. Cool. Pour into pastry-lined pie plate and dot with butter. Make a lattice top and arrange over filling. Bake in a 450F (230C) oven for 10 minutes; reduce heat to 350F (180C) and bake 45 minutes more. Cool before serving. Garnish with ice cream or whipped cream, if desired. Makes 6 servings.

Rhubarb Meringue Pie

4 cups (1 L) rhubarb, cut in quarter-inch (.5 cm) slices
1 1/2 cups (375 ml) granulated sugar
3 egg yolks
3 tablespoons (45 ml) milk
4 tablespoons (60 ml) all-purpose flour
1/2 teaspoon (2 ml) ground cinnamon
1 teaspoon (5 ml) vanilla extract

Meringue:
3 egg whites
1/4 teaspoon (1 ml) salt
1/4 teaspoon (1 ml) cream of tartar
1/3 cup (75 ml) granulated sugar

For pie: Combine rhubarb and sugar; let stand 15 minutes. In bowl, beat eggs lightly; add milk, flour, cinnamon and vanilla, beat. Stir in rhubarb mixture.

Line a 9-inch (23 cm) pie plate with pastry. Spoon in rhubarb mixture. Bake in a 350F (180C) oven for 40 to 50 minutes, or until filling is set. Remove pie from oven. Turn oven temperature to 400F (200C).

Make meringue: With mixer set at medium speed, beat whites for 20 seconds. Add salt and cream of tartar; continue beating 2 minutes, or until whites are light

continued on next page

Edna Staebler

■ At ninety-seven in 2003, Edna Staebler, of Waterloo, Ontario, may be the oldest of Canadian cookbook authors. She has earned national fame for documenting the wonderful good cooking of Ontario's Old Order Mennonites in her *Food That Really Schmecks* series. In her book, *Pies and Tarts with Schmecks Appeal* (1990), Edna says she counted at least sixty different rhubarb pie recipes when trying to choose the five she liked best. Rhubarb Meringue Pie is my choice for the best of the best.

and frothy. Gradually add sugar, increasing mixer speed to high and beat until whites are stiff. Do not overbeat. Spread meringue over pie, or pipe rosettes from piping bag. Return pie to oven and bake 6 to 8 minutes to brown meringue. Serve at room temperature. (If not using within 4 hours, store in refrigerator, removing half an hour before serving.) Makes 1 (9-inch/23 cm) pie, to serve 6.

Perfect Pumpkin Pies

How can we live in the same province with Howard Dill and let October go by without giving the pumpkin a nod? While Mr. Dill's champion giants may be overwhelming to any cook, we can always choose a less awesome specimen to prepare for tasty eating.

1 can (28-ounce/796 ml) pure pumpkin (not pumpkin pie mix) or 3 cups (750 ml) mashed cooked pumpkin
1 1/2 cups (375 ml) granulated sugar
1/4 cup (50 ml) packed brown sugar
1/3 cup (75 ml) all-purpose flour
1 teaspoon (5 ml) salt
1 teaspoon (5 ml) ground cinnamon
3/4 teaspoon (3 ml) ground ginger
1/2 teaspoon (2 ml) ground allspice
1/8 (.5 ml) ground cloves
Dash of ground nutmeg
2 eggs
1 1/2 cups (375 ml) canned evaporated milk
1 tablespoon (15 ml) butter or margarine
2 (8-inch/20 cm) baked pie shells
1 cup (250 ml) whipping cream, whipped, sweetened

In top of a double boiler, combine pumpkin, sugars, flour, salt, and spices. Beat with an electric mixer until blended. Beat in eggs and evaporated milk until blended. Cook over simmering water, stirring, until mixture thickens and loses its gloss. Remove from heat; stir in butter or margarine. Cool 5 minutes. Spoon mixture into pastry shells. Refrigerate several hours until firm, or up to 24 hours. Serve with whipped cream. Makes 2 pies, 6 servings each.

'Blue Ribbon' Chocolate Meringue Pie

I visited Meridee's Breadbasket in Franklin, Tennessee, on a Friday—the day its famous chocolate meringue pie is on the menu—and got there early before this delicious dessert sold out, as usually happens. They graciously shared the recipe.

1/4 cup (50 ml) butter
4 tablespoons (60 ml) cocoa powder
1 1/2 cups (375 ml) granulated sugar
1/3 teaspoon (1.5 ml) salt
1 1/2 (14-ounce/385 ml) cans evaporated milk
3 egg yolks, at room temperature
1 baked 9-inch (23 cm) pie shell
1/2 cup (125 ml) egg whites
1/4 teaspoon (1 ml) cream of tartar
1/2 cup (125 ml) granulated sugar (sift, if lumpy)

Melt butter in saucepan. Thoroughly stir in cocoa powder. Add 1 1/2 cups (375 ml) sugar and the salt; mix well. Gradually add evaporated milk, stirring until mixed. Cook slowly until mixture comes to a boil.

Slowly add half of hot mixture to slightly beaten egg yolks; add that mixture to remaining hot mixture. Cook, stirring, until mixture comes to a full boil for 2 minutes. Pour into baked pie shell.

In mixer bowl, beat egg whites and cream of tartar at high speed until foamy. Add 1/2 cup (125 ml) sugar, a tablespoon (15 ml) at a time, being sure each addition is well beaten. When all sugar is added, stir down any sugar on sides of bowl with rubber scraper. Continue beating until mixture is very stiff and has a glossy appearance.

Using the rubber scraper, seal all edges of pie with meringue, then fill in the middle. Make peaks or swirls to decorate. Bake at 325F (160C) for 15 minutes, until golden brown. Watch carefully. Your oven may run hot and meringue may bake faster. In that case lower temperature at least 25 degrees next time. Makes 6 to 8 servings.

Albertans Chef Hubert Aumeier and Cinda Chavich

■ There are probably no better spokespeople for Prairie cuisine than Chef Hubert Aumeier, of Canmore, Alberta, and Cinda Chavich of Calgary. In October 2000, the pair joined forces at a Northern Bounty conference in Jasper to demonstrate their knowledge of regional foods, both wild and cultivated. Hubert, master chef, restaurateur, and author, grew up on a small farm in Bavaria, and was already familiar with wild mushrooms, herbs, berries, and fruits before arriving in Western Canada. There he opened a restaurant featuring the abundant "wild" foods and setting the trend for the cooking of the Rockies. Cinda, the former food editor for the *Calgary Herald*, has authored three cookbooks, including *The Wild West Cookbook* and *High Plains: The Joy of Alberta Cuisine*, which won Cuisine Canada's prestigious Gold Award in 2002. Her Walnut Pie with Dried Berries was one of the special treats she prepared for conference delegates. It's very rich, so she suggests cutting it in small wedges, and topping with a dollop of lemon yogurt or mascarpone cheese.

Walnut Pie with Dried Berries

For the crust:
1 1/4 cups (300 ml) all-purpose flour
1 tablespoon (15 ml) sugar
Pinch of salt
1/2 cup (125 ml) cold butter
1 egg yolk
1 tablespoon (15 ml) milk

Combine flour, sugar, salt and butter in a food processor; process until crumbly (or mix in bowl with pastry cutter). Add egg yolk and milk; pulse until dough forms a ball. Wrap in plastic wrap and chill 1 hour or overnight. Roll out dough and line a tart or springform pan with removable bottom. Press to fill in cracks. Line with foil, weighting with 2 cups (500 ml) of dried beans or rice. Bake at 350F (180C) for 20 minutes. Remove foil, weights; bake 10 minutes more. Cool.

For the filling:
2 cups (500 ml) walnut pieces
4 eggs
1/2 cup (125 ml) granulated sugar
1 cup (250 ml) corn syrup
1/2 cup (125 ml) melted butter
1 tablespoon (15 ml) Grand Marnier or frozen orange juice concentrate
Grated zest of 2 oranges
1 teaspoon (5 ml) vanilla extract
Pinch of salt
1 1/2 cups (375 ml) dried cranberries or blueberries (substitute raisins or dried currants for a sweeter result)

Toast walnuts in oven on a baking sheet for 5 minutes. Cool. In a mixing bowl, whisk together eggs, sugar, syrup, melted butter, liqueur or concentrate, orange zest, vanilla and salt. Stir in cooled nuts and dried berries. Pour filling into prepared pie shell. Place on baking sheet and bake at 350F (180C) for 35 to 40 minutes, until filling is set.

For the fruit compote:
4 oranges
I cup (250 ml) fresh or frozen cranberries, saskatoons or blueberries
1/2 cup (125 ml) granulated sugar
1/2 cup (125 ml) orange juice
I tablespoon (15 ml) Grand Marnier or orange juice
Lemon yogurt or sweetened mascarpone cheese to garnish

Use a sharp knife to remove skin and pith from oranges. Working over a bowl to catch juices, cut flesh from membranes. Cook cranberries and sugar with orange juice, stirring over low heat for about 5 minutes, until berries soften and begin to pop. Remove from heat, stir in orange sections and Grand Marnier (or I tablespoon/15 ml orange juice). Serve slices of pie with chilled compote on the side. Makes 10 servings.

desserts

It might have been 150 years since Joseph Howe, Nova Scotia's best-loved politician and newspaper man, bragged to a British audience about the beautiful sight and smell of apple blossoms that give Nova Scotians an early spring boost. He said there was a valley in Nova Scotia where a man could walk for fifty miles and see nothing but apple blossoms. Old Joe might have been stretching the point a bit, since apple blossoms are with us for such a short time in early spring. But when they bloom, people come from near and far to see them, breathe in the aroma, and have their pictures taken under a blossoming branch.

Although August gives us a few early varieties, the Nova Scotia apple season really begins in mid-September with the Gravenstein, one of the old favourites that has survived the years of change. Along with the old-fashioned Gravenstein, which many claim to have the best flavour, is the Crimson Gravenstein, which offers the colour that some people desire on their apples. Both are excellent for eating fresh and cooking into pies, sauces, cobblers, and other desserts.

The Nova Scotia apple industry began when the Acadians planted the first apple trees sometime before 1609. But the first recorded apple harvest in Canada was at Annapolis Royal in 1633. Since then the industry has developed to such an extent that at one time, in the 1930s, almost half of the Canadian crop and more than sixty per cent of exported Canadian apples came from Nova Scotia.

Not so today. Because of shifts in areas of production, changing markets, and varieties grown, the industry has steadily declined. Nova Scotia now ranks fourth among Canada's apple-producing provinces. Yet, it is still one of Nova Scotia's major industries. Growers are gradually increasing the average yields by planting more productive orchards, and using new cultural techniques. Of the approximately three million bushels of apples harvested annually in Nova Scotia, fifty-five to sixty per cent goes to the processing market, with the remaining crop packed in polybags and sold on the fresh market. In recent years only three to five per cent of the total crop has been exported.

If you want to be sure you're buying local apples, watch the labels. Among the imported apples is the Jersey Mac, which might be mistaken for the McIntosh, Nova Scotia's most popular variety. Second on the popularity poll is the Cortland. A good dual-purpose apple, it makes a nice white sauce, and stores as long as the McIntosh. Third place goes to the Gravenstein, while the Red Delicious and the Northern Spy vie for fourth place. But these varieties should watch their backs, because the Ida Red is coming on strong.

On a couple of occasions while attending Northern Bounty conferences, I've shared a table with food and consumer consultant Shirley Ann Holmes, of Guelph, Ontario. The first was at a very formal dinner in Vancouver, when there were eight wine glasses at each place. Hardly room for the food, but somehow we managed. The second occasion was in Jasper, at a Prairie-style dinner featuring buffalo hump with forest mushrooms, and other wonderful entrees. Shirley Ann and I both marveled at the dessert, which, in the shape of a canoe, was a work of art. A professional home economist, Shirley Ann is the author of *Easy Bread Machine Baking*.

Hughena's Self-Saucing Apple Pudding

Hughena Hubley

■ A little bit of magic happens when Hughena Hubley of Halifax adds Nova Scotia Gravensteins to her favourite apple pudding. Although Cortlands and Northern Spys are good substitutes, the magic diminishes somewhat when McIntoshes are used—the pudding puffs up and looks great, but then deflates, along with the mood of the cook. Although the flavour doesn't disappoint, Hughena is a perfectionist and appearance is important to her. After Hughena's Self-Saucing Apple Pudding recipe ran in *The Chronicle-Herald* and *The Mail-Star* in September 2002, it garnered so much attention that Hughena was beginning to feel somewhat like a celebrity. She's had to make the pudding several times since then, but it's never a chore. It's so easy to make, she says, and is best served warm, although leftovers are also good cold. A scoop of vanilla ice cream or a spoonful of yogurt enhances the flavour.

Fruit Layer:
3 cups (750 ml) chopped tart apples
1/2 teaspoon (2 ml) grated nutmeg

Batter:
3 tablespoons (45 ml) butter
3/4 cup (175 ml) granulated sugar
1 cup (250 ml) all-purpose flour
1 teaspoon (5 ml) baking powder
1/4 teaspoon (1 ml) salt
1/2 cup (125 ml) milk

Sauce:
1 cup (250 ml) granulated sugar
2 tablespoons (30 ml) cornstarch
1 1/2 cups (375 ml) boiling water

Fruit layer: Spread apples in a 2-quart (2 L) casserole dish and sprinkle evenly with nutmeg.

Batter: Cream butter and sugar together. Combine flour, baking powder and salt; add to creamed mixture. Stir in milk. Spread evenly over apples.

Sauce: Combine sugar and cornstarch; sprinkle over batter. Pour boiling water over the sugar. Do not stir. Bake in a 375F (190C) oven for 50 to 60 minutes. Makes 6 servings.

Note: The recipe can be doubled, and Hughena sometimes makes one and a half times the amount and bakes it in a 13x9-inch (33x23 cm) baking dish, for 9 or 10 servings.

Easy Apple Strudel

Pastry for a single 9-inch (23 cm) pie crust
2 1/2 cups (625 ml) thinly sliced apples
1/2 cup (125 ml) raisins
1/3 cup (75 ml) granulated sugar
1/4 teaspoon (1 ml) ground cinnamon
1/4 teaspoon (1 ml) grated nutmeg
1/4 teaspoon (1 ml) ground cloves

Roll pastry into a 12x9-inch (31x23 cm) rectangle and place on a cookie sheet. Mix apples with raisins, sugar and spices. Place down centre of pastry. Cut side pastry edges into one-inch (2.5 cm) wide strips, cutting to within 1/2 inch (1 cm) of filling. Fold strips up over apples; press ends of strudel together to seal. Brush pastry with milk or beaten egg.

Bake in a 400F (200C) oven for 40 minutes or until pastry is golden and apples are tender. Cool slightly. Sprinkle with sifted icing sugar. Makes 4 to 6 servings.

Banana Flambé

■ The French word *flamber* means "to be in flame, to blaze." Foods are usually flamed just before serving, bringing a touch of glamour and drama to the table. An old hand at flaming foods with a flourish is Alan Johnston, a former executive chef at The Upper Deck and now chef/owner of MacAskill's Restaurant, Dartmouth. "What you want is a slow flame to burn longer, so don't have too hot a pan. Just light a match and stand back. You don't want to singe your hair as I have done."

1/4 cup (50 ml) unsalted butter
1/4 cup (50 ml) granulated sugar
2 large bananas, halved
1 ounce (30 g) Grand Marnier
1 ounce (30 g) brandy
Juice of 1 orange
Juice of 1/2 lemon
Vanilla ice cream

In a large sauté pan, melt butter and sprinkle with sugar. While stirring or moving the pan at all times, let this begin to caramelize at a low temperature to prevent burning. Add the bananas and citrus juices. Then flambé with the liqueur and brandy.

Remove bananas from pan and finish the sauce by letting it caramelize to a light syrup. Serve with ice cream. Makes 4 servings.

Blueberry Bread Pudding

2 tablespoons (30 ml) butter or margarine
4 eggs, beaten
2 1/2 cups (625 ml) milk
3/4 cup (175 ml) granulated sugar
2 tablespoons (30 ml) lemon juice
8 cups (2 L) French bread cubes (1/2 inch/1 cm)
2 cups (500 ml) fresh blueberries
1 teaspoon (5 ml) grated lemon rind
Custard Sauce (recipe follows)

Melt butter in a 13x9-inch (33x23 cm) baking dish; set aside.

In large bowl, combine eggs, milk, sugar and lemon juice; beat well. Add bread cubes and let stand for 5 minutes. Fold in blueberries and lemon rind. Spoon into prepared dish. Bake at 350F (180C) for 35 minutes or until lightly browned and puffed. Serve warm with Custard Sauce. Makes 10 servings.

Custard Sauce

2 eggs
2 tablespoons (30 ml) granulated sugar
Pinch of salt
1 cup (250 ml) milk, scalded
1/2 teaspoon (2 ml) vanilla
1/2 teaspoon (2 ml) grated lemon rind

In small mixer bowl, combine eggs, sugar and salt; beat well. Pour into top of a double boiler. Gradually add 1/2 cup (125 ml) scalded milk; add remaining milk, stirring constantly.

Bring water in bottom of double boiler to a boil. Reduce heat to low and cook custard over hot water, stirring occasionally, for about 15 minutes, or until mixture thickens. Cool slightly. Add vanilla and lemon rind. Makes 1-and-1/3 cups (325 ml)

■ When asked what the most popular chocolate dessert was at the now extinct Newsroom Restaurant on Argyle Street, Chef Bill MacKinnon said Mud Pie and Chocolate Orange Cream shared top billing, with the latter being the better.

Chocolate Orange Cream

4 ounces (125 g) semi-sweet baking chocolate
1/2 cup (125 ml) granulated sugar
2 tablespoons (30 ml) black coffee
1/4 cup (50 ml) Grand Curacao liqueur
1 teaspoon (5 ml) vanilla extract
2 cups (500 ml) whipping cream

In a double boiler, melt chocolate with sugar, coffee and liqueur. Be sure to stir mixture so the chocolate doesn't burn around the edges. When chocolate and sugar are completely melted, remove from heat and add vanilla. Chill, but stir once in awhile to prevent film from forming on the surface.

Meanwhile, whip the cream until very thick. Pour chocolate sauce into cream while whipping slowly. If allowed to thoroughly chill, it will become firm. Spoon into parfait glasses and garnish with a rosette of whipped cream. Makes 6 to 8 servings.

Strawberry Fritters

2 cups (500 ml) large fresh strawberries
three-quarters cup (175 ml) apricot jam
one-half cup (125 ml) almonds, toasted
1 cup (250 ml) fine salted cracker crumbs
2 eggs
Canola oil for deep frying

Wash berries first, then hull. Drain on paper towels until thoroughly dry. Force jam through a strainer; chop almonds very fine; beat eggs with a fork.

Dip berries in jam, then roll in almonds. When all berries are prepared in this way, quickly dip, two berries at a time, into beaten eggs and roll in cracker crumbs. Chill several hours in refrigerator.

When ready to serve, heat oil to 360F (185C), or until a cube of bread turns golden in 1 minute, add strawberry fritters (do not crowd) and cook until golden brown. Drain on paper towels. Serve plain or dipped in icing sugar.

Chef Jean-Luc Doridam

■ I thought I had died and gone to heaven. Such was my reaction to the first taste of Jean-Luc Doridam's chocolate mousse cake. A second taste reaffirmed the ethereal sensation, and with the third sampling, I knew this was a dessert to be enjoyed to the last spoonful. Previously pastry chef at the Halifax Sheraton Hotel, Jean-Luc is now bakery and pastry arts teacher at the Nova Scotia Community College, I. W. Akerley Campus.

Jean-Luc's Spectacular Chocolate Mousse Cake

Sponge Layer:
4 eggs
1/2 cup (125 ml) granulated sugar
1/2 cup (125 ml) all-purpose flour
Chocolate Mousse:
1/3 cup (75 ml) water
1/3 cup (75 ml) granulated sugar
8 egg yolks
10 (1 ounce/30 g) squares dark sweet chocolate
2 cups (500 ml) whipping cream, whipped

Glaze:
8 (1-ounce/30 g) squares dark sweet chocolate
1 cup (250 ml) whipping cream

To make sponge layer: Combine eggs and sugar and beat until light and fluffy. Stir in flour. Pour into a greased and floured 8-inch (20 cm) round cake pan. Bake in a 350F (180C) oven for about 30 minutes. Turn out and cool.

Cut a 1/4 inch (.5 cm) layer of cake and place it in bottom of an 8-inch (20 cm) un-greased spring-form pan. Save remaining cake for future use.

To make chocolate mousse: Bring water and sugar to a boil. Beat egg yolks until fluffy. Add sugar mixture to yolks and beat until mixture is cool. Melt chocolate; pour into egg mixture and blend well. Gently fold in whipped cream. Pour chocolate mixture over cake layer in spring-form pan. Chill until set.

Remove side rim from pan and cover chocolate mousse with chocolate glaze.

To make glaze: Bring cream to boil over low heat. Add chocolate and stir until it melts. Spread over top of chocolate mousse and store in refrigerator until needed. If desired, cake can be decorated with curls or shavings of white chocolate.

Note: This cake can be prepared ahead and stored for up to four days in the refrigerator or frozen for longer storage. Remove from freezer one hour before serving.

Chocolate Almond Cheesecake

If the way to a man's heart is through his stomach, you can be sure the short cut is paved with chocolate. This easy-to-prepare, luscious, creamy cheesecake was a favourite at Halifax's Silver Spoon Desserts (now closed). The almond flavour is more pronounced if the cake chills overnight. Garnish just before serving.

1 cup (250 ml) chocolate wafer crumbs (24 wafers)
1/4 cup (50 ml) butter or margarine
2 packages (8-ounce/250 g each) cream cheese, at room temperature
1 cup (250 ml) granulated sugar
1/3 cup (75 ml) unsweetened cocoa powder
2 eggs
5 tablespoons (75 ml) almond flavoured liqueur, divided
1/2 cup (125 ml) sliced almonds
1 cup (250 ml) whipping cream
Candied violets for garnish (optional)

Mix crumbs with butter until well moistened. Press onto bottom of a greased 8-inch (20 cm) spring-form pan. Refrigerate.

In large bowl, beat cream cheese, sugar and cocoa until blended. Add eggs and 3 tablespoons (45 ml) liqueur. Beat just until smooth. Turn into prepared pan and sprinkle evenly with almonds. Bake in a 375F (190C) oven for 35 minutes (do not open oven door during baking) or until sides are firm and slightly raised (centre will be soft).

Remove pan to a wire rack. While still hot, run a thin knife or spatula around edge of pan to loosen cake. Cool cake completely in pan before removing sides. Chill, covered, at least 4 hours before serving.

Meanwhile, in a small bowl combine whipping cream with remaining 2 tablespoons of liqueur; chill 1 hour. Beat until stiff peaks form. Pipe or drop spoonfuls around sides and in centre of cake. Garnish cream with some of the loose toasted almonds from cake and candied violets. Makes 10 servings.

■ The idea of having an official Apple Blossom Festival dessert, featuring apples as the main ingredient, was introduced in 1985, when the Aurora Inn in Kingston, Nova Scotia, was asked to develop a special dessert for the occasion. Apple Blossom Cheesecake was featured at the Aurora and several other valley restaurants. The recipe was developed by Amy Campeau; the following year, she developed another apple cheesecake to reign over dessert tables throughout the festival. In 1987, it was decided to allow valley restaurants to compete for the honour of submitting the official festival dessert. And that's the way it's been ever since.

When asked how she created three of the first four official desserts, Amy replied: "I bake a dessert about ten times in my mind, then I make it to see if it has the texture I'm looking for, the taste combination, and the appearance." These also happen to be the three criteria the judges look for in a winning dessert.

Apple Blossom Cheesecake

Crust:
1 1/2 cups (375 ml) all-purpose flour
1/8 teaspoon (pinch) ground cloves
1/4 teaspoon (1 ml) ground cinnamon
1 cup (250 ml) ground filberts
1/2 cup (125 ml) granulated sugar
1 teaspoon (5 ml) grated lemon peel
2 hard-cooked egg yolks, mashed
1 cup (250 ml) unsalted butter
2 raw egg yolks, lightly beaten
1 teaspoon (5 ml) vanilla extract

Filling:
1/2 cup (125 ml) apple juice
2 1/2 tablespoons (37 ml) unflavoured gelatin
1 pound (500 g) cream cheese
1 pound (500 g) creamed cottage cheese
6 tablespoons (90 ml) granulated sugar
6 tablespoons (90 ml) whipping cream
2 medium apples, cooked and sweetened with 1 teaspoon (5 ml)
   granulated sugar
1/2 teaspoon (2 ml) ground cinnamon
1/4 teaspoon (1 ml) ground allspice
1/4 teaspoon (1 ml) ground cloves
1/4 cup (50 ml) apple juice
3 or 4 nice red apples for top
Lemon juice
1 cup (250 ml) apricot glaze or warmed apricot jam, strained
Ground filberts for decorating sides

To make crust: Sift together the flour, cloves and cinnamon. Add filberts, sugar, lemon peel and mashed yolks. With a wooden spoon, beat in butter, raw egg yolks and vanilla. Continue to beat until mixture is smooth and doughy. Form into a ball, wrap and refrigerate one hour until it is firm.

Line bottom and sides of a 9-inch (23 cm) spring-form pan with silicon or heavy paper. Roll 1/3 of dough to 1/4 inch (.5 cm) thickness to fit over bottom. Bake in a 350F (180C) oven for 15 to 20 minutes, until lightly browned. Set aside to cool. (The remainder of dough may be used as needed. It will keep in the refrigerator for up to 2 weeks, but should be brought to room temperature before rolling.)

continued on next page

To make filling: Sprinkle gelatin over 1/2 cup (125 ml) apple juice and allow to soften. When softened, warm gelatin until it becomes liquid. Place cheeses, whipping cream, sugar, apples, cinnamon, allspice, cloves and 1/4 cup (50 ml) apple juice into a blender or food processor. Blend or process in short starts until mixture is smooth and creamy. Add gelatin. Pour mixture over cooled crust. Refrigerate for 3 or 4 hours.

Slice unpeeled apples very thin, and sprinkle with lemon juice to prevent them from browning. Arrange apples in circular pattern on top of cheesecake. Brush with glaze. Remove paper from sides. Add ground filberts to sides. Makes 10 to 12 servings.

Hazelnut Dacquoise

2 cups (500 ml) finely chopped hazelnuts (filberts)
1 1/4 cups (300 ml) granulated sugar, divided
1/4 cup (50 ml) cornstarch, divided
9 egg whites
1/4 teaspoon (1 ml) cream of tartar

Combine hazelnuts, 1/2 cup (125 ml) sugar and 2 tablespoons (30 ml) cornstarch; set aside. Combine remaining 3/4 cup (175 ml) sugar and 2 tablespoons (30 ml) cornstarch; set aside.

Beat egg whites and cream of tartar until frothy. Gradually beat in sugar and cornstarch mixture until stiff peaks form. Fold hazelnut mixture into meringue. Spread batter in a greased foil-lined 15x10x3/4 inch (40x25x2 cm) jelly roll pan. Bake in a 350F (180C) oven for 20 to 30 minutes or until lightly browned. Cool on wire rack.

Turn out of pan; peel off foil. Cut crosswise into three equal portions. Fill and frost layers with Cocoa Buttercream (recipe follows). Garnish with chopped and whole hazelnuts.

Cocoa Buttercream

2 cups (500 ml) icing sugar
1/2 cup (125 ml) cocoa powder
1 cup (250 ml) butter (do not use margarine)
1 1/2 teaspoons (7 ml) vanilla extract
6 egg yolks

Sift together icing sugar and cocoa. Cream butter until light; beat in cocoa mixture and vanilla. Add egg yolks, one at a time, beating well after each addition. Makes about 4 cups (1 L). Use to fill and frost Hazelnut Dacquoise. Refrigerate any leftover dessert.

The '21' Club's Rice Pudding

At New York's famous '21' Club, where influential business executives, politicians, celeb-rities, and socialites dined, the most popular dessert was rice pudding.

3/4 cup (175 ml) uncooked rice
4 cups (1 L) milk
2 cups (500 ml) whipping cream, divided
1 cup (250 ml) granulated sugar, divided
1/2 teaspoon (2 ml) salt
1 vanilla bean
1 egg yolk
1 1/2 cups (375 ml) sweetened whipped cream, divided

Combine rice, milk, 1 3/4 cups (425 ml) cream, 3/4 cup (175 ml) sugar, salt and vanilla bean in large saucepan. Bring to a boil. Reduce heat to medium-low and cook for 1 hour, or until thickened, stirring frequently. Remove from heat. Blend yolk with remaining cream and sugar. Stir into rice mixture. Cool.

Stir 1 cup (250 ml) whipped cream into pudding. Spoon into 10 individual oven-proof dishes or a 2-quart (2 L) soufflé dish or shallow baking dish. Spread remaining cream over top. Place pudding under preheated broiler for 1 minute, or until lightly browned. Serve at room temperature or chilled. Makes 10 servings.

Noel Woolgard and Cheryl Tardif at the T&W Saskatoon Berry Farm in Victoria Vale, Nova Scotia

■ For a taste of the Prairies, try…where else? Victoria Vale in Nova Scotia's Annapolis Valley. Saskatoon berries, once plentiful on the prairies and a dietary staple for Plains Indians and pioneers, are being cultivated on North Mountain near Middleton. The T&W Saskatoon Berry Farm in Victoria Vale is owned and operated by Saskatchewan-born Noel Woolgar, who, with his Ottawa-born wife Cheryl Tardif, produces organically-grown saskatoons, blueberries, and raspberries for the U-pick market. Nearby, in Prince Albert, Nova Scotia, is the delightful tea room called Daydreams and Destiny, where saskatoons are served in season.

Saskatoon Berry Cobbler

Berry mixture:
10 cups (2.5 L) saskatoon berries
1/2 cup (125 ml) water
1 1/2 cups (375 ml) granulated sugar
1/4 cup (50 ml) lemon juice
1/2 cup (125 ml) melted butter
Pinch of salt

Biscuit topping:
2 cups (500 ml) all-purpose flour
1 tablespoon (15 ml) baking powder
2 tablespoons (30 ml) granulated sugar
1/4 teaspoon (1 ml) salt
2 tablespoons (30 ml) butter
1/3 cup (75 ml) shortening
1 cup (250 ml) milk
2 teaspoons (10 ml) granulated sugar
Ice cream, optional

In large saucepan, simmer saskatoons in water for 10 minutes. Add 1 1/2 cups (375 ml) sugar, lemon juice, melted butter and pinch of salt. Bring to a boil, then pour into a 13x9 inch (33x23 cm) pan. Place in a 400F (200C) oven until bubbles appear around edges.

Meanwhile, prepare topping: In bowl, combine flour, baking powder, 2 tablespoons (30 ml) sugar, and 1/4 teaspoon (1 ml) salt. Cut in butter and shortening to the consistency of small peas. Add milk all at once, tossing quickly to make a soft and sticky batter.

Drop batter by spoonfuls onto the hot berry mixture. Sprinkle with 2 teaspoons (10 ml) sugar. Bake for 25 to 30 minutes longer, until top is golden and berries are bubbly. Serve with a scoop of ice cream, if desired. Makes 12 servings.

Deluxe Strawberry Pavlova

If you can make meringue, you can make this elegant dessert.

4 eggs, separated
1 teaspoon (5 ml) vanilla extract
1/4 teaspoon (1 ml) cream of tartar
1/4 teaspoon (1 ml) salt
1-and-1/3 cups (325 ml) granulated sugar, divided
1/3 cup (75 ml) lemon juice
1 cup (250 ml) whipping cream
4 cups (1 L) sliced strawberries

Line a cookie sheet with foil. Draw a 9-inch (23 cm) circle on foil.

In large glass or metal bowl, beat egg whites, vanilla, cream of tartar and salt at high speed until soft peaks form. Gradually beat in 1 cup (250 ml) sugar, 2 tablespoons (30 ml) at a time, beating well after each addition. Continue beating until stiff, glossy peaks form.

Spoon meringue onto prepared cookie sheet, shaping it within the circle and mounding higher around the edge. Bake in a 250F (120C) oven for 75 to 90 minutes, until crisp on the outside and firm to the touch. Turn off heat and allow to cool in oven with oven door propped open.

Meanwhile, in a heavy saucepan, whisk together egg yolks, remaining 1/3 cup (75 ml) sugar and lemon juice. Cook over low heat, stirring constantly, for 5 to 6 minutes until thickened and smooth. Cover surface directly with plastic wrap. Cool.

Whip cream until stiff; fold in cooled lemon mixture. Just before serving, spread whipped cream mixture over meringue. Serve with strawberries. Makes 6 to 8 servings.

Note: To make things even easier when entertaining, the meringue shell can be made up to several days ahead and kept in an airtight container in a cool place.

Chef Maurizio Bertossi

■ Da Maurizio has been called
the best restaurant in Nova
Scotia, not only by the Herald's
restaurant critic Stephen Maher,
but by others who have reason
to know. Da Maurizio is owned
and operated by the husband
and wife team of Maurizio and
Stephanie Bertossi, who also
own Il Mercato Ristorante and
the elegant Bish World Cuisine.
Originally from northern Italy,
Chef Maurizio but has been
dishing up fine food in Halifax
since 1984. It was only natural
then that I turn to him for an
authentic tiramisu recipe. There
are many imitations out there
but nothing compares with
Maurizio's divine dessert.

Maurizio Bertossi's Own Tiramisu

*Tiramisu should be served very cold. It will keep in the refrigerator for twenty-four hours,
but any longer will make it soggy. This recipe can be halved for six servings.*

6 eggs, separated
1 cup (250 ml) granulated sugar
1 pound (450 g) fresh Italian mascarpone cheese
1 pound (450 g) ladyfingers, savoiardi-style
1/2 cup (125 ml) espresso coffee
1/2 cup (125 ml) brandy
2 ounces (60 g) shaved chocolate or semisweet cocoa powder

In small bowl of electric mixer beat egg yolks and 1/2 cup (125 ml) sugar until
smooth and fluffy. Carefully fold in mascarpone, folding gently until all lumps are gone.
Beat egg whites until stiff; add remaining sugar and beat until glossy. Add to
mascarpone mixture, folding gently to a smooth, fairly stiff cream.
To assemble: Use two 12-inch (30 cm) spring-form pans, 2 inches (5 cm) deep.
Arrange layers of savoiardi on bottom of pans. Sprinkle with 1/4 cup (50 ml) of
combined espresso and brandy, to soften the biscuits. Add layer of mascarpone
mixture, filling in all the gaps. Repeat procedure until all ingredients are used, ending
with mascarpone. Sprinkle with shaved chocolate if serving within 1 hour, or refrigerate,
covered, and add cocoa or chocolate just before serving. Makes 12 servings.

Chocolate Filled Cream Puffs

*French in origin, cream puffs may appear intimidating but they are nothing more than a
simple cooked mixture of water, butter, flour, and salt into which eggs are beaten. Mounds
of the puff paste or pâté a choux, the French term, are placed on a cookie sheet and
then into a hot oven, where they automatically puff to form wonderful golden brown puffs.*

1 cup (250 ml) water
1/2 cup (125 ml) butter
1/4 teaspoon (1 ml) salt
1 cup (250 ml) all-purpose flour
4 eggs
Chocolate Cream Filling, recipe follows
Chocolate Glaze, recipe follows
Fresh strawberries, optional

Heat oven to 400F (200C). In medium saucepan combine water, butter and salt. Bring to a rolling boil. Add flour all at once and stir vigorously over low heat about 1 minute or until mixture leaves the side of the pan and forms a ball.

Remove from heat and cool slightly. Add eggs, one at a time, beating with a spoon until smooth and velvety. Drop by scant 1/4 cupfuls (50 ml) onto ungreased cookie sheet, about 3 inches (8 cm) apart. Bake 35 to 40 minutes or until puffed and golden brown. Remove from oven and cool on wire racks.

Slice off small horizontal portion of tops; reserve. Remove any soft filaments of dough. Fill with Chocolate Cream Filling. Replace tops. Drizzle with Chocolate Glaze; refrigerate. To serve, garnish with fresh strawberries, if desired. Makes about 12 cream puffs.

Chocolate Cream Filling

1/2 cup (125 ml) sugar
1/3 cup (75 ml) all-purpose flour
1/2 teaspoon (2 ml) salt
2 1/2 cups (625 ml) milk
2 egg yolks, slightly beaten
1 cup (250 ml) semi-sweet chocolate chips
1 tablespoon (15 ml) butter or margarine
2 teaspoons (10 ml) vanilla extract

In medium saucepan combine sugar, flour and salt. Gradually add milk and cook over low heat, stirring constantly, until mixture boils. Boil and stir for 2 minutes; remove from heat.

Gradually stir about half of the hot mixture into egg yolks, then return to saucepan. Cook and stir 1 minute longer. Remove from heat and stir in chocolate chips, butter and vanilla. Stir until mixture is smooth. Pour into a medium bowl; place plastic wrap directly onto surface. Cool; refrigerate. Makes about 3 cups filling.

Chocolate Glaze

In a small bowl, combine 1/2 cup (125 ml) semi-sweet chocolate chips and 1 tablespoon (15 ml) vegetable shortening; melt in microwave on high about 1 minute. Stir; continue to microwave on high about 30 seconds or until chips are softened and melt after stirring. Or, place in a pan of hot water being careful not to get water into the chocolate; stir until smooth.

sauces and dressings

W hether tossing a green salad, marinating vegetables, fish, meat, or poultry, or serving an antipasto platter, you can add your signature to basic vinaigrette with a choice of flavourings. Vinaigrette, also known as French dressing or oil and vinegar dressing, offers so many variations that it's easy to come up with your own specialty. You just start with a mixture of oil, vinegar, salt, and pepper, and take it from there. There are variations even in oils and vinegars. Some cooks say olive oil is the only way to go. Others prefer a less flavourful oil, such as olive light or peanut. But don't be intimidated; an excellent vinaigrette can be made with the more common and less expensive vegetable oils that are always on hand, including the highly monounsaturated Canadian product, canola oil. The type of vinegar will also alter the taste of vinaigrette. Some experts insist that balsamic vinegar is the best. Other good choices include red or white wine vinegars, tarragon and other herb vinegars, and cider vinegar.

When making vinaigrette, the standard ratio is three parts oil to one part vinegar. Again, personal taste is a factor. You can perk up a bland salad by increasing the proportion of vinegar. Or, if you want the oil to predominate, use a ratio of four parts oil to one part vinegar. Flavourings can be as subtle or dramatic as imagination allows. Garlic, while optional in some recipes, is a must in others. The easiest way to crush a clove of garlic is to sprinkle some salt on a chopping board, place the garlic on the salt, and crush with the broad side of a chopping knife, mixing the salt with the garlic as it is pressed. The salt acts as an abrasive and helps to crush the garlic. Fresh herbs are a natural for vinaigrette. To extract the most flavour from the herbs, warm the oil before adding a few sprigs of tarragon, basil, dill, parsley, or whatever you prefer. Allow the oil to cool before proceeding with the dressing. If fresh herbs are not available, substitute dried herbs crushed to a powder. Seeds, such as poppy or celery, also add variety to vinaigrette, and if you like the tang of citrus, replace the vinegar with lemon juice and toss in a little orange, lemon, or lime zest (grated rind).

Vinaigrette is usually made in small amounts just before using, although some cooks like to keep a week's supply in a covered jar in the refrigerator. To dress a salad, use only a small amount. As little as two tablespoons (30 ml) is often enough to coat the leaves lightly in a salad for six. Since dressing will not adhere to wet leaves, thoroughly dry greens after washing.

Not only is vinaigrette the classic dressing for salads, it also makes a flavourful topping for cold vegetables, including asparagus and artichokes. Use it, too, to marinate raw or blanched vegetable pieces, or fish; brushed on chicken or beef after grilling; tossed with diced fresh tomatoes; or brushed on slices of crusty bread and baked in a hot oven until lightly browned.

Pat Crocker

■ When culinary herbalist Pat Crocker, of Hanover, Ontario, shared a conference breakfast table with Margaret Fraser, Margo Embury, and others, I seized the opportunity to settle a question I had been asking for years. "How do you pronounce herb?" Pat, who knows everything that needs to be known about herbs, uses the "h." Everyone else agreed.

Craig Claiborne's Basic Vinaigrette

2 tablespoons (30 ml) vinegar, preferably balsamic
2 tablespoons (30 ml) Dijon mustard
6 tablespoons (90 ml) olive oil
Salt and freshly ground pepper to taste
1 teaspoon (5 ml) minced garlic

In a bowl, stir vinegar and mustard with a wire whisk. Gradually add oil, whisking rapidly. Stir in salt, pepper and garlic. Makes 1/2 cup (125 ml).
Variation: Add 2 tablespoons (30 ml) finely chopped shallots.

Caesar Salad Vinaigrette

2 cloves garlic, minced
1/4 cup (50 ml) canola or olive oil
2 tablespoons (30 ml) lemon juice
Salt to taste
3/4 teaspoon (4 ml) ground black pepper
1/4 teaspoon (1 ml) dry mustard
1/4 teaspoon (1 ml) sugar
5 tablespoons (75 ml) grated parmesan cheese

Combine ingredients in a jar with tight-fitting cover. Shake well. Store in refrigerator until needed. Shake well before using. Makes about 1/2 cup (125 ml)

Greek-style Dressing

1/4 cup (50 ml) oil
1/2 cup (125 ml) red wine vinegar
2—3 tablespoons (30—45 ml) honey
3/4 teaspoon (4 ml) salt
1/8 teaspoon (.5 ml) dry mustard
1 teaspoon (5 ml) mint, crushed
1/8 teaspoon (.5 ml) each oregano, thyme and anise seed, all crushed

Combine ingredients in jar with tight-fitting cover. Shake well. Store in refrigerator and shake again before using. Makes about 1 cup (250 ml).

Anita Stewart

■ Ask Anita Stewart if there's such a thing as Canadian cuisine and you'll get more than a hot appetizer. Give her a few minutes and she'll orate a coast-to-coast meal, complete with a list of fine Canadian wines. In half an hour, she'll hold you spellbound as she unfolds the history of what comprises classic Canadian food and drink. There's no one better qualified to discuss the subject than this energetic food and travel writer, cookbook author, lecturer, radio commentator, and champion of Canadian food culture. And she makes it all so interesting: "We're not a melting pot," she says, lifting us above the mundane. "We're a smorgasbord."

Dill Hollandaise

Created by Chef Gerard AuCoin, this recipe appears in Anita Stewart's The Flavours of Canada.

> 3 egg yolks
> 1/4 cup (50 ml) chopped fresh dill
> 4 teaspoons (20 ml) lemon juice
> 2 teaspoons (10 ml) water
> 1/2 teaspoon (2 ml) dry mustard
> 1/4 teaspoon (1 ml) salt
> 1/4 teaspoon (1 ml) cayenne pepper
> 1/2 cup (125 ml) unsalted butter, melted

In blender, combine yolks, dill, lemon juice, water, mustard, salt and cayenne. Blend at low speed 5 to 10 seconds. With machine running, gradually pour in half of melted butter. Increase speed to high; gradually pour in remaining butter. Makes 1 cup (250 ml)

Orange Yogurt Dressing

This dressing goes well with pasta. Most pasta salads taste better if they are dressed and then chilled for at least an hour to allow flavours to blend.

> 1 cup (250 ml) plain yogurt
> 1 1/2 teaspoons (7 ml) grated orange rind
> 1/4 cup (50 ml) orange juice
> 1 tablespoon (15 ml) canola oil
> 1/2 teaspoon (2 ml) salt
> 1/2 teaspoon (2 ml) celery seed
> 1/4 teaspoon (1 ml) curry powder
> 1/4 cup (50 ml) toasted sliced almonds (optional)

Whisk ingredients together; gently stir into prepared pasta. Chill at least an hour. Serve garnished with almonds, if desired. Makes about 1 1/4 cups (300 ml).

■ I met June Roth in June 1984, during the newspaper food editors and writers conference in Montreal. After the conference we shared a taxi to the airport; believe it or not, most of the conversation still centred on food. I was interested to hear about her latest book, *The Pasta-Lovers Diet Book*, which had just recently come off the press. An author and syndicated columnist living in New Jersey, Roth has always faced the occupational hazard of having to be on a perpetual diet. Her solution to the cook's dilemma was to devise a well-balanced eating plan which, she said, is not a fad diet, but is "fun, filling and fat-blitzing." Although many diets shun high carbohydrate pasta, June said that including moderate portions of pasta is a way of meeting biochemical needs while losing weight. One of the requirements is low-calorie sauces, such as her bolognese sauce, which contains only 58 calories per serving.

June Roth's Bolognese Sauce

4 ounces (125 g) fresh mushrooms, sliced
1 onion, diced fine
1 garlic clove, minced
1 cup (250 ml) tomato paste
one-quarter teaspoon (1 ml) honey
one-half teaspoon (2 ml) dried basil
Dash of freshly-ground black pepper

Sauté mushrooms, onion and garlic in a nonstick frying pan, adding a tiny bit of water to make stirring easier. Let water evaporate as vegetables become limp. Add tomato paste, honey, basil, and pepper; cook for 5 minutes, stirring occasionally. Serve over pasta. Makes 2 servings of 58 calories each.

Note: The sauce will keep for one week in the refrigerator.

Slow Simmered Spaghetti Sauce

With a slow cooker, you can let spaghetti sauce simmer all day and all you have to do to get a quick meal on the table is cook the pasta. This sauce can be frozen in airtight containers for up to two weeks.

2 cloves garlic, minced
1 large onion, chopped
2 (28-ounce/796 ml) cans Italian-style tomatoes, undrained and chopped
1 (14-ounce/398 ml) can tomato sauce
2 (5 1/2 ounce/156 ml) cans tomato paste
2 to 3 teaspoons (10—15 ml) dried basil
2 to 3 teaspoons (10—15 ml) dried oregano
1/2 teaspoon (2 ml) dried crushed red pepper

Combine all ingredients in slow cooker. Cover and cook on high for 6 hours. Serve over spaghetti, chicken or pork. Makes 2 1/2 quarts (2.5 L).

Sweet and Sour Dipping Sauce

Every cuisine has its own characteristics, no matter how subtle. And while Vietnamese cooking is greatly influenced by other cultures, including Thai, Chinese, and French, it manages to retain a delicate texture and taste all its own. The ingredient credited with setting Vietnamese cuisine apart is the indispensable salty, pungent fish sauce called nuoc mam.

1/4 cup (50 ml) sugar
1/4 cup (50 ml) white vinegar
1/4 cup (50 ml) chicken broth or water
1/4 teaspoon (1 ml) chili sauce or Tabasco sauce
2 tablespoons (30 ml) soy sauce
2 tablespoons (30 ml) nuoc mam (Vietnamese fish sauce)
1 tablespoon (15 ml) tomato paste
1 tablespoon (15 ml) cornstarch
1 teaspoon (5 ml) grated fresh gingerroot
1 tablespoon (15 ml) canola oil
2 garlic cloves, chopped very fine

In a small bowl combine all ingredients except oil and garlic. Stir until cornstarch is well dissolved.

Heat oil in a small saucepan over medium heat. When oil is hot, add garlic and fry until golden, about 15 seconds. Stir sauce mixture; immediately pour into the saucepan. Cook over medium heat, stirring until thickened, about 5 minutes. Serve warm. Makes 1 cup (250 ml).

Note: If making ahead, cool sauce completely, then refrigerate in a covered jar until needed; it will keep up to 1 month. Reheat before using. It's at its best served warm, not piping hot.

Chocolate Fudge Sauce

1/2 cup (125 ml) cocoa powder
1 cup (250 ml) granulated sugar
1 cup (250 ml) light corn syrup
1/2 cup (125 ml) light cream
3 tablespoons (45 ml) butter
1/4 teaspoon (1 ml) salt
1 teaspoon (5 ml) vanilla

Combine all ingredients except vanilla in a saucepan; boil 5 minutes. Remove from heat and stir in vanilla. Makes about 2 cups (500 ml). Serve hot or cold over ice cream, cakes, brownies, puddings, or other desserts.

Caramel Pecan Sauce

Whether it's a Christmas pudding waiting to be dressed, or pancakes, ice cream, or other desserts, this tasty and easy-to-make sauce fits the bill.

1/2 cup (125 ml) packed brown sugar
1 tablespoon (15 ml) cornstarch
2/3 cup (150 ml) milk
2 tablespoons (30 ml) light corn syrup
1/4 cup (50 ml) chopped pecans or walnuts
2 tablespoons (30 ml) butter or margarine
1 tablespoon (15 ml) rum or brandy

Combine brown sugar and cornstarch in a saucepan. Stir in milk and corn syrup. Cook stirring, until mixture is thickened and bubbly. Cook ,and stir 2 minutes more. (Mixture may appear curdled during cooking, but don't worry, it will turn out fine.)

Stir in chopped nuts, butter and liquor. Remove sauce from heat and cover surface with clear plastic wrap. Cool slightly before serving. Makes about 1 1/2 cups (375 ml).

Apricot Sauce

If you like to keep your pancakes basic, any number of sauces or toppings can be poured over them for additional interest and variety.

2 teaspoons (10 ml) cornstarch
1 (14-ounce/398 ml) can apricot halves, drained, juice reserved
1 cup (250 ml) orange juice
2 tablespoons (30 ml) butter
1/4 teaspoon (1 ml) ground ginger
1/2 cup (125 ml) raisins, optional

In a medium-size saucepan, blend cornstarch with just enough apricot juice to make a smooth paste. Stir in remaining apricot juice, orange juice, butter and ginger. Bring to boil over medium heat and simmer gently, stirring frequently, for 5 to 10 minutes until sauce is thickened.

Slice apricots into wedges, and fold, along with the raisins, if using, into the sauce. Serve warm over pancakes. Makes about 2 cups.

Note: This sauce can be made ahead, covered and refrigerated until needed. Reheat slowly, stirring occasionally.

Wild Blueberry Sauce

1/3 cup (75 ml) granulated sugar
1 tablespoon (15 ml) cornstarch
1/2 cup (125 ml) water
1 teaspoon (5 ml) lemon juice
1 1/2 cups (375 ml) wild blueberries

In a saucepan, combine sugar and cornstarch. Add water and lemon juice. Bring to a boil, stirring constantly. Reduce heat and simmer until thickened and clear. Add blueberries and simmer 2 minutes more. Cool before serving. Sauce may be stored for up to 3 weeks in the refrigerator. Makes about 1 and 2/3 cups (400 ml)

jams and preserves

Often, when jam-makers get into discussions, they break into two camps: those who use commercial pectin and those who don't. The common question asked of the natural-pectin boosters is: "How do you get a set?" While some put it down to luck, others say it's all in the boiling. One woman says she never has a set problem when she uses commercial pectin. Another claims the natural pectin in under-ripe fruit does the job quite nicely, thank you.

Pectin is a gummy carbohydrate that occurs naturally in fruits, especially in the pulp and skin. It helps jams, jellies, and marmalades to form a semi-solid jell. But pectin only works when it is precisely balanced with proper amounts of acid and sugar. That is why it is important not to tamper with recipes. Sugar is a preservative, not just a sweetener, and if a recipe calls for lemon juice, it's because it needs acid. Some fruits contain more acid than others. Those with high pectin content include apples, crabapples, cranberries, currants, gooseberries, grapefruit, grapes, kiwifruit, lemons, limes, oranges (highest in sour varieties, such as Seville), and quinces.

Low-pectin fruits include apricots, blueberries, cherries, figs, nectarines, peaches, pears, pineapples, raspberries, and strawberries. Rhubarb, the vegetable used as a fruit, also falls into this category. Low-pectin fruits need added pectin to guarantee a good set. This can be done either by combining a high-pectin fruit with a low-pectin fruit, or by adding commercial pectin.

Another point that could be made by the pro-commercial pectin group is that the same amount of fruit yields almost double the amount of jam. As well, freezer-type, no-cook jams can't be made without it.

Certo, a commercial producer of pectin, offers these helpful tips to jam- and preserve makers:

For freezer jam, use jars or plastic containers no larger than a 2-cup (500 ml) capacity.

When chopping fruits in a food processor, be careful not to purée them; otherwise they may not set.

Because strawberries can be over-liquefied in a food processor or blender, they should be crushed with a potato masher.

Use perfect, ripe berries. Over-ripe fruit can lead to a softer set, while under-ripe fruit lacks juice, creating a stiff set.

Pour jellies into warm jars as quickly as possible. If the jelly cools it may not set properly.

Never reduce the amount of sugar. The sugar and fruit balance is critical for a proper set.

Always use the pectin product indicated in a recipe—each product uses different proportions of ingredients.

Never double a recipe for jams or jellies.

Spiced Apple and Red Pepper Jelly

4 cups (1 L) chopped sweet red peppers
2 teaspoons (10 ml) dried crushed chili pepper flakes
1 cup (250 ml) apple juice
1/2 cup (125 ml) apple cider vinegar
6 cups (1.5 L) granulated sugar
6 cinnamon sticks
6 strips fresh lemon peel
2 pouches Certo liquid fruit pectin

Purée sweet red peppers in a food processor or blender. Line strainer or colander with cheesecloth. Strain enough juice to make 1 1/4 cups (300 ml).

Combine pepper juice, pepper flakes, apple juice, vinegar, sugar, cinnamon and lemon in a saucepan. Bring to a full boil. Immediately stir in liquid fruit pectin. Bring to a full rolling boil and boil hard for 1 minute, stirring constantly. Remove from heat and skim off foam.

Using sterilized tongs, carefully place a cinnamon stick and lemon strip in each of six warm sterilized (8-ounce/250 ml) jars. Pour hot jelly quickly into warm jars filling up to 1/4 inch (5 mm) from rim. Seal while hot with sterilized 2-piece lids with new centres. Makes 6 cups (1.5 ml)

Strawberry Jam Using Frozen Berries

After a hot day of picking strawberries in the fields, it's far easier to freeze the berries and leave the jam-making for a cooler day when you're not so tired. You have the option of freezing the berries whole, or slicing them before freezing, which only means they'll thaw faster.

4 cups (1 L) thawed and mashed frozen strawberries
4 cups (1 L) granulated sugar
1/4 cup (50 ml) lemon juice

Place two small plates in freezer to chill for set testing. Put mashed berries, sugar and lemon juice in a deep stainless steel saucepan with a heavy bottom. Stir over low heat until sugar dissolves. Increase heat to high and bring to a rolling boil. Boil hard, uncovered, for 10 minutes, stirring often. Be careful of jam splattering.

Remove from heat. Drop a little jam onto one of the chilled plates and return to freezer for 2 minutes. Test for set by pushing your finger through the chilled jam. If it wrinkles, it has reached its set. If not, return jam to heat and cook a little longer. Test again.

Skim and stir jam for 5 minutes, before filling sterilized jars. Seal with a light coating of paraffin wax, breaking any air bubbles if they form, and tilting jars slightly to seal securely. Makes about 5 (8-ounce/250 ml) jars.

■ There I was, choosing my herb plants at the Halifax Farmers Market when an attractive young woman saunters in and picks up the last pot of French tarragon. "Are you going to make tarragon vinegar?" asked the vendor. No, she said, she made an excellent onion vinegar. When you have something that delicious, why switch? As the two went on to discuss the pros and cons of fresh herbs, my tuned-to-food ear picked up some key phrases—wild mint jelly, pear butter, pickled grapes, spiced gooseberries, the green ones, so good with meats. Soon, I had forgiven the shopper for taking the French tarragon and had joined the conversation.

Kim Sloan of Halifax liked to preserve the unusual, having first become interested in her mother's kitchen. "Preserving is an acquired art," she said. "You need a bit of imagination as you try to predict what a recipe will taste like. For example, fig and rhubarb are flavours and textures that support each other wonderfully." Where are you now, Kim Sloan? Are you still making those incredibly rich Peach Cantaloupe Preserves?

Kim's Peach Cantaloupe Preserves

6 peaches, peeled, pitted, and chopped in medium pieces
1/2 cantaloupe, peeled, seeded, and chopped in medium pieces
2 small oranges, peeled, sectioned and seeded
Sugar

Measure fruit. Add 2/3 cup (150 ml) of sugar for each cup of fruit. Let stand several hours. Cook until fruit is transparent and tender, and syrup is thick. Pour into hot sterilized jars and seal. Makes at least three (8-ounce/250 ml) jars.

Gooseberry Jam

2 quarts (2 L) gooseberries
2 cups (500 ml) water
8 cups (2 L) granulated sugar

Wash, top and tail gooseberries. Place them in a deep stainless steel saucepan with a heavy bottom. Add water and cook gently for 20 minutes or until soft and mushy.

Meanwhile, place sugar in a heatproof bowl and warm in a 250F (120C) oven.

Add warmed sugar to the gooseberry mixture, and dissolve slowly, stirring, and then boil rapidly until the jam gives a good jell test. (Put a little jam on a cold plate, place in the freezer compartment to cool it quickly. Run your index finger through the centre. If the jam is ready it will crinkle slightly and remain separated. It will also form a firm drop on your finger.)

When jam is ready, skim and pour into hot, dry jars. Cover and seal.

■ In the summer of 1999, my husband Laurie and I made a trip to the Boates Farm in Woodville, Nova Scotia, to see their cider-making operation. Impressed with the pure apple cider made from whole apples rather than peelings and cores, we also warmed to the hospitality of Keith and Charlotte Boates. As we sat sipping cold cider on the verandah of the 150-year-old house, Charlotte insisted that I bring home some of her pre-serves. Among them was a jar of tomato jam, which can be served as a spread or as relish with cold meats.

Charlotte Boates' Ripe Tomato Jam

8 cups (2 L) peeled, seeded and chopped ripe tomatoes (about 12 large)
2 1/2 cups (625 ml) granulated sugar
2 cups (500 ml) apple cider vinegar
1 teaspoon (5 ml) ground cinnamon
1 teaspoon (5 ml) ground cloves
1 teaspoon (5 ml) salt

To peel tomatoes: cover with boiling water and let stand for 1 minute, then plunge into ice cold water for 1 minute (the skins will practically slip off).

Coarsely chop tomatoes and combine with sugar in stainless steel or enamel preserving kettle or large saucepan. Boil for 1 hour, stirring occasionally.

Add vinegar, spices, and salt, and boil, stirring often, until setting point is reached. When mixture forms a good set (see note), ladle into hot sterilized jars to within 1/2 inch (1 cm) of top rim (head space). Remove air bubbles, wipe jar rims, cover with 2-piece lids (following manufacturer's directions), and process in a boiling water bath for 10 minutes. Makes 6 (8-ounce/250 ml) jars.

Note: To test for set: Put 2 small plates in freezer. When ready to test, remove pot from heat, spoon 1/2 teaspoon (2 ml) of mixture onto one cold plate; put in freezer for 2 minutes, then push your finger through the jam. If it wrinkles, you've got a "set"; if not, return pot to heat and cook a few minutes more. Test again.

Rose Murray

■ Elizabeth Baird once said that the very best place to be is in Rose Murray's kitchen. Some great cooking happens there. Rose, who lives in Cambridge, Ontario, with her husband Kent, has authored eight cookbooks, the latest of which is *A Year in My Kitchen*. She has also contributed to more than forty others, including the popular *Canadian Living* series. Now, that's a lot of cooking to pack into a twenty-five-year period. But the thousands of recipes she has developed for her cookbooks and food articles have earned the trust of those who have come to rely on her.

Having studied cooking techniques at schools in Paris, Costa Rica, and Hong Kong, Rose is never intimidated by any cooking task. She even did all of the catering for her daughter's wedding. At a delightful dinner in Jasper, when I found myself seated between Rose Murray and Rose Olsen (of the Saskatchewan Turkey Producers Marketing Board), I couldn't help asking, "What does that make me? The thorn?" Rose's pumpkin marmalade recipe is from *Canadian Christmas Cooking*.

Rose Murray's Pumpkin Marmalade

14 cups (3.5 L) cubed pumpkin or 1 medium-large pumpkin
8 cups (2 L) granulated sugar
3 oranges
3 lemons

Remove rind and seeds from pumpkin. Cut flesh into 1/2 inch (1 cm) cubes. Mix pumpkin and sugar together in a large preserving kettle. Stir well to dissolve the sugar. Cover and let sit overnight.

Next morning, remove pumpkin from the juice with a slotted spoon and set aside. Cook the pot of juice over high heat. Bring to a boil, then reduce heat to medium-high and boil gently, uncovered, for 20 minutes to reduce the liquid.

Meanwhile, remove outer rind (zest) of the oranges and lemons; set zest aside. Remove all the bitter white membrane underneath and discard. Grind the zest and fruits in a grinder with a medium blade, or in a food processor fitted with a steel blade. Add pumpkin, citrus fruits and rind to the boiling juice. Gently boil everything together for 1 1/2 to 2 hours, uncovered, until the marmalade thickens and pumpkin is translucent. (The marmalade will be a rich golden-brown colour.) Stir very frequently, especially near the end of cooking time.

Remove from heat. Let the marmalade cool very slightly while you skim off any foam from the top with a metal spoon (this will prevent the fruit from floating to the tops of the jars). Ladle into hot sterilized jars and seal with a thin layer of melted wax. Makes 10 (8-ounce/250 g) jars.

Pickling

Pickling is both art and a science, using salt and acid to prevent the growth of micro-organisms. The trick is to have a product that is crisp, crunchy, colourful and flavourful months after you put it in the jar. Here are some tips from the Food Advisory Division of Agriculture Canada (now defunct).

Use the best, firm-type, freshly picked fruits and vegetables for pickling.

Sort cucumbers and other vegetables for size.

Remove blossom end (the end opposite the stem) from cucumbers to prevent soft pickles.

Clean all produce in several changes of water, but do not soak.

Do not tamper with salt in a recipe. Salt is both a preservative and flavouring. Remember to use pickling salt.

Commercial vinegar provides the acetic acid to kill bacteria, yeast and molds. Most recipes use 5 per cent strength vinegar.

Sugar provides sweetness and draws out juices from fruits and vegetables, making pickles firmer.

Fresh spices give the best, pungent flavours. Use whole spices as ground spices may cloud the brine.

Tangy Apple Cranberry Mincemeat

Mincemeat has a long history, having been developed as an alternative method of preserving meat, other than the usual smoking and drying procedures. Like many other foods, mincemeat developed political overtones. Puritans even tried, unsuccessfully, to prohibit their pastors from eating it. But all of that's in the past. Whatever "devils" were thought to dwell within the mixture of meat, fruits and sugar, have long since been exorcised, and the heavy meat content has also been diminished, if not done away with completely.

6 cups (1.5 L) chopped, peeled apples
5 cups (1.25 L) packed brown sugar
4 cups (1 L) grape or apple juice
4 cups (1 L) cranberries
3 cups (750 ml) raisins
3 cups (750 ml) currants
1 1/2 cups (375 ml) cider vinegar
1 tablespoon (15 ml) ground cinnamon
1 teaspoon (5 ml) grated nutmeg
1 teaspoon (5 ml) ground allspice
1/2 teaspoon (2 ml) ground cloves

Combine all ingredients and bring to boil, stirring constantly. Reduce heat and simmer, uncovered, until thickened (about 1 hour). Pour into hot sterilized jars, and seal. Or, cool, pack in freezer containers and freeze at 0 degrees F (-18 C). May be stored for one year. Makes about 3 quarts (3 L).

Mustard Corn Relish

3 cups (750 ml) fresh corn cut from the cob or canned corn kernels
1 large onion, chopped
1 cup (250 ml) chopped celery
1 small green pepper, chopped
1/4 cup (50 ml) chopped pimiento
2 teaspoons (10 ml) coarse salt
1 tablespoon (15 ml) cornstarch
1 tablespoon (15 ml) dry mustard
1 teaspoon (5 ml) turmeric
2 cups (500 ml) vinegar
1 cup (250 ml) granulated sugar
1 teaspoon (5 ml) mustard seed

Combine all ingredients in a deep stainless steel saucepan with a heavy bottom; simmer for 30 minutes or until mixture thickens, stirring often. Pour into hot sterilized jars and seal. Makes about 3 pint-size (500 ml) jars.

■ People have been puckering up with pickles since long before Peter Piper ever picked his famous peck. Before the advent of refrigeration, and eventually the freezer, pickling was the most used method of keeping vegetables through the winter. It became a matter of great pride to our foremothers to turn out the best pickles in the county, and they took seriously their efforts to bring home the red ribbon from the county fair.

Some things never change. Women still vie for the coveted ribbon at fairs all over the province. Lorna Trimper's Bread and Butter Pickles, Esther Beck's Chow Chow, and Pauline Swain's Mustard Pickles took prizes at the Digby County Exhibition, the Pictou County and North Colchester Exhibition, and the Shelburne County Exhibition (respectively) in 1984.

Lorna Trimper's Bread and Butter Pickles

16 cups (4 L) washed and thinly sliced cucumbers
6 medium onions, peeled and sliced
1 green pepper, chopped
1 red pepper, chopped
1/3 cup (75 ml) coarse salt
3 cups (750 ml) white vinegar
5 cups (1.25 L) granulated sugar
1 1/2 teaspoons (7 ml) turmeric
1 1/2 teaspoons (7 ml) celery seeds
2 tablespoons (30 ml) mustard seeds

Combine cucumbers, onions, green and red peppers and place in layers alternately with salt in a large kettle. Mix contents of one tray of ice cubes through cucumber mixture and empty a second tray of ice cubes over the top. Let stand 3 hours. Drain well and return to kettle.

In a bowl combine remaining ingredients. Add to cucumber mixture and heat to the boiling point. Place in sterilized jars while hot. Seal. Makes 10 to 12 pint (500 ml) jars.

Esther Beck's Chow Chow

4 quarts (4 L) green tomatoes, chopped
2 quarts (2 L) onions, chopped
1/4 cup (50 ml) coarse salt
4 cups (1 L) granulated sugar
2 tablespoons (30 ml) pickling spice tied in a gauze bag
1 teaspoon (5 ml) dry mustard
3 cups (750 ml) white vinegar

Put tomatoes and onions in a large kettle, cover with the salt and let stand overnight.

In the morning, drain well and return mixture to kettle. Add sugar, mustard and spice bag. Taste, and add salt (if needed). Stir in vinegar. Cook until clear (tomatoes will be soft). This takes about 1 hour. Bottle while hot in sterilized jars. Seal. Makes 7 or 8 pint (500 ml) jars.

Pauline Swain's Mustard Pickles

3 quarts (3 L) cucumbers, peeled, seeded and chopped into 1/2 inch
  (1 cm) pieces
1 quart (1 L) onions, chopped into 1/2 inch (1 cm) pieces
1 quart (1 L) cauliflower, cut in 1-inch (2.5 cm) pieces
1 quart (1 L) chopped celery
1 sweet red pepper, chopped
4 cups (1 L) granulated sugar, divided
1 quart (1 L) white vinegar, divided
3/4 cup (175 ml) all-purpose flour
1 tablespoon (15 ml) turmeric
1 tablespoon (15 ml) mustard seed
1 tablespoon (15 ml) salt

Put cucumbers, onions, cauliflower, celery, red pepper, 3 cups (750 ml) of the sugar, and 3/4 cup (175 ml) of the vinegar into a large kettle and bring to boiling point.

Make a paste of 1 cup (250 ml) of sugar, the flour, spices and remaining vinegar. Add to pickles and simmer 30 to 45 minutes. Do not let it boil. Bottle while hot. Makes 10 to 12 pin (500 ml) jars.

■ Linda Ritchie of Antrim, Halifax County, makes the best cucumber relish in Canada. After first entering her Million Dollar Relish in the Halifax County Exhibition at Middle Musquodoboit in August 1985, Linda was confident she had a winner. In fact, it was good enough to win the red ribbon and first place money at the Halifax County Exhibition as well as a qualifying place in the regional competition where it was judged against entries from all the Maritime provinces. Again, Million Dollar Relish came up the winner, qualifying it for a berth in the Allen's/Agriculture Winter Fair Canadian Home Pickling Championship, held in Toronto. Here it was judged against national competition winners from Quebec, Ontario, and Western Canada—and came up the winner.

Linda Ritchie's Champion Million Dollar Relish

6 pounds/3 kg (8 large) cucumbers, deseeded but not peeled
2 pounds (1 kg) onions
2 red peppers
1 green pepper
8 cups (2 L) hot water
1/2 cup (125 ml) salt
4 cups (1 L) white vinegar
6 cups (1.5 L) granulated sugar
1 tablespoon (15 ml) turmeric
2 tablespoons (30 ml) mustard seed
1 tablespoon (15 ml) celery seed
3 heaping tablespoons (45 ml) cornstarch

Put cucumbers, onions, red and green peppers through a food chopper and let stand overnight in a brine made of the hot water and salt. In the morning, drain well and add dressing made of vinegar, sugar, turmeric, mustard seed, and celery seed.

Bring to a boil. Thicken with cornstarch, which has been dissolved in a little cold water. Cook slowly for 20 minutes after cornstarch is added. Pour into hot sterilized jars and seal. Makes about 10 pint (500 ml) jars.

Ellie Topp

Margaret Howard

■ When I am asked a question about preserving that I can't answer, I turn, as I do with any subject, to the experts. My constant friends in this department are Ellie Topp and Margaret Howard, who co-authored *Put a Lid on It!* and *The Complete Book of Small-Batch Preserving*. These books tell all you have to know about the latest and safest methods for pickles, jams, and other preserves.

Here are Ellie and Margaret's Steps for Perfect Processing:

20 minutes before processing: Partially fill a boiling-water canner with hot water. Place the number of clean mason jars into the canner needed to hold the quantity of finished food prepared in the recipe. Cover and bring water to a boil over high heat. This step generally requires 15 to 20 minutes, depending on the size of your canner.

5 minutes before processing: Place snap lids in hot or boiling water according to manufacturer's directions.

Filling jars: Remove jars from canner and ladle or pack the food into hot jars to within one-half inch (1 cm) of top rim (head space). If the food is in large pieces, remove trapped air bubbles by sliding a rubber spatula between glass and food; readjust the head space to one-half inch (1 cm). Wipe jar rim to remove any stickiness. Centre snap lid on jar, apply screw band just until fingertip tight.

Garden Patch Salsa

To make the transition from mild to medium to hot salsa, gradually leave more seeds and membranes in the jalapeno peppers. That's where most of the heat is stored.

6 tomatoes, peeled, diced
4 jalapeno peppers, seeded, minced
2 cloves garlic, minced
1 cup (250 ml) chopped onion
1 cup (250 ml) shredded carrot
1 cup (250 ml) shredded zucchini
1/2 cup (125 ml) chopped sweet green pepper
1/2 cup (125 ml) chopped sweet yellow pepper
1/2 cup (125 ml) chopped Italian (flat-leaf) parsley
1/2 cup (125 ml) white vinegar
1/3 cup (75 ml) tomato paste
1/4 cup (50 ml) chopped fresh oregano OR 1 tablespoon (15 ml) dried
1/2 teaspoon (2 ml) pickling salt

Place all ingredients in a large stainless steel or enamel saucepan. Bring to a boil over high heat, reduce heat and simmer, uncovered, for 30 minutes or until thickened.

Remove hot jars from canner and ladle salsa into jars to within 1/2 inch (1 cm) of rim (head space). Process for 20 minutes for half-pint (250 ml) and pint (500 ml) jars. Makes 5 and 1/2 cups (1.375 L).

recipe index

alphabetical index